NOVA SCOTIA

A COLOUR GUIDEBOOK
5TH EDITION

Stephen Poole a
Photographs b

FORMAC PUBLISHING COMPANY LIMITED
HALIFAX

CONTENTS

Formac Publishing Company Limited acknowledges the support of the Cultural Affairs Section, Nova Scotia Department of Tourism and Culture. We acknowledge the financial support of the Government of Canada through the Book Publishing Industry Development Program (BPIDP) for our publishing activities.

For publisher information and photo credits, please see page 208.

National Library of Canada Cataloguing in Publication
Poole, Stephen, 1963-
    Nova Scotia colourguide / by Stephen Poole and Colleen Abdullah; photography by Keith Vaughan. — 5th ed.

(Colourguide series)
Includes index.
ISBN 0-88780-583-3

    1. Nova Scotia—Guidebooks. I. Abdullah, Colleen II. Title. III. Series.

FC2307.P66 2003   917.1604'4   C2003-900465-1
F1037.7.P66 2003

CONTENTS

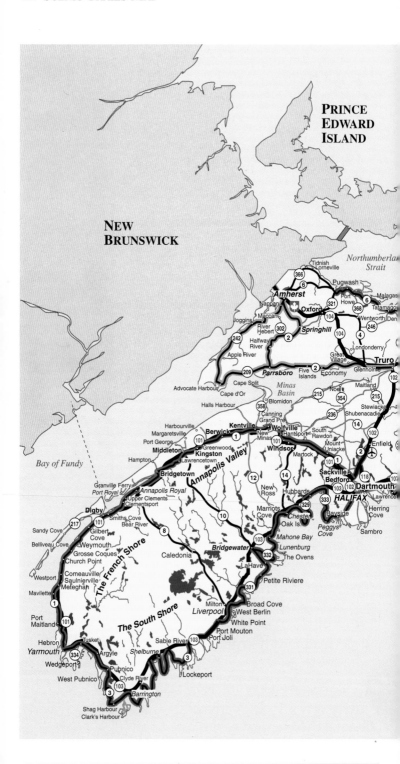

N 0 10 20
km

Cape North
Meat Cove
Bay St. Lawrence
Dingwall
Smelt Brook
Pleasant Bay
New Haven
Neils Harbour

Cape Breton Island

Cheticamp

Ingonish

Margaree Harbour

Indian Brook
North East Tarbotvale
Margaree
Englishtown
162
Sydney Mines
Broad Cove
Margaree Forks
Goose Cove
St Ann's
North Sydney
Sydney
Glace Bay
Inverness
223
125
255
Mira
Mabou
Nyanza
Baddeck
327
22
Louisbourg
Port Hood
Whycocomagh
Shunacadie
Eskasoni
Big Pond
19
Iona
4
Bras d'Or Lake
105
Orangedale
Marble Mountain
Roberta
Fourchu
Craigmore
Dundee
St. Peters
Port Hastings
4
104
River Bourgeois
Ardoise
D'Escousse
Arisaig
245
337
Bayfield
104
Port Hawkesbury
206
Petit-de-Gras
Monastery
Arichat
Caribou
St John
6
Pictou
Trenton
New Glasgow
104
7
316
Boylston
344
Atlantic Ocean
Westville
Stellarton
247
Lochaber
Guysborough
16
Canso
Aspen
316
316
7
211
Tor Bay
Sherbrooke
Isaacs Harbour
Upper Musquodoboit
Liscomb
Mills
Port Bickerton
224
uodoboit
The Eastern Shore
Ecum Secum
7
Sheet Harbour
Tangier
Spry Harbour
Clam Harbour

GETTING AROUND

CABOT TRAIL

Though Nova Scotia is one of Canada's smallest provinces, its land mass is equal to the combined area of Massachusetts, New Hampshire and Vermont, so a visitor can easily fill a day or two in one location, or spend weeks exploring the countryside and enjoying its many attractions.

Shaped somewhat like a lobster found off its coast, Nova Scotia stretches 730 kilometres from Yarmouth to Sydney. You can drive this in under eight hours along new highways, but plan to take the older, more scenic routes, for a relaxing drive, with plenty of opportunities for sightseeing, and for visiting interesting local museums and shops. For those with limited time, however, the 100-series highway routes, which extend to all areas of the province, are an excellent way to reach particular destinations in a hurry. While they bypass the picturesque villages, many of them offer panoramic vistas not seen on older routes.

AMHERST ENTRY POINT

Most motoring visitors enter the province at Amherst, at the border point with New Brunswick. A trip through the Wentworth Valley via the Cobequid Pass toll highway is the usual route to the central point of Truro, or take the lower route, winding around Folly Lake. Then you can follow the TransCanada Highway to scenic Cape Breton Island, or branch off to the metropolitan area of Halifax-Dartmouth. If time is limited, a couple of days can be enjoyed taking in the sights of the cities and their museums, but be sure to include a drive to spectacular Peggys Cove. Day trips can be planned to the South Shore or Annapolis Valley, but it's better to plan two or three days to make the loop along one route to Yarmouth, following the shoreline one way, and driving through the province's agricultural heartland on the other.

If Cape Breton is your destination, and time is limited, follow the TransCanada to Baddeck, where you can make a stop at the Alexander Graham Bell Museum, and then head for the Cabot Trail, taking the counter-clockwise route from Ingonish to Cheticamp. If additional days can be scheduled, be sure to include a visit to Fortress Louisbourg and the Glace Bay Miners' Museum on the east side of the island.

YARMOUTH ENTRY POINT

Arriving at Yarmouth by ferry from Maine, you are faced with the choice of following the Lighthouse Route (see p. 94) along the province's scenic South Shore, or taking the Evangeline Trail (see p. 114) along the French Shore and through the pastoral Annapolis Valley. If a decision is difficult, enjoy the best of both worlds by taking either route about half way, then cutting across country to enjoy contrasting scenery. Depending on your schedule, you might plan one to three days to enjoy charming villages and historic sites. Both routes have a wealth of history to exhibit, opportunities for recreation, and spectacular scenery to enjoy.

HALIFAX ENTRY POINT

The Halifax metro area (see p. 75) demands at least a day for sightseeing, but two or three days would be better, especially if you didn't include a side trip to Peggys Cove on the way from Yarmouth. You will want to visit Halifax Citadel National Historic Site, stroll along the waterfront, and do some shopping at the Historic Properties. Evening entertainment might include taking in a play at Neptune Theatre, or experiencing Shakespeare By The Sea in Point Pleasant Park. A water excursion on Halifax Harbour and the Northwest Arm adds a different perspective to your visit.

Plan a day or two for the drive to Cape Breton, taking in some sights along the way, like historic Sherbrooke Village on Marine Drive (see p. 141). After crossing the Canso Causeway, follow Route 4 through St. Peter's and along the Bras d'Or Lakes. Perhaps you will have time for tea at Rita's Tea Room in Big Pond.

A couple of days in Cape Breton will leave you wanting to stay longer, but from Sydney you can visit Fortress Louisbourg (see p. 162), and take in the Miners' Museum in Glace Bay (see p. 168) in one day. The Cabot Trail (see p. 146) can be done in a day, but you will want to make a list of things to do, and places to stop, on your next trip. An overnight stay at Baddeck, or perhaps Cheticamp or Margaree, will let you enjoy a taste of the Celtic or Acadian culture of those areas.

THE FERRY ARRIVING IN YARMOUTH HARBOUR

If you have to head for home, take another day to make your way to Amherst, enjoying the byways of the Sunrise Trail (see p. 135) or the Glooscap Trail (see p. 130).

Visitors beginning their Nova Scotia tour at Halifax have the opportunity to adjust their schedule by planning two to three days exploring the Annapolis Valley and South Shore. A day could be enjoyed along Marine Drive, and if more time is available, a visit to Cape Breton should be planned.

LAND AND SEA

BY ROBERT J. MCCALLA AND AL KINGSBURY

KEJIMKUJIK NATIONAL PARK

Spectacular scenery, a rich blend of history and culture in seaside villages and vibrant metropolitan areas, and a full calendar of festivals and events combine to offer the visitor to Nova Scotia an unforgettable experience.

Located on Canada's East Coast, within a day's drive of the United States border, and just hours from the major airports in Boston and New York, Nova Scotia prides itself as being "Canada's Ocean Playground," with its 7450 kilometres of beaches, coves, salt marshes, headlands and cliffs. Its geology, climate, plants and animals — as well as its peoples — all have been shaped by the sea.

Nova Scotia is part of the Appalachian Region, which extends from the southeastern United States to Newfoundland in the northeast. Along the Atlantic coast, rugged beauty, like the mass of granite rising from the sea at Peggys Cove, draws thousands of visitors each year. By contrast, Cape Breton Island and the northern mainland, along the Northumberland Strait, boast some fine beaches.

ROCKHOUNDING AT JOGGINS

The world's highest tides have worn spectacular sea cliffs along the shores of the Bay of Fundy. Its effects are most dramatic at Advocate Bay, along Cape Chignecto (see p. 132) and in the area of Cape Split which divides the Minas Channel from the Minas Basin. Millions of years ago, this

area was swamp land, where deposits of organic matter later became coal, to be mined at Joggins, Springhill, and in communities in Pictou, Inverness and Cape Breton counties. You can tour underground coal seams at the Springhill Miners' Museum (see p. 131) and the Miners' Museum at Glace Bay (see p. 168). Embedded within the sedimentary rocks is an excellent record of past plant and animal life. The areas around Joggins and near Parrsboro are famous for fossils (see pp. 132–133).

The province's land surface has been scarred by glaciers at least four times during the last 100,000 years, leaving behind deposits of drumlins (egg-shaped hills) and erratics (large boulders).

The melting of the glaciers caused a rise in sea level which flooded the shoreline, creating deep bays and sheltered harbours along the Atlantic coast. Halifax Harbour, one of the world's finest, owes its existence to both glacial erosion and a rise in sea level.

TIDAL RIPS AT CAPE SPLIT

TIDES

Coastal Nova Scotia is influenced by the twice-daily ebb and flow of the tides. These effects are most spectacular in the upper reaches of the Bay of Fundy where the tidal range has exceeded 16 metres, and huge mud flats are exposed at low tide. Several companies take advantage of the upriver surge of tidal waters by providing white-water rafting excursions on the Shubenacadie River. This phenomenon, known as a tidal bore, can be seen along many of the rivers that flow into Cobequid Bay and the Cumberland Basin.

TIDES DRAMATICALLY CHANGE THE BAY OF FUNDY SEASCAPE

CLIMATE

Nova Scotia has a modified continental climate. Once again, the sea exerts its influence, making winters warmer and summers cooler than in the Canadian interior. The same effect takes place within the province; temperatures become more continental as you move away from the coast. And while you can blame the ocean for Nova Scotia's cold, damp springs (the sea is slow to warm), it is also responsible for our fine autumns (it takes just as long to cool).

Precipitation is plentiful and evenly distributed throughout

the year. On average, Halifax records precipitation on 153 days of the year.

The Cape Breton Highlands and southwestern mainland receive more moisture than the northern mainland and the Annapolis Valley, mainly because of onshore winds.

FLORA

The forests of Nova Scotia are mixed, typical of the Acadia Forest found throughout the Maritime provinces. Softwood — mostly balsam fir, red, white and black spruce, and white pine — are generally found in poorly drained areas, while the hardwoods — mainly red maple, yellow birch, sugar maple, and white birch — prefer drier ground. During autumn, many Nova Scotian hillsides blaze with colour as hardwood leaves turn from soft greens to vivid yellows, oranges and reds. The most dramatic display of fall colour is along Cape Breton's Cabot Trail.

The natural open spaces in Nova Scotia — the salt marshes, bogs, coastal dunes, shallow lakes and ponds, stream banks and barrens — have their own distinctive plant communities. In the salt marshes, for example, angiosperms, algae and grasses trap sediment and help in the transition of the marsh from a saltwater environment to a freshwater one. You'll find many of these marshes in the Minas Basin and Chignecto Bay, although large areas, like Grand Pré, have been converted to dykeland.

BIRDS AND MAMMALS

With its diverse landscape and strategic position along the Atlantic flyway, Nova Scotia hosts a wide variety of birds. Some, like jays, grouses and sparrows, are typical of boreal forest regions. Others create more of a stir. Bald eagles and osprey can be found close to marine and freshwater feeding areas, particularly in the more remote areas of the northern mainland, and on Cape Breton Island. Eagle tours are provided in Cape Breton's Bras d'Or Lakes region (see p. 158).

In August, huge flocks of shorebirds (sandpipers, plovers and phalaropes) gather in the upper reaches of the Bay of Fundy to feed on the nutrient-rich mudflats before resuming their southward migration (Evangeline Beach, near Grand Pré, is a crowded stopover). They can also be found at Brier Island, where they take advantage of nutrient upwelling, and along the Atlantic coast in sheltered harbours with exposed mudflats and salt marshes.

FIELDS IN THE ANNAPOLIS VALLEY

The best place to observe seabirds — razorbills, guillemots, kittiwakes, cormorants, and puffins — is at Hertford and Ciboux, tiny islands off the coast of Cape Dauphin in Cape Breton. The "Bird

Islands" are protected sanctuaries and can only be reached by boat tours that leave from Big Bras d'Or.

Nova Scotia's land mammals range in size from the mole to the moose. Moose and deer are found throughout the province. Other species (skunks, for example) that are found on mainland Nova Scotia are not present on Cape Breton Island. A relatively recent arrival, the coyote is the most vilified of Nova Scotia's mammals, given its penchant for killing sheep.

Marine mammals, including seals, whales, porpoises and dolphins, are among the province's most popular attractions. Numerous species of whales visit Nova Scotia's coastal waters. The Bay of Fundy, near Brier Island, is a good place to see fin and humpback whales; pilot and minke whales are often sighted in the Gulf of St. Lawrence, especially along the west coast of Cape Breton Island.

NOVA SCOTIA IS HOME TO A WIDE VARIETY OF BIRDS AND ANIMALS: PILOT WHALES NEAR CHETICAMP (TOP) OWL (ABOVE), GULL (BELOW), BALD EAGLE (BELOW), WHITE-TAILED DEER (BOTTOM)

SETTLEMENT

The prehistoric evidence of native settlement is sparse. At the time of European contact an estimated 3000-3500 Mi'kmaq were living in the area that is now Nova Scotia, New Brunswick and Prince Edward Island. In Nova Scotia the largest concentration was probably on Cape Breton Island.

European exploration of Nova Scotia may have included the Norse, but there is no hard evidence to show this. Certainly, the English and Portuguese had explored the coast by the beginning of the 16th century.

The story of European settlement starts with the French at Port Royal in 1604 and includes the Acadian population which numbered 13,000 at the time of their deportation in 1755. The story of subsequent immigration (and the return of the Acadians) is told in the following chapters.

Today, more than 900,000 people live in Nova Scotia. Although close to 350,000 live in Halifax Regional Municipality, Nova Scotia is mainly a rural and small-town area. Even the urban communities are small. Truro has fewer than 12,000 people; Yarmouth, in southwest Nova Scotia, has a population of only 7500; Amherst, at the border with New Brunswick, has fewer than 10,000; Lunenburg's population is under 3000; and 115,000 reside in Cape Breton Regional Municipality.

There are more than 70 cultural groups in the province (identified by mother tongue), but the vast majority of people trace their roots to the British Isles. Nova Scotia's telephone books are full of Scots' surnames, especially on Cape Breton Island and along the Northumberland Shore. Still, other peoples — the Mi'kmaq and Acadians are most visible — have retained strong cultural identities that will certainly enrich your visit to Nova Scotia.

GENEALOGY

TERRY PUNCH

Nova Scotia was home to Canada's first French settlement four centuries ago, and several waves of people — English, Blacks, Scots, Germans, Irish and Dutch — have followed, so it's not surprising that many descendants of those immigrants are being drawn to the province each year in search of their family roots. Residents, too, have developed a keen interest in genealogy, and have put extensive efforts into compiling, preserving and cataloguing data. As a result, there are many sources of research available to people trying to trace their roots that can be used both before and during a visit to the province.

Details critical to finding family links are name, place and date (within two to three years) of births, deaths and marriages. If a place within Nova Scotia is not known, religion or ethnicity might help to localize a family. My book *In Which County? Nova Scotia Surnames from Birth Registers; 1864 to 1877*, gives the distribution of 5,000 surnames. And before you do too much work, you should check Allan E. Marble's *A Catalogue of Published Genealogies of Nova Scotia Families*. Perhaps your family has been done before, and you will need only the published information to update your branch of the family tree.

In Nova Scotia, no government records of births and deaths were kept prior to 1864. In a few areas, township books help, and an incomplete set of marriage licences exists, going back to 1763. Otherwise, church registers, newspaper notices or headstone data must be used. Government records prior to 1908 can be viewed at the Nova Scotia Archives & Records Management. Records after that date are available through the provincial Deputy Registrar-General, who should first be contacted regarding fees and other details.

Church records can be an invaluable resource for genealogical research, and many of these are available in Nova Scotia. Members of the Church of Jesus Christ of Latter Day Saints (Mormons) microfilmed many church records, and these are accessible through their worldwide library system. The Nova Scotia Archives and Records Management (NSARM) has many pre-1908 church registers, especially Anglican, Methodist and Presbyterian ones, and other records are in church repositories or in local custody. Typically, registers open in the 1800s, although some start decades earlier. Catholic records of the French era (pre-1755) are best explored through the Centre d'Etudes Acadiennes at New Brunswick's Université de Moncton.

Many headstone inscriptions have been transcribed, and the results are often available at NSARM or with local historical or genealogical societies. Most surviving inscriptions date from after 1840, and these are particularly useful for deaths in the 1875-1950 period. Death and marriage notices in newspapers favoured anglophones, the prominent and Protestants until about 1850, when coverage grew increasingly general. The NSARM has microfilm of most of the old newspapers, and data from the Halifax press (1769-1854) has been published by the Genealogical Association of Nova Scotia. Other information available at the archives includes census data, poll tax records, land grants and deeds, and probate records.

Township books were kept in areas settled by New Englanders in western Nova Scotia. These generally covered births, marriages and deaths from the 1760s to the 1820s. They often recorded only those families having shares in the township, neglecting minorities, transient families and immigrants.

The major repository in the province is NSARM on University Avenue in Halifax. It is closed to the public on Sundays and public holidays, and Saturdays on holiday weekends, so Americans should note that three Canadian holidays differ from their own: Victoria Day (the first Monday before May 25), Canada Day (July 1), and Thanksgiving (the second Monday in October).

The provincial organization for family history is the Genealogical Association of Nova Scotia. It publishes *The Nova Scotia Genealogist*, an annual list of members' interests, readers' queries, book reviews, interesting short articles and other useful information.

Other active organizations that can be of help to anyone researching their family roots can be founding in the Listings section at the end of this book. Further particulars of existing records and where to find them can be obtained by consulting two standard works I've written about the subject: *Genealogist's Handbook for Atlantic Canada Research* and *Genealogical Research in Nova Scotia*. They are available at the archives and at many local libraries.

PIONEER SETTLEMENT

MUSEUMS

NIKKI MITCHELL AND COLLEEN ABDULLAH

OX TEAM AT ROSS FARM

Nova Scotia is an interesting old place. Its modern history is diverse, abundant and, by New World standards, long. The area has witnessed some cataclysmic events in the evolution of the earth. Fascinating stories of the ages before human settlement are visible in its rocks and land formations. The history of its first people, the Mi'kmaq, stretches back 16,000 years, to the end of the Ice Age. Europeans visited Nova Scotia as early as the 11th century, and came to stay in 1605. Thankfully, the riches of the past have been collected, treasured and preserved and are now artfully and creatively presented at more than 100 museums in Nova Scotia.

Credit for this good stewardship belongs to the provincial and federal governments, and to local community groups as well as philanthropists and enthusiasts who have helped preserve fragments of social and natural history. A Nova Scotia Museum Pass, (available at museum.gov.ns.ca, by calling 1-800-632-1114, or at any Nova Scotia Museum site) is a great bargain, especially for families, ($37.50 per adult; $75 per family) and will admit you to all 26 Nova Scotia Museum sites. Parks Canada administers several important National Historic Sites in the province, including the Halifax Citadel and Fortress Louisbourg. There are also many excellent community museums. Check before you go out of your way to visit a museum, as many are only open during the summer season.

If you are coming to Nova Scotia by ferry, you can get your first history hit as soon as you disembark in the old seaport of Yarmouth. Kids love fire trucks. Get their vacation off to a roaring start at the Firefighters' Museum of Nova Scotia. Here, you'll find a rare collection of firefighting memorabilia from the 19th and early 20th centuries, including leather water buckets and antique toy fire engines. While you're in town, the award-winning Yarmouth County Museum is worth a walkabout.

The stories of Nova Scotia's earliest settlers unfold along the Evangeline Trail. Along the Acadian Shore you will witness evidence of the faith, industry and tenacity of Nova Scotia's 17th-century French settlers. Beautiful St. Mary's Church in Church Point/Pointe de l'Eglise is the largest wooden church in North America (56 metres from floor to steeple). The church houses le Musée Ste-Marie, comprised of church artifacts such as vestments, furnishings, documents and photographs. Further along is another large, impressive church — St. Bernard Church — a Gothic structure of granite, with a small museum.

When you arrive at the graceful old town of Annapolis Royal, you can stretch your legs on the earthworks of Fort Anne National Historic Site, which affords great views of the Annapolis Basin. The gunpowder building is the only surviving structure of the first 1708 French fort. The museum in the officers' quarters (circa 1797) presents a chapter in the struggle between France and Britain for supremacy in the New World. An amazing tapestry represents 400 years of the area's history.

Nearby, Port Royal National Historic Site is a reconstruction, based on a detailed drawing by Samuel de Champlain, of Canada's first European colony — a fur-trading post established here in 1605. High wooden walls around the habitation bring to mind the dangers of fierce weather, the intrusion of wildlife and fear of the wilderness. Inside the habitation, costumed interpreters perform the daily chores that made it possible for the French to maintain a European lifestyle.

Also on the Evangeline Trail is the Prescott House Museum, in Starrs Point, home of the Honourable Charles R. Prescott, a Halifax merchant who became a horticulturalist, introducing new varieties of apples to the Annapolis Valley. He helped establish the Fruit Growers Association. The house (circa 1814) is now part of the Nova Scotia Museum. The heritage perennial gardens are delightful.

Past Wolfville is the Grand-Pré National Historic Site, which commemorates the deportation of the Acadians in 1755. The site paints a vivid picture of the lives of the first French settlers around Minas Basin. As a

FIREFIGHTERS
MUSEUM,
YARMOUTH

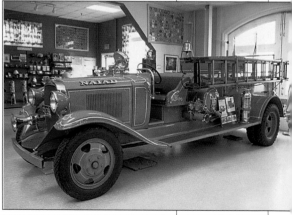

prelude to your visit, you might read Longfellow's epic poem *Evangeline*, or the novel *The Sea is So Wide* by Evelyn Eaton, both fictional stories based on the tragic events of 1755. Acadian families can find their ancestors' names on the lists in the church at Grand Pré.

The town of Windsor claims bragging rights to being the birthplace of Canada's great game on ice. At the Hockey Heritage Centre fans can see wooden pucks, handmade, one-piece hockey sticks and early memorabilia of the game. Also in Windsor are two Nova Scotia Museum sites — the mid-Victorian Haliburton House, former home of Thomas Chandler Haliburton, writer of the famous Sam Slick stories, and the late-Victorian Shand House.

The Glooscap Trail leads you along the Fundy shoreline. Here's history of another, and much older sort — the history of ancient rocks and life forms. Go to the Joggins Fossil Centre for an excellent collection of 300-million-year-old fossils and some explanation of the geological phenomena in this area. Afterwards, take a guided tour of the nearby fossil cliffs.

The Fundy Geological Museum at Parrsboro is a great place to take young dinosaur enthusiasts. There are some Jurassic tales here to tell the kids back home.

Nova Scotia has an extensive shipbuilding heritage. Huge wooden vessels were built on the beaches of this shore. The Age of Sail Heritage Centre at Port Greville highlights the history of lumbering and shipbuilding with artifacts and hands-on exhibits. On the other side of Minas Basin, you can learn more about this important industry at the Lawrence House Museum in Maitland.

AGE OF SAIL HERITAGE CENTRE, PORT GREVILLE

Go deep into a dark coal mine at the Miners' Museum in Springhill. The coal-mining town has seen more than its share of tragedy. Learn about the stories of heroism and survival around the chilling disaster of 1891, the 1916 subterranean fire, the 1956 explosion and the major "bump" in 1958.

There aren't many places where you can still see a huge Scottish granite millstone in action, but at the Balmoral Grist Mill Museum you can watch how it's done and sample toasted oats that have been ground the same way as they were in 1784. Freshly ground flour and baked goods are sold at the museum shop. The idyllic brookside setting is a great location for a picnic.

At Pictou's Hector Heritage Quay, costumed guides and exhibits let you feel the hardships of the 1773 voyage that brought early Scottish settlers to "New Scotland." Step aboard the full-size replica of the ship *Hector* and

FORTRESS OF LOUISBOURG

imagine yourself crossing the Atlantic in the crowded space below decks.

In nearby Stellarton, the Nova Scotia Museum of Industry celebrates 200 years of progress with more than 18,000 artifacts and many interactive exhibits. It is built over the famous Albion mine. The museum helps explain technology and the province's industries, past, present and the future.

Across the Canso Causeway in Cape Breton there are some very fine museums, beginning in Baddeck, with the Alexander Graham Bell National Historic Site. The well-designed museum deserves a half-day visit. It shows the diverse interests and accomplishments of the man behind the telephone, Alexander Graham Bell. Most of Bell's later years were spent in Baddeck, and the museum demonstrates the impressive breadth of his inventiveness, including his method for teaching speech to the deaf, his giant kites, airplanes and hydrofoils. The view of the Bras d'Or Lakes from the museum is breathtakingly beautiful.

At Fortress Louisbourg National Historic Site, you will be transported back to 1744. Dozens of costumed actors portraying townsfolk and soldiers carry on as if the 21st century weren't just beyond the site's walls. The fortress is best experienced over a full day. You can buy a hefty loaf of bread from the baker who assures you that it's the same as the soldiers ate, except for the absence of floor sweepings formerly added to augment the flour. Wet your whistle in a lively tavern, wander through the period homes, watch women at work in the authentic kitchen gardens. Sit up on the ramparts at the back of the fortress and take in the bird's-eye view of the harbour and town, with the children at play and the soldiers doing their drills.

On the other side of the island, the Ceilidh Trail promotes, preserves and presents its music-making heritage at the Celtic Music Interpretive Centre in Judique. Enjoy live music, vintage recorded music and collections of musical family histories. The biggest fiddle in the world makes for a fun photo opportunity.

When you return to the mainland, take the ruggedly beautiful Marine Drive for a very different view of Nova Scotia. Along the way, stop at the Lighthouse Interpretive Centre at Port Bickerton, where the lore of the lighthouse and the lightkeeper is kept alive. The lighthouse gives a great view of the sea and community.

Sherbrooke Village is a must-see. Like Louisbourg, it is a living history museum, depicting rural life in Nova Scotia between 1860 and the First World War. Visit a weaver's cottage, a blacksmith's shop, a doctor's office and the home of an affluent master mariner as they looked 100 years ago.

The Fisherman's Life Museum in Jeddore Oyster Pond is a little gem. An early 1900s inshore fisherman, his wife and his family of nine daughters lived here. Women of the eastern shore tell stories of the family and how they lived, as they bake, tend the garden and preserve its wonderful produce, just as it was done several generations ago. The pump organ in the parlour, the hooked mats and the embroidered samplers all bring the close-knit family into focus.

In Halifax, be sure to visit the Maritime Museum of the Atlantic. Many are unaware of Halifax's close connection to the *Titanic* disaster. It was from Halifax that search and recovery operations were conducted. The museum has the world's largest collection of wooden artifacts from the *Titanic* (sit in a replica deck chair from the *Titanic* for a great souvenir photo). The powerful exhibit, "A Moment in Time," captures the devastation wrought by the Halifax Explosion of 1917. Exhibits on the Age of Sail, shipwrecks and the navy are part of the big picture of a great port city in a maritime province.

Halifax is crowned by the star-shaped Halifax Citadel National Historic Site. The Citadel is surrounded by a dry defensive ditch: don't fall in! But do stand on the earthen ramparts for great views of the city and harbour. Constructed between 1828 and 1856, the Citadel is a fine example of a bastioned fort of the "smooth bore" era. The site's newest exhibit, *Fortress Halifax — Warden of the North*, describes Halifax and its defences. In summer, students portray soldiers of the Royal Artillery and the 78th Highlanders of 1869 and fire the noonday gun. Fun to watch — but cover your ears.

Discover the natural wonders of Nova Scotia at the Museum of Natural History. Get close to models of a life-sized whale, soaring eagles, a moose, a puffin colony and of Canada's oldest dinosaurs. See a busy beehive (located safely behind glass).

Many Canadians have a neighbour who came to Canada as a war bride, or had a great uncle who went off to war, or knows a family who came to Canada as refugees. A gateway to North America for more than a million people, Pier 21 National Historic Site recollects the experiences of many individuals who arrived between 1928 and 1971. The facility houses interactive displays and artifacts, touching first-hand accounts, and exhibits celebrating the ethnic diversity and cultural heritage of Canada.

HALIFAX CITADEL NATIONAL HISTORIC SITE

If you are touring the South Shore, there are a couple of museums you really shouldn't miss. Even if the Lighthouse Route isn't on your agenda, you can make an easy day trip from Halifax to New Ross and the town of Lunenburg a World Heritage Site.

In 1816, William Ross, an army captain, and his wife Mary arrived in Nova Scotia with 172 disbanded soldiers to take up

ROSS FARM
MUSEUM, NEW ROSS

lands granted to them by the Crown. Today, the Ross Farm Living Museum of Agriculture is alive with costumed heritage interpreters who take you back to the early 1800s at a vintage store, the Ross farmhouse, barns and workshops, a village school, a blacksmith's shop and a cooper's shop. The farm is populated with heritage animals — horses, cows, oxen, sheep, pigs and poultry. The baby farm animals are always popular with children. Kids who have never seen a cow up close can try to milk one. Slightly older children (and their grandparents) might enjoy demonstrations of spinning, flax processing, bread making, yarn dying and woodworking.

In Lunenburg, the Fisheries Museum of the Atlantic is one of the Nova Scotia Museum's largest and most popular sites. *Bluenose* buffs will enjoy the exhibit of memorabilia and photos of the famous schooner built here. Old salts will tell you all you want to know about lobster fishing and demonstrate fishing skills. There's an exhibit on Lunenburg's rum-running days and a wonderful aquarium with peep holes at just the right level for pint-sized observers. You can board the schooner *Theresa E. Connor*, and see what the life of a Grand Banks fisherman was like.

If you are carrying on to Yarmouth, stop in at Liverpool. The Sherman Hines Museum of Photography and Galleries is the only museum of photography east of Montreal and contains artifacts dating from the beginnings of photography in the Maritimes, as well as vintage photographs by Karsh, Notman, MacAskill, Hines and others. The Queens County Museum and Perkins House give important insights into colonial life and times.

For nearly 80 years, the Barrington Woolen Mill Museum supplied yarn for fishermen's warm woolies. Its carding machines, spinning mule, loom twister and skeiner remain in their original places. There are also exhibits on raising sheep on the islands offshore and on wool processing, and demonstrations of hand spinning.

Nova Scotians have a right to be proud of the museums in their communities. Large and small, these sites provide entertainment and education to people of all ages. Many of them are run by volunteers and all of them try to give an authentic glimpse into the region's social and natural heritage.

FISHERIES MUSEUM
OF THE ATLANTIC,
LUNENBURG

Art and Crafts

Nikki Mitchell

Chris Colwell Pottery

Nova Scotia is more than seafood, shouts of *"sociables"* in pubs and lively fiddle music. It's fertile ground for some of the country's best visual arts. Canada's ocean playground is home to numerous talented artists, designers and craftspeople.

With the help of the Studio Rally map, these artists and craftspeople can be found in their studios, workshops and sheds. Studio Rally was created by Adriane Abbott and Beverly McClare 11 years ago as a way to stitch together the disparate locations of hidden talents.

Grunt Glass

"Many craftspeople were taking their crafts to Canadian cities and getting a great reputation for being talented craftspeople located in Nova Scotia, but visitors to the province couldn't find us," explains Abbott. "We felt that we should capitalize on the talent that we have here in Nova Scotia."

The land is dotted with hundreds of independent craftspeople and artists. It's a matter of locating their work spaces to get a glimpse and a shopping opportunity. The Studio Rally map leads you to 111 studios that feature diverse creations — traditional landscape paintings, contemporary fashion, funky pottery, hand-blown glass vessels, mailboxes adorned with whimsical barnyard creatures and much more. The free guide illustrates and describes the work of each participating artisan. Choose a region to visit and you'll be sure to find welcoming people who will gladly show you their latest works.

Every year on the first weekend of October (unless it falls on a holiday weekend), all studios on the map throw open their doors to welcome visitors and demonstrate their talents. Most of the studios are open year-round, however, so take a fun Sunday drive off the beaten path to sneak into the artists' world. It's a good idea to call before you stop in, though. The artists' studios often double as their homes, so it's best to catch them when they're not taking the kids to soccer or sorting their laundry.

TANGLED GARDEN

JOY LAKING
WATERCOLOUR

If you are driving the Evangeline Trail into the Annapolis Valley region, go to Grand Pré's Tangled Garden for a visit to the studio, garden and gallery to see Beverly McClare's sculptures of natural materials and George Walford's paintings. While you're there, sample some of the Tangled Garden jams and jellies and then pop out to the garden to appreciate the source of the ingredients! The neighbouring town of Wolfville is home to Frank Hill, a "bodger" — a crafter of Windsor chairs and tables who uses hand tools and techniques. Sara Nadeau's oil paintings depict her love of animals, food and wine, and stretch between realism and symbolism. In Annapolis Royal, the Annapolis Region Community Arts Council operates an artist-run centre and community cultural resource. Artist's talks, workshops and a used bookstore make this a welcome place to stop. At Yarmouth, visit a recently opened branch of the Art Gallery of Nova Scotia.

Along the Glooscap Trail is Raspberry Bay Stone, a perfect summer stop in the community of Bass River. Wander through Heather Lawson's gardens to see the hand-carved stone pieces dotting the grounds. Also located near Bass River is Joy Laking, a watercolour painter and printmaker whose works of villagescapes, interiors, salt marshes and lyrical flower portraits have been exhibited in major public collections. West of Parrsboro, you'll find ArtWare, Krista Wells's collection of colourful polymer clay and mixed media masks, décor, clocks and jewellery, and her line of block prints.

Heading to Lunenburg for the day? En route, stop in

LEATHER WORKER JOHN ROBERTS, INDIAN BROOK

WILLIAM ROACH

Mahone Bay to see Tom Ward's internationally exhibited realist watercolours. The Moorings Gallery & Shop Limited in Mahone Bay features the work of Maritime artists — paintings, jewellery, sculptures, carvings, stained glass and more. When in Lunenburg, visit Nova Terra Cotta Pottery for Joan Bruneau's thrown and altered earthenware of rich surfaces and distinct shapes. Lunenburg's Houston North Gallery celebrates Inuit people and their art, and shows Nova Scotian artists whose work harmonizes with the featured Arctic prints and sculptures. The truly adventurous should press on and head further along the South Shore to Shelburne County's Tudor Tile for Rebecca Tudor's handmade, custom-designed ceramic tiles, which are inspired by the land and seascape surroundings. Have lunch at Charlotte Lane Café & Crafts located in the historic waterfront properties.

The Sunrise Trail leads to the town of Antigonish, which boasts the painting talents of Anna Syperek, Gillian McCulloch and Alice Reed. V. L. MacLean's studio of original hand-pulled prints and paintings is also in the area. The Lyghtesome Gallery is a good place to see the region's talent. The gallery has a long-standing reputation for promoting local artists through its monthly exhibition schedule.

MI'KMAQ
QUILLWORK CRADLE

When travelling Cape Breton's Cabot Trail, stop for a visit at the Ross House Studio, located in a group of historic buildings in Margaree Harbour, where limited edition prints and art of Maritime subjects can be found. Sunset Art Gallery in Cheticamp is the studio of William Roach, a local folk artist — and a real character! He welcomes visitors anytime in the summer, and by appointment in the off-season, to view his spirited painted wood carvings. Take a look at John C. Roberts' leather goods, which range from bags, buckets, belts and bowls to wallets, aprons and dog leashes. The town of Baddeck is another artisan hotspot. Stop in to see Burland Murphy's nature-inspired work in a variety of media, Carol and Gordon Kennedy's Iron Art & Photographs: Working Forge & Gallery and Claire Ryder's sculptures, which are carved into found and fallen wood. If making a visit to Louisbourg, take a side road to Grey Seal

23

ART GALLERY OF NOVA SCOTIA

Weaving Studio in Point Michaud to see a large loom in a small cabin with a great view of the Atlantic.

The Studio Rally map is best suited to those with wheels, since solitude-seeking artists often live on the roads less taken. But for those who are visiting Halifax, all you need is time, a sense of adventure and the wherewithal to walk the hilly city. Painter Justin Augustine's studio is located downtown, where you'll find paintings that depict young blacks transfixed in otherworldly spaces. Elizabeth Goluch's Lizzy Bugs will make friends out of entomophobes. Her studio is filled with metal insects — from sculptures of giant articulated praying mantis to earrings of sterling silver bees.

If you take a stroll along the city's picturesque harbourfront docks, continue walking south to the Pier 21 Arts Annex building. Though not all of the studios are open to the public, Jeffery Cowling Architectural Interior Accessories welcomes visitors to the Arts Annex. Stop in to see his wooden architectural boxes, which are also containers for documents, jewellery and CD collections.

Halifax has several galleries and museums that provide a solid cross-section of local art and crafts. A visit to the Art Gallery of Nova Scotia will give you a feel for the diversity of talent and the work of local folk and contemporary artists. Be sure to stop into the AGNS Gallery Shop to support the gallery and local artists. Studio 21 features the work of local and nationally recognized artists in three galleries within its warehouse space close to the redeveloped Pier 21 area. Zwicker's Gallery, Eastern Canada's oldest commercial art gallery, carries original oil and watercolour paintings, drawings, sculpture and prints by over 80 Maritime and other Canadian artists. The Secord Gallery offers traditional and modern works — paintings, drawings, original prints and photographs. Argyle Fine Art represents regional, national, international, historic and contemporary artists. To get the scoop on emerging artists, go to YHZ Gallery and ViewPoint Gallery, an artist-run co-operative exhibiting fine art

photographers and printmakers.

Just a short drive from Halifax, you'll come upon a cluster of studios along Purcells Cove Road. Joy Pennick's jewellery and metalworks, Mindy Moore's pottery for tea and garden, Kathy Brown's seacoast-inspired watercolours and Sally Ravindra's stoneware and porcelain vessels are all minutes away from one another.

The rich tradition of art and crafts in Nova Scotia is greatly supported by the strength of local organizations, including the Nova Scotia Designer Crafts Council, Visual Arts Nova Scotia, the Nova Scotia Centre for Craft and Design and the Nova Scotia College of Art and Design.

MI'KMAQ BASKET WORK

Adriane Abbott describes the universal Studio Rally experience: "When you visit artists in their environment you have absolutely fantastic experiences with the creators, which enhance your appreciation for something that you otherwise may not have immediately gravitated towards. Or, you'll need to purchase work because you'll want to have something to commemorate the experience — to acquire an authentic souvenir."

For a copy of a Studio Rally map, stop by any tourist information desk in Nova Scotia, call (902) 889-9000 or download a copy of the map at www.studiorally.ca. Call 1-800-565-0000 or visit novascotia.com for information on more artists and craftspeople in Nova Scotia. See the Listings section of this book for the addresses and phone numbers of the artists mentioned above.

SHOW OF HANDS, HALIFAX

THEATRE

LINETTE CHIASSON

ORDER OF GOOD CHEER, PORT ROYAL

The theatre community in Nova Scotia has always been abundant and strong. With more than 30 working venues and a list of companies that grows longer every year, actors, directors and playwrights are flocking to the province, producing works that are commanding international attention.

The first theatrical production in Nova Scotia (and, arguably, in the New World) was a masque devised by Marc Lescarbot, a settler at Port Royal, in 1606. The theatrical tradition of the area is continued to this day at King's Theatre, site of the Annapolis Royal Summer Theatre Festival, held each year in July and August.

SCULPTURE AT NEPTUNE THEATRE

The numerous theatre festivals in Nova Scotia constitute a good reason for a trip just in themselves. Festival Antigonish is a popular event, with attendees from around the globe — a treat for any theatre lover and set in a jewel of a town. The Liverpool International Theatre Festival, held at the Astor Theatre every other May; the Atlantic Theatre Festival in Wolfville, which spans from June to September; and the Chester Theatre Festival at the Chester Playhouse in July and August are all worth checking out. The Internet is an invaluable tool when

planning a festival expedition, with listings and information about plays and show times.

The Halifax Fringe Festival is an excellent opportunity to see some new and innovative pieces. Because the fringe festival draws from local, national and international companies, it provides a diverse range of styles. It also gives a rare opportunity for up-and-coming artists from the area (and smaller established companies) to showcase their work. Fringe prices are so reasonable it's well worth seeing half a dozen performances.

The recently renovated Neptune Theatre started life in 1915 as the Strand Theatre vaudeville house, but since 1963 the company has been producing shows almost year-round. The Fountain Hall main stage is a grand space with beautiful acoustics, while the smaller DuMaurier studio provides a more intimate setting. With the addition of the DuMaurier studio series, the Neptune season offers a fine mix of old and new works with an emphasis on Canadian content. Ticket prices are available on the theatre's website, but if you're not able to book ahead, a limited number of rush tickets are sold a half hour before most performances for about half price. Both of the Neptune venues also serve as host theatres for touring productions and smaller companies, so it's worth calling the box office ahead of time to find out what's happening when you're going to be in town.

While in the metro area, there are a host of other companies and venues to see — most notably Shakespeare by the Sea, set against the natural beauty and fantastic forts and ruins around Point Pleasant Park. The company's season is in the summer only, and audience sizes can be limited, so call well in advance for

NEPTUNE THEATRE

SHAKESPEARE BY THE SEA

information and reservations. Year-round, check out Dartmouth-based Eastern Front Theatre located at Alderney Landing, a fun few minutes on the ferry from downtown Halifax. This is the area's only professional company whose mandate places emphasis on producing plays of regional provenance and social relevance. It's a short walk from here to Crichton Avenue where the Dartmouth Players, an amateur company which attracts some fine local talent and provide solid entertainment. The Theatre Arts Guild is a Halifax institution and has been presenting good entertainment to theatre-goers at its Pond Playhouse for many years.

Keep your eyes peeled, and peruse *The Coast* (a free Halifax weekly) for complete entertainment listings, as there are many smaller companies in the metro area that produce shows on a less regular schedule. Names to watch for include the Irondale Ensemble (alternative), Jest in Time, Zuppa Circus, Bunnies in the Headlights, Exodus Theatre (historical drama) and Two Planks and a Passion (a touring company dedicated to bringing theatre to the masses). Daltheatre, the Dalhousie University theatre department, runs an interesting season from the Sir James Dunn Theatre in the Dalhousie Arts Centre — also the home of the Rebecca Cohn auditorium. Year-round fun can be found at Halifax's two most popular dinner theatres — Historic Feast Dinner Theatre and Grafton Street Dinner Theatre, both within the downtown core. Don't forget to make reservations. Keep an eye on Theatre Nova Scotia's website at www.theatrens.ca for frequently updated information about productions in Halifax and across the province.

For a true taste of Nova Scotia culture and history, don't miss the summer performances of *Évangéline* at Université Ste-Anne. This musical is based on Longfellow's famous poem, with shows in Acadian French and English. The story is so familiar and the staging so evocative that this piece is really best experienced in its original tongue. If you don't have much French but can't make an English show, simultaneous translation headsets are available for a small additional fee.

NEPTUNE THEATRE

Mermaid Theatre, an internationally acclaimed touring puppet theatre based in Windsor, is targeted for children, but is equally magical for adults. It's well worth a trip from anywhere in the province.

If your taste runs to unusual venues, you shouldn't miss the Ship's Company Theatre in Parrsboro. The theatre is housed

in a converted car ferry, the MV *Kipawo*, and the performances are just as innovative. For more historic savour, there's the Savoy Theatre in Glace Bay, built in the 1920s in the manner of a Victorian show house. Although extensively renovated in the 70s, the theatre maintains all of its original period charm. It hosts a wide range of touring performances and cultural activities, including the original Cape Breton Summertime Review, with comedy and music blended in perfect proportion. The Savoy is developing its own in-house theatre company, which should be up and running soon.

With so much to choose from, theatre aficionados will have no difficulty finding exciting productions across the province. The key is to keep abreast of the many new companies, productions and venues popping up all the time. Check websites, ask at your place of accommodation, and pay attention to signs and posters. For more information on how to contact the companies mentioned here (and others), see the Listings section of this book.

SHIP'S COMPANY THEATRE, PARRSBORO

MUSIC

ANTHONY RING

Nova Scotia is alive with the sound of music. The province for all seasons is also the province for all sounds. From pop music to Celtic swing, down-home bluegrass to hard-core jazz — touring Nova Scotia can be an eclectic symphony of sounds.

One of the headliners in this soundscape is Symphony Nova Scotia — the only professional full-time orchestra east of Quebec City — which presents an exciting repertoire mixing classical with contemporary music. The orchestra's season runs from mid-September to early May. Symphony musicians can be heard throughout the year in several smaller ensembles which perform at venues all over the province. The Rhapsody Quintet plays a Palm Court repertoire and the Blue Engine String Quartet features women composers and innovative arrangements, including Leonard Cohen songs. SuddenlyLISTEN plays improvisational music led by the symphony's principal cellist. Under the direction of Maestro Bernhard Gueller, Symphony Nova Scotia's programming reaches beyond the core repertoire to include local artists such as John Gracie, Lennie Gallant and Rita MacNeil. Much of the credit for the creative partnerships with Maritime musicians goes to local conductor/arranger Scott Macmillan, who has worked with the orchestra for almost two decades. His highly acclaimed Celtic Mass for the Sea and MacKinnon's Brook Suite have been featured nationally on CBC and sold throughout the world. The orchestra's website is www.symphonynovascotia.ca.

Complementing the orchestra's program, in late May

and early June the Scotia Festival of Music launches a world-class chamber music series in Halifax with artists of exceptionally high calibre. The two-week festival presents excellent concerts and an opportunity for Nova Scotian musicians to participate in master classes. The festival also features an artist-in-residence program that has brought in such prestigious talent as the Prazak Quartet and Philip Glass.

For 10 months of the year the St. Cecilia Concert Series (www.stcecilia.ca) brings a very wide range of performers to Nova Scotia audiences at a number of venues in the Halifax region. The series features diverse talents — from the internationally-acclaimed Vancouver Chamber Choir, the classical Chinese *erhu* of George Gao, to local amateur instrumentalists. During the summer months, visitors will be delighted to find Music at the Three Churches in Mahone Bay, Musique Saint Bernard on the Acadian Shore and Musique Royale at various historic venues around the province. These classical concert series engage musicians from across Canada.

Each area of Nova Scotia offers its own musical pedigree: in Cape Breton, the fiddle shares the stage with Celtic singers; in southwest Nova Scotia, Acadian musicians blend Louisiana cajun, modern folk and fiddle tunes for a distinctive and lively sound. Each community has its own stellar entertainers: for example, fiddler Buddy MacMaster is king of the Ceilidh Trail, and from the French-speaking communities in the district of Clare comes the celebrated group Blou.

Community dances are popular all over Nova Scotia, but few can compare with the Mabou Family Square Dance. A tradition for more than 20 years, this community ceilidh is a weekly event all year round. The musicians range from stars such as Natalie MacMaster to gifted youngsters who are itching to get in the spotlight. People at all levels of dancing ability are welcome to participate. You can learn the steps from seasoned regulars.

Communities such as Italy Cross in the Bridgewater area have found their own way to bring Canadian talent to their villages. Seaside Folk, a non-profit organization of music fans, hosts monthly concerts at the Italy Cross fire

THE RHAPSODY QUINTET

GROU TYME FESTIVAL, HALIFAX

hall featuring performers as diverse as Scotland's Battlefield Band to local favourites such as Ian Janes.

In late May, the Apple Blossom Festival in the Annapolis Valley, an annual event since 1933, mixes pageantry with music. Well-known Canadian music performers, including the Bare Naked Ladies and Atlantic Canada's Great Big Sea, have appeared on stage at the festival.

All the pomp and circumstance of the province's rich military history comes alive at Halifax's Metro Centre the last week in June, with the Nova Scotia International Tattoo. Nova Scotia's spine-tingling massed pipes and drums share the floor with the best international military bands at one of the world's most prestigious musical events.

On Cape Breton Island, the tempo picks up in June, especially in Port Hawkesbury. With a weekly ceilidh at the Creamery (Tuesdays, mid-June to first of October) and free Granville on the Green concerts (Sundays, July and August), the port town is making a strong case as the musical capital of the Island. Each of these events hosts some of the region's best songwriters and musicians.

Bluegrass is blooming in Nova Scotia. Communities like Bridgewater, Avon Valley and Stewiacke have built amazing concerts and camping festivals spotlighting the

LUNENBURG FOLK HARBOUR FESTIVAL

unique down-home sounds of this provincial treat. In summer, concerts are advertised in the local newspapers, tourist bureaus and on community cable channels.

One of the best places to enjoy the music scene is in downtown Halifax. *The Coast,* a weekly newspaper found all over the city, gives details on the what and where of live music, be it pop, jazz, fusion, hard-core rock or anything in between. The Marquee Club on Gottingen Street has built a reputation as one of the best clubs in eastern Canada, featuring such acts as Joel Plaskett and Blue Rodeo. Halifax also hosts the best pub scene in Canada. Mainstays such as the Lower Deck and Peddler's Pub hold Sociables on Saturday nights with groups like McGinty and Barnacle.

FIDDLER ASHLEY MACISSAC

The Atlantic Jazz Festival, which takes place in early July, is the place to see solo artists and ensembles from Canada and the international scene. In addition to free jazz during the day on Spring Garden Road, the festival hosts events in many different venues, including the Casino and Hell's Kitchen.

Another banner event is held in the town of Canso on Marine Drive, a three to four-hour drive from Halifax. The Stan Rogers Folk Festival, named for one of the country's best-loved folk musicians, can lay claim to being one of Canada's best folk festivals. Every year many artists drive to this east coast port to entertain a large crowd of folk lovers.

Nova Scotia has a rich history of community spirit and entrepreneurism. Two music festivals in August exemplify these characteristics: the Lunenburg Folk Harbour Festival and the New Glasgow Jubilee both show what small communities can do. Lunenburg hosts folk musicians from various parts of the world in a fishing town steeped in history. The Jubilee, set against the backdrop of the beautiful New Glasgow riverfront, offers the best in East Coast and Canadian talent ranging from pop to Celtic.

The festival season draws to a close in October with the internationally acclaimed Celtic Colours International Festival in Cape Breton. The traditional Celtic program draws enthusiastic crowds to listen to the likes of Slainte Mhath and Rita MacNeil. A musical gem, Celtic Colours shines amidst the jewel tones of Cape Breton Island in its autumn splendour.

Music has always been an important part of the Nova Scotian way of life and Nova Scotia has made important contributions to world music, including opera singer Portia White and Springhill's star Anne Murray. Performers always find a warm reception in the province, and formal concerts, outdoor festivals and ceilidhs are enthusiastically attended by people of all ages.

For details about music festivals and events call 1-800-565-000 or ask at a local visitor information centre.

DINING

BY ELAINE ELLIOT

With an abundant supply of local fresh fruit, produce and seafood, Nova Scotia's chefs are waiting to treat you to memorable dining experiences. While it is true that we have restaurants and fast food eateries with names familiar to anyone living in North America, I invite you to choose local, one-of-a-kind establishments and savour our regional cuisine.

Seafood is our forté. Seventy percent of our visitors order seafood, and the menus around the province offer a generous selection. Atlantic lobster, the king of the crustacean family, is very popular. Dining on lobster should be a casual affair. It is, after all, a hands-on experience. Choose a table overlooking the sparkling Atlantic waters at the Quarterdeck Grill at Summerville Beach or visit the Lobster Pound and Restaurant at Halls Harbour on the Bay of Fundy. At the Pound, meals are served outdoors, picnic style, overlooking the ever-changing tides in this picturesque village. Throughout the province, locals celebrate the advent of lobster seasons with church or community suppers. A visit to any tourist information centre

HADDON HALL, CHESTER

should provide details of times and places. For the faint of heart who cannot bear to tackle the whole lobster, choose a lobster roll — a soft bun stuffed with lobster meat, a feature on menus throughout the province.

World-renowned Digby scallops, North Atlantic crab, farm-raised Atlantic salmon and blue mussels, haddock, halibut and swordfish are but a few of our other seafood dining options. Succulent scallops are featured on most menus, and while some may be content with the simple sautéed version, look for innovative adaptations of this delicious bivalve. Swiss born chef Alex Jurt of Restaurant Le Caveau at Domaine de Grand Pré Winery prepares his scallops in a subtle curry sauce, while at Dartmouth's La Perla Restaurant, chef James MacDougall serves his scallops with an Italian flair. Cultivated mussels are large and tender, and are served steamed in the shell or in chowders.

BLUENOSE LODGE, LUNENBURG

Be sure to sample planked salmon, a specialty at Liscombe Lodge on the province's eastern shore. There, diners are invited to watch each evening as the chef arranges the hot embers, bastes his fish with butter, and turns the planks to ensure an evenly cooked fish. Cedar-planked salmon is not to be confused with "cold smoked" salmon, a delicacy known around the world as Nova Scotia smoked salmon, used mainly in appetizers or perhaps in a pasta sauce. Smokehouses are scattered along the province's shores and many, such as Willy Krauch's Danish Smokehouse at Tangier or St. Marys River Smokehouse at Sherbrooke welcome visitors and ship worldwide.

Halifax and Dartmouth offer the most diversified food experiences in the province. Here, you will find intimate restaurants tucked in 19th-century buildings competing with upscale dining rooms, and most are a short walk from

BELOW: RESTAURANT LE CAVEAU AT DOMAINE GRAND PRÉ

downtown hotels. Sample Canadian cuisine at Chives Bistro or Maple; visit any of the various ethnic restaurants for Indian, northern Italian, Hungarian, Korean, Japanese and Greek fare. Several restaurants such as the Cheapside Café at the Art Gallery of Nova Scotia, Sweet Basil Bistro or the Economy Shoe Shop offer fashionable lighter dishes, such as vegetarian, pasta and stir-fry combinations.

As you enjoy the spectacular scenery of the South Shore, be sure to sample its regional cuisine. Chunky chowders from Mahone Bay's Innlet Café, succulent rack of lamb from Lunenburg's Lion Inn or a seasonal fruit dessert at Charlotte Lane Café in Shelburne — whatever you choose, you can be assured of excellence. Meander through the Annapolis Valley and savour seasonal fruits and vegetables. Vine-ripened strawberries become delightful desserts at Wolfville's Blomidon Inn, while blueberries are incorporated into dressings, sauces and desserts at Between the Bushes, a neat little café located, aptly, between the bushes at a commercial blueberry farm. Be sure to try a slice of pie made with early Gravensteins or an apple crisp prepared from freshly picked MacIntosh apples. And for a truly Acadian experience, visit Café Christofe at Grosses Coques, where chef Paul Comeau will introduce you to fricot, fish cakes and rappie pie.

No holiday to Nova Scotia is complete without a visit to Cape Breton Island, and you should plan on spending at least three or four days enjoying the magnificent scenery and sampling the distinctively Scottish fare. Look for porridge or bannock breads, surprisingly tasteful presentations of root vegetables and local lamb. Gowrie

JOST VINEYARDS,
MALAGASH

CHEAPSIDE CAFÉ,
HALIFAX

House Country Inn in Sydney Mines and Duncreigan Country Inn in Mabou both offer exquisite fine dining. Duncreigan's companion establishment, the Mull Café and Deli, is an ideal choice for family dining.

Fine dining is never complete without a glass of wine. Ask the restaurateurs to suggest a local wine, from Jost Vineyards in Malagash, Grand Pré Winery near Wolfville or Sainte Famille Wines, in the Windsor area. Enjoy a fruity dessert wine from Lunenburg County Winery, Newburne, or Telder Berry Winery of Nine Mile River. Visit a brew-pub that crafts its own beers such as Rosie's in Kentville and Wolfville, Granite Brewery in Halifax, or sample Stutz Cider from Grand Pré Winery.

Advanced planning is the key to a good vacation. If travelling with children, look for establishments offering services and menus adapted to little ones. The Old Orchard Inn in Greenwich, Oak Island Resort at the Western Shore and Inverary Resort in Baddeck are ideal family destinations. Call before you begin a foray into the countryside as many rural inns and restaurants are seasonal, operating from early May through October. A few offer limited public dining, others have one seating; some do not serve liquor. Consider your expectations, check menus on web pages or ask your innkeeper to recommend regional dining specialties. Reservations for peak travel times, such as July and the height of fall foliage viewing, are strongly suggested.

GOWRIE HOUSE COUNTRY INN

Fairs, Festivals and Events

Alan Lynch

Dragon boat Festival

Nova Scotia is Canada's party province. It's been a party place since Samuel de Champlain launched a dining club, the Order of Good Cheer, as a way to break up the winter boredom of 1605. Champlain's idea set the tone for Nova Scotia's passion for fairs, festivals and food. Nova Scotians use any excuse to eat, drink and be merry.

As if to prove the gregarious nature of Nova Scotians, the province's calendar is crammed with over 700 fairs, festivals and special days. Many festivals are inspired by the bountiful fruits of Nova Scotia's fertile land and generous sea. There's the Apple Blossom Festival in the Annapolis Valley held in late May; maple syrup festivals in Dean and Maplewood in early spring, and wine festivals in Falmouth, Lunenburg and Malagash in early fall. There are a staggering number of strawberry socials, lobster suppers, chowder festivals, and bean and sausage or ham and scalloped potato dinners. These events are fantastic bargains for residents and visitors alike, with plates stacked high by cooks used to feeding farm hands and fishermen.

Agricultural exhibitions take place throughout the summer. Three of the largest are the South Shore Exhibition (late July to early August), the Nova Scotia Provincial Exhibition at Bible Hill (late August) and Nova Scotia's oldest, the Hants County Exhibition in Windsor (mid-September). These exhibitions have all the traditional elements: fruit, vegetable and flower competitions, quilt shows and livestock displays. The ox-pulls are the main attraction at the "Big Ex" in Bridgewater. Teams of these impressive beasts pull three times their weight. The Maritime Fall Fair is held in October just outside Halifax, where small children love to pet young farm animals and the horse jumping events are always popular.

The fishery is the focus for many other community events across the province. There's the Pictou Lobster Carnival in mid-July, Digby Scallop Days, the Economy Clam Festival and the Louisbourg Crab Festival in August. In mid-August, Lunenburg hosts the Nova Scotia Fisheries Exhibition and Fishermen's Reunion. A number of fishermen's competitions take place at these festivals, including net mending, fish filleting, scallop shucking and the hotly contested dory races.

OX-PULL, SOUTH SHORE EXHIBITION

When Nova Scotians do move away from the table, they celebrate with some blockbuster events. The Nova Scotia International Tattoo is a musical extravaganza held at Halifax's Metro Centre in late June to early July. It is the largest military tattoo in North America, with over 2,000 performers. The Atlantic Jazz Festival in late July draws crowds to the downtown area. For 10 days in early August, Halifax hosts the International Buskers' Festival, which showcases 50 street performers from around the world. The buskers are a favourite with children. The Mahone Bay Wooden Boat Festival (end of July) has a parade, music, seafood and boat-building demonstrations on the water's edge. The highlight of the three-day event is the "Fast and Furious" competition in which teams build and then race unique wooden boats, often with hilarious results. The Lunenburg Folk Harbour Festival is four days of international folk music in the historic surroundings of this world heritage town. At the Clam Harbour Beach Sandcastle Contest, fantastical sand sculptures crowd out plain sandcastles.

NOVA SCOTIA TATTOO PARADE

Some of Cape Breton Island's stunning celebrations include the Fête de Saint Louis — a baroque-styled celebration at the Fortress Louisbourg that ends with an antique fireworks display that recreates the great siege of the fortress, and the Celtic Colours International Festival, a week-long celebration of Celtic music, with over 300 concerts held across the Island. During the summer months, watch for smaller musical surprises like the regularly scheduled ceilidhs held Tuesdays in Mabou and Wednesdays in Judique. Ceilidhs are impromptu musical evenings of toe-tappin' wild fiddles, throbbing bodhrans (flat Irish hand drums) and plaintive bagpipes, mixed with step dancing and singers.

Nova Scotians also celebrate the diverse cultures that make up the population of the province. Mi'kmaq traditions are demonstrated at the Millbrook First Nations Powwow in August. Black Loyalists are remembered in January in Amherst. Haligonians eagerly anticipate the Greek Festival in early June, which kicks off a summer season of feasting and festivity. The Multicultural Festival on the Dartmouth waterfront in mid-July is an opportunity to hear world music while munching your way through a global food court. There's a Polish festival in Sydney. There are a dozen special events celebrating our Acadian heritage and population, such as Musique de la Baie, a summer-long music festival throughout the District of Clare, Journées Acadienne de Grand Pré (a music and

GROU TYME FESTIVAL, HALIFAX

APPLE BLOSSOMS

cultural fair), Fête National des Acadiens in St. Bernard, Festival de l'Escaouette in Cheticamp and the Grou Tyme Acadian Festival in Halifax (more music and food). One of the biggest, the Festival Acadien de Clare, includes games, traditional dances, an ox-haul, fishing tournament and many other community-based activities that last a whole week in early July.

The culture of one of the largest groups of settlers, the Scots, takes over a number of open spaces in summer to hold highland games, where you'll see traditional heavy events such as the caber toss, when a telephone-pole-sized log is tossed end-over-end. These games also include traditional dancing and pipers. So, if you can't live without a touch of the tartan, look for the Gathering of the Clans in Pugwash (Canada Day), Festival of the Tartans in New Glasgow (July), the Inverness Gathering (July), Clan Celebrations at the Highland Village in Iona (late July to early August) and the Halifax Highland Games and Scottish Festival (July). The Antigonish Highland Games, the oldest (since 1861) and largest highland games held outside Scotland, are the best bet. Each August, the Gaelic College of Celtic Arts and Crafts at South Gut, St. Anns, in Cape Breton, holds the Gaelic Mod, a weekend of Gaelic language and song.

CABER TOSS, ANTIGONISH HIGHLAND GAMES

Watch for numerous other celebrations and fairs based on Nova Scotia's traditional music, culture, crafts and culinary specialties, as well as its natural history. There's also a wealth of music, theatre, dance and visual arts festivals — and many others that are just an excuse to have fun. It's been 400 years since explorer Samuel de Champlain founded the Order of Good Cheer and Nova Scotians are still partying, proving that having fun never goes out of fashion.

INTERNATIONAL BUSKER FESTIVAL, HALIFAX

For specific times and information about these fairs and festivals, and for a full list of all 700 events held annually consult the *Nova Scotia Doers' and Dreamers' Guide*, visit www.novascotia.com/whattodo or call 1-800-565-0000. You can also pick up a copy of the *Nova Scotia Festival and Events Digest* at a visitor information centre.

GOLF

ELEANOR ANDERSON

HIGHLAND LINKS, INGONISH

With just the right mix of classic and contemporary designs, breathtaking scenery, warm hospitality and affordable golf, Nova Scotia is your perfect choice for a golf vacation.

Rolling landscapes and seaside vistas are a highlight of the more than 60 golf courses found throughout Nova Scotia. Most courses offer the challenging game that golf enthusiasts are seeking yet provide layouts that can appeal to the novice golfer. The golf season typically runs from May through to October, with an average of 5 to 10 inclement days per season. The *Nova Scotia Golf Travel Guide* identifies the golf courses that welcome green-fee play. Pick up a copy at visitor information centres and travel information kiosks throughout the province. Approximate fees range between $13 and $35 for 9 holes and from $29 to $125 for 18 holes.

Golf courses throughout the province are easily found by following the blue highway signs bearing a golfer symbol. Peak season times (July and August) should be booked well in advance to avoid disappointment. Optimal tee times are before 10 am, with weekends busier than the weekdays. On Monday to Thursday afternoons most courses have tee times available on shorter notice.

Whether it is a tee time you require or you need to rent clubs, or if it's golf clinics and lessons you seek, you will be surprised at the range of services offered at most clubs. Well-appointed pro shops are the norm across the province: they can meet your immediate requirements and provide you with great souvenirs.

Many accommodation operators, both large and small, across Nova Scotia offer golf as part of their accommodation packages. They will often arrange tee times and include some meals. Each package has varying

NORTHUMBERLAND LINKS, NEAR PUGWASH

characteristics and should be clarified upon booking. Keltic Lodge is located next door to the Highlands Links and offers "Drive and Dream" golf packages, which include one-night resort accommodation, breakfast, one round of golf and an electric cart for under $140 per person. Rates are subject to change and are higher in peak season.

Additional golf packages are offered through experienced accommodation operators such as White Point, The Pines Resort and Cape Breton Resorts, whose "Ultimate Golf Package" includes three nights accommodation in properties across Cape Breton Island and a round at each of the Fabulous Foursome golf courses — all for under $400. The annually produced golf travel guide provides a list of numerous golf/accommodation packages.

Some travel and tour agents offer fly-drive packages from Toronto, Montreal and most other major centres in North America. These include Maxxim Vacations at www.maxximvacations.com and Golf Can at www.golfcan.net.

Golf in Nova Scotia can be challenging, with courses cut from unforgettable landscapes; most are built with a view of one of the world's greatest water hazards, the Atlantic Ocean. Golfers of all skill levels will enjoy a diversity of courses from the classic Stanley Thompson-designed Highlands Links to the gem of southern Nova

Scotia — The Pines Resort Golf Course. Highlands Links, dramatically cut from the highlands of Cape Breton, is ranked the 69th best golf course in the

TOP: BELL BAY
ABOVE: CHESTER
GOLF COURSE

world by *GOLF Magazine*, and ranked the number one public course by *SCOREGolf* magazine. It's well worth driving the meandering but modern highway up Smokey Mountain, each kilometre adding to your anticipation as you get closer to this true links course. Framed by the rugged Atlantic coastline and the mountainous contours of the Cape Breton Highlands, the brilliance of Stanley Thompson's design invites all to experience and enjoy his legacy. At the other end of the province is The Pines, carved out of a superb setting through an evergreen forest. Many professional golfers consider this to be one of the most challenging and picturesque golf courses in the country.

OSPREY RIDGE

Golf in this vibrant seaside province has advanced in

recent years with the opening of other championship layouts, such as the impeccable Glen Arbour Golf Club, located just outside of Halifax, and Baddeck's Bell Bay Golf Club, which *SCOREGolf* ranked the number one most underrated golf course in Canada

in 2002.

The Pines, Highlands Links, Bell Bay and Glen Arbour are the more familiar names to visiting golfers. However, there are many other must-play experiences. These include the Graham Cook-designed Osprey Ridge 18-hole golf club, which offers a blend of links and parkland golf as well as outstanding panoramic vistas from many of the tees, and Granite Springs — just 25 minutes from Halifax on the way to Peggys Cove (Route 333). This memorable course features granite outcroppings, which make for an interesting and sometimes challenging round. Continue on to Peggys Cove, perhaps the most photographed harbour in the world, and a must on any visitor's itinerary.

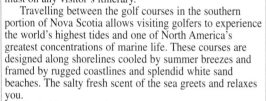

GLEN ARBOUR

Travelling between the golf courses in the southern portion of Nova Scotia allows visiting golfers to experience the world's highest tides and one of North America's greatest concentrations of marine life. These courses are designed along shorelines cooled by summer breezes and framed by rugged coastlines and splendid white sand beaches. The salty fresh scent of the sea greets and relaxes you.

Nestled in the Acadian community of Clare, the Clare Golf & Country Club welcomes visitors with its charming rustic clubhouse and a truly challenging layout for golfers of all abilities. For a completely different golf experience, visit the delightful nine-hole facility at White Point, a golf club and cozy resort complete with sandy beaches, gourmet dining room, tennis courts and high-quality accommodations. Other South Shore golf courses to include on your itinerary are the historic Chester and River Hills in Shelburne.

The entertainment capital of the province, Halifax offers gourmet dining, endless shopping and nightlife galore. Lucky for you that Nova Scotia's capital city has wonderful golf as well. New and enhanced courses around which to plan your golf vacation include Glen Arbour (ranked number 64 in Canada by *SCOREGolf*), which is challenging yet rewarding regardless of your skill level, and Granite Springs. Closer to Dartmouth, the Links at Montague offers an executive nine-hole experience that should not be missed. This course is the designated national training centre for Atlantic Canada by the Royal Canadian Golf Association and has an "old

DUNDEE RESORT AND GOLF CLUB

world" flavour and ambience with its old restored rock fences and classically designed clubhouse.

A burgeoning golf cluster is being nurtured in the centre of the province. Less than an hour's drive from Halifax, Truro is a bustling urban centre with shopping, restaurants, festivals and, of course, lots of great golf to choose from. Whether you book your tee time with the oldest course in the province, the Truro Golf Club, located most appropriately on Golf Street close to downtown, or venture to the surrounding areas and visit Mountain Golf Club, or the delightful nine-hole offerings at Greenfield or River Run, you will not be disappointed. The central location and hospitality to be found will make you glad you came—and brought your clubs!

Touring the scenic shores of Northumberland Strait, you will come upon the oceanside Northumberland Links. This Scottish links-style course offers spectacular seascapes and a view of all three Maritime provinces.

As you travel further north in Nova Scotia, the landscape becomes more rugged and a mystical island awaits. On Cape Breton Island there are three things you will always remember — the majesty of the land, the friendliness of its people and the great golf. Nova Scotia's masterpiece is home to a masterpiece in golf… Cape Breton Island's Fabulous Foursome. The fall is a great time to experience some of the finest golf and scenery Atlantic Canada has to offer. Panoramic landscapes painted in spectacular autumn colours surround the Bell Bay Golf Club, Dundee Resort & Golf Club, Le Portage Golf Club and Highlands Links. Ranked the 29th best golf destination in the world by *Golf Digest*, there are opportunities for a memorable round for both novice and championship players alike. Most accommodation providers offer room and green-fee rates and make these arrangements on behalf of their visitors. Individually, these courses offer challenging and unique golfing experiences, and collectively, they make up the ultimate golfing destination.

In Nova Scotia, you are never more than a one-and-a-half- to two-hour driving distance between golf courses. The pristine natural beauty found across the province is simply not to be missed. From the Bay of Fundy to the majesty of the Cape Breton Highlands, the viewscapes are unspoiled and unmatched. Nature is treasured in Nova Scotia, as evidenced by Highlands Links being the first course in Atlantic Canada to hold the designation of "Certified Audubon Cooperative Sanctuary."

Golf in Nova Scotia includes excellent nine-hole facilities that attract golfers and families to value-priced, well-groomed fairways. Putting greens and driving ranges are common and easy to locate. The selection of nine-hole courses offering great, and affordable, play includes Sackville Golf Course just outside Halifax and Truro's Greenfield, plus many more throughout the province. This may be just what the visiting golfer is looking for.

While in Nova Scotia, not only can you experience some of the best golf in North America but you can do so while enjoying lobsters fresh from the sea and boiled to perfection, delicious sweet treats of home-grown blueberries and strawberries, and of course, an ale or two.

Do you still ask, "Why is Nova Scotia such a great place to golf?" The quantity, quality and diversity of the golf courses coupled with the endless options for touring, tasting and immersing oneself in the past and present make a Nova Scotia golf vacation a perfect choice.

The *Nova Scotia Golf Travel Guide* contains course profiles and information such as yardage/slope, hours of operation, practice greens, teaching pros, pull or electric carts, food and beverage services, rates and contact information. For a free copy of the guide or more information on golf in Nova Scotia, visit www.golfnovascotia.com or www.golfcapebreton.com. For golf and accommodation packages in Nova Scotia, contact 1-800-565-0000 or visit www.novascotia.com.

CYCLING

DALE DUNLOP

APPROACHING FRENCH MOUNTAIN, CABOT TRAIL

Nova Scotia has been a popular destination for cyclists and cycling tours for many years. Although most of the touring is on roadsides rather than specially constructed bicycle paths, there is no problem finding paved byways in scenic areas that see a minimum of auto traffic. Nova Scotia motorists are generally polite and mindful of cyclists. Nova Scotia's temperate climate makes for pleasant cycling six months of the year. When it does get particularly hot, choosing a route that skirts the ocean usually ensures that you'll get a cooling onshore breeze.

When considering where to cycle, any one of the

province's designated scenic routes is a good place to start. The Lighthouse Route along the South Shore is popular because it follows the coast very closely and has many interesting historic towns such as Chester, Mahone Bay and Lunenburg at which to spend the night. The portion of the Evangeline Trail that traverses the Annapolis Valley is equally popular for its gentle pastoral landscape, fine inns and fine dining. Those looking for a challenge should consider the Cabot Trail, which is strenuous, but rewards strong legs and lungs with spectacular seascapes and highland

TOURING GROUP WITH *BLUENOSE II*, LUNENBURG

valleys. The loop around the main island of Isle Madame, also on Cape Breton Island, provides a complete contrast of gentle cycling and captivating scenery. For a real off-the-beaten-path cycling experience, Marine Drive follows the twisting and rolling route along the coast from Halifax to Cape Breton Island, passing through some of the most remote and well-preserved fishing villages in all of Canada. Stop at any harbour along the way — Ship Harbour, Spry Harbour, Sheet Harbour, Isaacs Harbour — for a glimpse into the past and a good night's rest.

Those who prefer to do their cycling in day trips from a central base have two outstanding choices in Nova Scotia. Lunenburg, a UNESCO World Heritage Site, offers not only a great base to come home to each night, but an amazing number of interesting coastal peninsulas to explore on day trips. For over a hundred years, the Blue Rocks peninsula has been a favourite with artists and photographers who delight in its tiny colourful fishing shacks which sit upon the unusual blue polished slate shoreline. In contrast, First Peninsula and Second Peninsula are more pastoral, with tranquil coves in a time-forgotten setting. The Lunenburg Bike Barn on Blue Rocks Road offers a variety of rentals and plenty of suggestions for day trips in the area.

Many paved roads radiate out through the countryside from the college town of Wolfville, making it an equally popular choice as a base. In late spring, the apple blossoms are in full bloom and a trip through the rolling hills of the Gaspereau Valley, just outside of town, will provide a memorable day's outing. Those up for a more strenuous day should consider climbing North Mountain to the look-off for amazing views of the Minas Basin and the patchwork quilt of fields and orchards far below. From here, continue to Scots Bay, with its agate-strewn beach and the entrance to the hiking trail at Cape Split. After descending the mountain, return via the series of roads that follow the red sandstone shoreline back to Wolfville.

For more information on Nova Scotia cycling, check out Bicycle Nova Scotia on the web at www.bicycle.ns.ca or pick up a copy of *Nova Scotia by Bicycle* by Walton Watt. Those interested in taking a cycling tour of Nova Scotia with a Nova Scotia-based company should consider Freewheeling Adventures at www.freewheeling.ca, which has been building a solid reputation for many years. Should it be necessary to have your bike serviced, there are repair shops in almost all localities. An up-to-date listing can be found under the Atlantic Canada Cycling directory at www.atl-canadacycling.com. To find out about the many top-quality bicycle rentals throughout the province, see the Equipment Rentals section of *Nova Scotia Doers' and Dreamers' Guide* .

BOTTOM: TOURING CYCLISTS AT MAHONE BAY

HIKING

DALE DUNLOP

Nova Scotia, with its many distinct geographic regions in a compact area, offers a wide variety of hiking trails that should appeal to hikers of all skill levels and experience. Over the past decade, the number of kilometres of trails has increased dramatically, particularly with the opening of large portions of the TransCanada Trail. Hiking as a recreational pastime is exceeded perhaps only by sea kayaking as a sector of rapid growth in Nova Scotia's tourist industry.

With over 7,000 kilometres of coastline hikes — whether over the rugged granite outcrops on the Atlantic, atop the heights of highland Cape Breton or at the base of the fantastic seascapes of the Fundy coast — are extremely popular.

On the eastern shore's Marine Drive, head for Taylor Head Provincial Park where a series of trails lead out to a rugged, windswept headland overlooking the clear, cold waters of the Atlantic. On the South Shore, do not miss St. Catherines River Beach at Kejimkujik Seaside Adjunct. This trail crosses a coastal barren to arrive at a spectacular white sand beach where seals and seabirds frolic just offshore. On the Fundy Shore, there are a number of great hiking sites, including the recently opened Cape Chignecto Provincial Park in one of the most remote areas of the province. This park features strenuous wilderness trails that make their way up and over coastal hills to secluded

CAPE BRETON HIGHLANDS

ROCKHOUNDING NEAR PARRSBORO

CAPE BRETON HIGHLANDS

valleys, deserted settlements and tiny coves not accessible along the shore. Serious hikers can make a triangular loop of the park that can take up to a week. Those less daring might prefer to hike along the beach to Red Rocks and other very unusual and rare rock formations. At Five Islands Provincial Park, trails follow the top of the Fundy cliffs to a series of look-offs over such well-known landmarks as the Old Wife and Red Head. The very popular Cape Split Trail follows the spine of this peninsula, which juts out into the Bay of Fundy to its very tip from where the tremendous force of the tides can be viewed first-hand.

Cape Breton Island offers a myriad of coastal hiking opportunities, in particular Cape Breton Highlands National Park, one of the oldest in Canada's park system. Offering over 25 trails of varying length and difficulty, it is hard to recommend just a few. But do not miss Middle

ECONOMY FALLS

Head Trail, which starts right behind Keltic Lodge and wends its way to the tip of Middle Head where great views of the sea and highlands can be seen in all directions. Also of note are the Skyline Trail, which, as its name suggests, climbs high above the waters of the Gulf of St. Lawrence; the Coastal Trail, which explores hidden coves and a waterfall along a gentle portion of the park; and Franey Mountain Trail, which climbs very steeply to one of the best viewpoints in the province. Here, eagles and hawks often soar hundreds of metres below you as they rise up on the thermals from the valley below. Not to be overlooked are the Mabou Highlands and Cape Smokey Provincial

Park, which provide trails and vistas equal to the national park but with fewer people.

Aside from coastal hikes, Nova Scotia has some great hikes to waterfalls, including Economy Falls and Wards Falls in the Bay of Fundy area and Uisage Bahn, Beulach Bahn and Mary Ann Falls, all in Cape Breton. To help you explore the tranquility of inland Nova Scotia, Kejimkujik National Park has more than a dozen hikes that parallel the Mersey River and the many lakes in this place of understated beauty.

AUTUMN ALONG THE COAST

People who prefer their hiking on the less strenuous scale have numerous venues from which to choose — many on reclaimed railbeds that now form part of the TransCanada Trail system. These trails are uniformly flat and well maintained to the point that some of them are suitable even for strollers. Some of the best sections of these railbed trails are the Mabou Harbour Trail in Cape Breton; the Musquodoboit Railway Trail on the eastern shore; the Salt Marsh Trail, which starts just outside the Halifax metropolitan area; and the St. Margarets Bay Trail, which skirts the bay of that name between Halifax and Hubbards. All in all, there is definitely something for everyone on the hiking trails of Nova Scotia.

Those with a serious interest in hiking have a number guidebooks from which to chose, including two by Michael Haynes, whom most consider the dean of Nova Scotia hiking. His *Hiking Trails of Nova Scotia* and *Hiking Trails of Cape Breton* are revised regularly and provide detailed descriptions of over 70 trails. There are also a number of local and international companies that feature hiking tours of Nova Scotia. One reputable Nova Scotia company that has been in business for many years is Scott Walking Tours. You can check them out at www.scottwalking.com.

BEACHES

COLLEEN ABDULLAH

FIDDLER AT QUEENSLAND

ROCK FORMATIONS ON THE MINAS BASIN

Nova Scotia is a seaside adventure. Visitors come to be invigorated by the fresh salt breeze, to be soothed by the murmur of the waves and to savour that sand-between-the-toes feeling. You will want to spend your time here in close communion with the sea — in it, on it, by it. You can't get a much closer salt water experience than at one (or several) of the 400-odd accessible beaches that scallop the 7,000-kilometre-long coastline of this almost-island province.

You don't have to be a beach bum or a bathing beauty to enjoy the sand, the surf and the sea. Nova Scotia's beaches are as varied as its geography. Young or young-at-heart, sociable or solitary, athletic or aesthetic — whatever your age or inclination, Nova Scotia has a beach experience for you.

Junior geologists and paleontologists will have a heyday at beaches along the shores of the Minas Basin, where gemstones, minerals and fossils are constantly liberated from the cliffs by the Fundy tides. Rockhounding on the beaches at Blomidon Provincial Park and Scots Bay on the Evangeline Trail may yield agates and amethysts. In the Parrsboro area of the Glooscap Trail, where

QUEENSLAND BEACH

Jurassic Age dinosaur bones have been discovered, you might see a real dig in progress on the beach at Wasson Bluff.

At Five Islands, you can dig up some lunch. That's right! Clam digging is great fun for the whole family. See a squirt and dig like fury. If you brought a camp stove along, you can steam or grill them on the spot. On the same shore at Economy, when the Fundy tide is out — and it goes waaay out — you can walk for (what seems like) miles on the ocean floor. The cool red sand flats are great therapy for the foot-weary. The Fundy tides come in very swiftly, so make sure you can get safely back to terra firma ahead of them.

If you are seeking peace and solitude, snuggle into the lee of a warm sand dune with a good book. Sand Hills Beach Provincial Park near Barrington, or Carters Beach at South West Port Mouton are perfect. Beaches set the scene for romance. Honeymooners and lovers stroll along a water's edge bathed in moonlight, lost in dreams and each other. You'll feel like the only people in the world at Ingonish Beach near Keltic Lodge.

SURFERS AT
LAWRENCETOWN

Little kids can amuse themselves for hours observing starfish, jellyfish, sea urchins and periwinkles in sun-warmed tide pools at Hirtle and Crescent beaches on the South Shore, Bayswater on the Aspotogan Peninsula and Rushton Beach near Tatamagouche. Big kids, too, like to pick up shells, pretty pebbles and interesting bits of driftwood. Mavillette Beach on the Acadian Shore is a good place to beachcomb for lovely shells deposited on the shore by the tide.

Bird watching is a bona fide beach activity. Nova Scotia is almost completely surrounded by water — ergo lots of sea and shore birds. At Taylors Head on Marine Drive you can see a variety of sea ducks and shore birds. The beach at Gulf Shore Provincial Park on Wallace Bay is a good starting point to observe the more than 160 bird species recorded in the area. Many beaches have signs marking nesting grounds of the endangered piping plover. During nesting season, stick to boardwalks or marked paths and you may be rewarded with a glimpse of this rare little shorebird.

The ocean is capricious and can go from calm to choppy in pretty short order. Some revel in the excitement

MELMERBY BEACH

of wild seas and white caps. When the surf's up, local and itinerant surfers head for Lawrencetown Beach, just outside Dartmouth (which, incidentally, has several supervised beaches on lakes within its boundaries). Scuba diving is popular at Terence Bay. Children delight in the age-old games of jumping waves and racing them up the shore at Queensland on St. Margarets Bay, a convenient drive from Halifax.

If you insist on being a traditionalist and *must* swim in the ocean, there are actually some very fine beaches ideally suited to that purpose, with change houses, lifeguards and, most importantly, warm water. On the Sunrise Trail, Melmerby Beach, not far from New Glasgow, is a great place to break the journey enroute to or from Cape Breton. This one is apt to be relatively crowded on weekends, but the Northumberland Shore sports many other warm-water (and less peopled) beaches, including supervised Heather Beach. On Cape Breton Island, the beaches along the Ceilidh Trail also benefit from the warming effects of the Gulf Stream. There is a nice supervised beach at Inverness.

Braver souls may relish a dip in the ocean on the eastern shore where the waters are bracing but the beaches are spectacular. Martinique has almost 5 kilometres of fine white sand and you might be the only soul in sight. If you time your trip for mid-August, you could participate in the annual Clam Harbour Beach Sandcastle and Sculpture Contest. You can join in or stroll the beach and judge for yourself. This lovely fine-sand beach is supervised and has full amenities. There is a whole string of gorgeous fine white sand beaches along the Lighthouse Route — Summerville, Rissers, and at Lockeport there are five, including the famous Crescent Beach, featured for years on the $50 bill. A few cautionary words — never underestimate the power of the ocean. Do not swim where yellow signs warn of dangerous currents. Strangers to the seaside may not be aware that on foggy or hazy days at the beach, the sun can still scorch the skin. Put on your sunscreen and wide-brimmed hat. Make sure you have shirts for the children. For a complete list of supervised beaches, contact the Nova Scotia Lifeguard Service at (902) 477-6155.

You can drive right up to the edge of some beaches, jump out of the car and into the water. Others are the reward at the end of a pleasant hike like St. Catherines River Beach at Kejimkujik Seaside Adjunct, a naturalist's dream. Some beaches are on islands and make a nice sailing or sea-kayaking destination. If you are touring Nova Scotia by car, there is no better place to stretch the legs and clear the head than a beach (and there is sure to be one handy). Stop for a picnic. Spread out your car rug, or if you're squeamish about sand in your sandwiches, many beaches offer picnic tables. There are dozens of little provincial and community parks with picnic tables and a beach. These are well indicated with signs on the highways. In Northern Cape Breton, you might encounter a fishing boat arriving at Neils Harbour with a catch of king crab. If you can prevail upon the fisherman to part with a few, take yourselves along to Black Brook on the Cabot Trail and cook them up at picnic facilities overlooking a fine beach. Now there's a picnic. Kids getting fractious? Hit the beach near you with buckets and spades — or reasonable facsimiles. Cool travel-weary bodies and tempers with a refreshing dip and a race up and down the edge of the wave-packed water's edge.

Many accommodations offer front-row beaching. The Quarterdeck at Summmerville Beach and Salty Rose at Rose Bay come to mind as good examples. MacLeod's Cottages at Petite Riviere and White Point Beach Resort have been favourites with families for generations. By the Dock of the Bay Cottages at Margaretsville are mere steps from the water. An early walk along the shingle will set you up for a busy day's sightseeing.

If you fancy camping at the beach, there are many provincial beach parks with camping

CRYSTAL CRESCENT BEACH

facilities. Thomas Raddall Park at East Side Port L'Hebert, with secluded campsites and white sand beaches, and Caribou and Munroes Island near Pictou, with its red sand and warm water, are good choices. For RVers, there is a great spot right across the road from Louis Head Beach near Sable River on the Lighthouse Route. To find and book beachside accommodations, check the Nova Scotia travel guide entitled *Nova Scotia Doers' and Dreamers' Guide* or call 1-800-565-0000.

If you are based in Halifax, there are beautiful beaches within a short drive of metro. Conrads Beach and Rainbow Haven outside Dartmouth, and Crystal Crescent just beyond the fishing village of Sambro are popular beaches within easy access of the city.

Take a dip, take a hike, take a break at one of Nova Scotia's beautiful beaches — or two, or three. And take home a healthy glow, a relaxed body, a head full of precious memories (and a little salt water in your veins) from Canada's ocean playground.

BEACHCOMBING AT CHESTER

SAILING

MICHAEL ERNST

As a sailing destination, Nova Scotia offers thousands of kilometres of beautiful, natural, accessible coastline, dotted with innumerable small harbours, sheltered coves and uninhabited islands with sandy beaches. "The sailing here is better than Chesapeake Bay," commented one of our sailing companions. It was a sunny day, winds steady at 12 knots, beautiful scenery, clear waters and very few boats on the horizon. A typical Nova Scotia summer day. Yes, the sailing *is* good!

Nova Scotia is renowned for its many and varied sea birds, and sailing is a great way to observe them, along with seals, porpoises and, in some areas, whales. Our summers are usually dry and warm with steady southwesterly winds, and we can sail comfortably from June to October. And when the day's sailing is done? There are fine onshore amenities including quality accommodations, restaurants and unique cultural experiences.

Nova Scotia's history has been written by the sea. It is a rich mixture of sea battles, shipwrecks, privateers, buried treasure and ghosts. Nova Scotians have been going down to the sea in ships since the province was first settled. The Mi'kmaq arrived over 10,000 years ago. They lived on the coast during the summers, and travelled the waters by birch bark canoe. The first European visitors may have been Vikings, a Scottish prince named Henry Sinclair in

SAILBOATS IN CHESTER HARBOUR

HMS *ROSE* IN HALIFAX HARBOUR

1398 or John Cabot in 1497. Permanent European settlements were established in the early 17th century, and over the next hundred years the province changed ownership between the French and English four times. During the American Revolutionary War, and the War of 1812, many battles were fought along the coast. Nova Scotia's coast was also a haven for privateers and the cause of thousands of shipwrecks.

Sailing is part of the Nova Scotian culture — it's in our bones and blood. Recreational sailors started flocking to Nova Scotia in the 1920s and 30s. Yacht clubs scattered throughout the province provide locals and summer residents with high-quality competition and onshore amenities. The number of visiting yachts increases annually, and marina facilities are being developed to keep pace with the demand. The majority of visitors on cruises are from the US and Canada, but Nova Scotia is also being recognized internationally as a sailing destination. These visitors are attracted by the quality of our sailing areas, warm summers, fair winds and our rich and diverse culture.

Any visitor who wants to sail can enjoy our wonderful province in a variety of environments and sailing craft. Sailing operators offer a wide range of activities that will meet practically all tastes.

If you have never sailed before but yearn to try, you can cruise with an experienced skipper. Someone else can do the work while you savour the salt air and the scenery, or you may want to take the helm and help sail the boat.

You may want sailing lessons, but are only going to be in Nova Scotia for a short vacation. Some providers will offer this opportunity to individuals and families. For visitors who plan to spend the summer, or several weeks, at one location, you could check out the availability of lessons for adults or kids at the nearest yacht club.

Whatever option you choose, being properly equipped is important. Hat, sunblock, sunglasses, summer clothing, sweater, rain jacket and non-slip shoes are essential items.

Being properly prepared can make for a more pleasurable sailing experience.

If you are a seasoned sailor and plan to sail your own boat, or charter, Mahone Bay and the Bras d'Or Lakes may have what you are looking for.

Nova Scotia is approximately 34,000 square kilometres in area — about the same size as Belgium. With approximately 7,000 kilometres of coastline, the sailing is quite spread out. This is a brief summary of what visitors can expect.

Halifax, with the second largest natural harbour in the world, has very strong links to the province's maritime history. Learn about this history and such famous events as the sinking of the *Titanic*, the Halifax Explosion and sea battles of the world wars at the Maritime Museum of the Atlantic located on the city's waterfront. Close by are sailing tours that provide a unique way to explore the harbour. The tall ship *Silva* (Canadian Sailing Expeditions) and the *Mar II* (Murphy's on the Water), both offer short cruises. The *Bluenose II*, a replica of Canada's most famous sailing vessel, usually spends a few weeks of the summer in Halifax and offers sailing cruises to the public. The schedule changes every summer, but up-to-date information can be found at www.bluenose2.ns.ca.

Just an hour southwest of Halifax is Mahone Bay, named after the scenic village located at its head waters. Beautiful scenery, sheltered waters, fair winds and warm summer weather make the bay a sailor's paradise. This area was a haven for privateers during the many wars between France and England in the 17th and 18th centuries. Local legends tell of raids, buried treasure and ghost ships. There are over 100 islands in Mahone Bay. Many are uninhabited and have small beaches — great stopping places for picnics and exploration. The most famous is Oak Island, where the longest on-going treasure hunt in the world has been taking place since 1795.

Three sailing companies operate in Mahone Bay and provide cruises, lessons and rentals. Sail Mahone Bay has a fleet of small dayboats and sailing cruisers available for charter, lessons and cruises for family groups. Sou'west Adventures, based

WOODEN BOAT FESTIVAL, MAHONE BAY

at the Oak Island Resort offers Canadian Yachting Association cruising qualification courses. If you are looking for a live-aboard cruise, then Discovery Charters in Chester will provide this experience on its 11-metre yacht.

Two boating events of importance in Mahone Bay are Chester Race Week, the largest keel-boat regatta in Eastern Canada, and the Mahone Bay Wooden Boat Festival. The festival is a celebration of the area's shipbuilding heritage through music, water and shore-based activities — great fun for sailors and landlubbers alike.

In nearby Lunenburg, there are sailing cruises of this historic harbour on the *Eastern Star*, a 14-metre ketch. These tours leave from the wharf near the Fisheries Museum of the Atlantic — a must for anyone interested in boats and the sea. *Bluenose II*, which was built here, offers cruises when it is in port.

On Cape Breton Island, a three-hour drive from Halifax, the Bras d'Or Lakes claim to offer the finest sailing in the world. This warm, inland saltwater sea is approximately 600 square kilometres in size with breathtaking scenery, sheltered waters and islands (and no fog). Visiting yachts can access the lakes through the historic St. Peter's Canal. Cape Breton Lake Charters provide bareboat charters and learn-to-sail vacations on cruising yachts. There is also the chance to sail the Bras d'Or on the *Elsie*, a classic wooden yacht once owned by Alexander Graham Bell, and now operated by Cape Breton Resorts. Further north you can "See the Whales by Sail" on a traditional schooner, the *William Moir*, leaving from Dingwall Harbour. This is a great way to experience these sea creatures and view the wonderful bird life of the coast.

The freedom of the sea, the excitement of a lively boat responding to a brisk wind, the challenge of navigation and learning every time you sail — these are a few rewards of this great sport. Whether you are an old salt or a novice,

DORY RACING, MAHONE BAY

Nova Scotia can offer great sailing opportunities. The serenity of our waters, the beauty of the environment, the encounters with wildlife, the sense of exploration and the knowledgeable professional guides will provide memories that will make you want to set sail for Nova Scotia again and again.

SEA KAYAKING

SCOTT CUNNINGHAM

Sea kayaking has become increasingly popular in recent years, and Nova Scotia, with its countless harbours, headlands, inlets and islands, offers a world-class destination. Our meandering shoreline is extensive (over 7,000 kilometres), access is easy (nowhere are you more than 55 kilometres away) and the contrasts are exceptional. Within a short time you can travel between paddling venues as diverse as the rugged Atlantic coast and the sandy beaches of the Northumberland Strait, or between the highlands of Cape Breton and the tides of the Bay of Fundy. There is something for paddlers of every taste and skill level. You will find protected day trips for the beginner as well as challenging multi-day routes, and everything in between. And you can explore all this in relative solitude, because with so much waterfront, there is plenty of space to find a spot for yourself.

My favourite realm, and my home, is along the rugged eastern shore, where an isolated band of islands stretches from Clam Harbour to Canso. This forgotten wilderness forms a compelling mix of natural and human history. Some of these outposts are just tiny specks, scarcely breathing air at high water,

EAST COAST OUTFITTERS

OAK ISLAND

while others are huge forest-covered expanses that dominate the horizon, and beckon to the inquisitive traveller. Explore abandoned lighthouses and shipwrecks, uncover those vanishing signs of our own transient history, or camp on a deserted isle where your only companions are the seals and the sea birds. There are no bridges or ferries to this archipelago, and few fishing or pleasure craft—only a dramatic and pristine isolation far from the summer bustle. Tangier is an ideal place from which to start. This is where Coastal Adventures, the pioneer in sea kayaking in the province, is located and offers day trips, extended tours and courses.

At the other end of the province, near Yarmouth, the glacier-sculpted Tusket Islands are very different from the resistant bedrock outposts of the eastern shore. Fishermen still use them as a base during lobster season, much as their ancestors did for centuries. At other times, they are also deserted. Elsewhere along the South Shore, there are dozens of idyllic places to put in and explore, including the Kejimkujik Seaside Adjunct, the LaHave Islands, Blue Rocks, Mahone Bay and Prospect, and a number of operators to help you out (Mahone Bay Adventures, Rossignol Surf and Kayak, East Coast Outfitters). Even Halifax, with its eclectic waterfront and harbour islands, merits a visit by kayak.

On Cape Breton Island, the paddling possibilities are also numerous, both along its rugged east coast and on the more protected Bras d'Or Lakes. However, the gem is certainly the Highlands. This majestic plateau occupies the northwestern tip of the island, where it rises abruptly from the Gulf of St. Lawrence, and it is particularly imposing when viewed from the perspective of a sea kayak. Sea spires, caves and a colourful geology decorate the perimeter, while the Cabot Trail winds out of sight and sound far above. Rich deciduous valleys alternate with barren vertical cliffs, washed by waterfalls. Here, you will certainly spot bald eagles and seals. If lucky, you will also paddle with the whales, as I have done many a time. By mid-summer, the water can warm up considerably, but this is an open coast and experience is advised. Outfitters offering trips here include Cape Breton Sea Coast Adventures, Coastal Adventures and North River Kayaks.

The Bay of Fundy is perhaps our most distinctive region. The highest tides ever recorded on earth wash these shores, sculpting cliffs and inundating massive salt marshes and mud banks with surprising speed. Experience is essential, but novices can take advantage of a knowledgeable outfitter (Coastal Adventures and Hinterland Adventures both run tours here). Cape Chignecto, which juts into the bay separating the Minas Basin from Chignecto Bay, is the jewel of the Fundy. This is the boundary where Africa was thrust up against North America eons ago, and where the details of a cataclysmic upheaval can be read in rock strata of the exposed escarpment. Even for those with little knowledge of geology, the striking array of colours, textures and forms is fascinating. The abrupt cliffs, numerous pinnacles and sea caves combine with tides exceeding 12 metres to create a spectacular land/seascape. In the remote river valleys, remnants of a lost era, play hide and seek among the shifting gravel. This is where some of our largest wooden vessels were constructed during the Age of Sail. Elsewhere in the bay, along the Minas shore, the layered sandstones and dark basalt of the Five Islands and Economy Mountain offer another intriguing destination.

If you arrive early in the season, when the Atlantic coast may be draped in fog, or if the Highlands and the Fundy are too exposed for your taste, you should try the

LOW TIDE ON THE MINAS BASIN

YOUNG KAYAKERS AT TERENCE BAY

North Shore. Along the Northumberland Strait, you will be treated to the warmest salt water north of the Carolinas and, after numbing your toes in the Atlantic, this can be a real pleasure. Fog has been banned, and the miles of sandy shores and salt marsh estuaries offer protected paddling for the entire family. Kayakers are not the only ones who enjoy soaking up a few summer rays, and this shore has become a mecca for the vacation crowd. However, secluded corners can still be found. Outfitters along this coast include Shoreline Adventures and Coastal Spirit Expeditions.

There are many other exciting areas of our coastline to entice you and your sea kayak. A comprehensive guide (for example, *Sea Kayaking in Nova Scotia*, available at most bookstores) should have detailed descriptions of over 40 routes. Bring your own boat and paddle on your own, or accompany a local outfitter (the *Nova Scotia Doers' and Dreamers' Guide* lists over 25), who can introduce you to the biology, geology and human history of this fascinating environment where the land meets the sea. Happy paddling!

MAHONE BAY

BIRDING

JOAN WALDRON

Nova Scotia has endless beaches, tucked-away fishing villages, hundreds of years of culture and a special natural beauty. With its rich marshlands, forests and lakes at every turn, it has perfect habitats for all kinds of birds. Whether the birds visit your backyard feeder, scurry around you on the beach or add to the sounds of nature on a stroll through the woods, you may wonder what kind they are, and whether they are local or just visiting. Some 305 birds have been listed in the province, with about 50 of these noted as regular strays or seldom seen. The avid birder may seek these rarities. For example, the rare Bicknell's thrush spends its summers in the Cape Breton Highlands; Canada's only breeding American oystercatchers have spent the past few years with their families on Cape Light, just off the fabulous birding area, Cape Sable Island. Visiting birders may want to see birds that Nova Scotians take for granted, such as the magnificent osprey, the provincial bird, which is commonly seen around beaches and harbours. Seabirds abound off Nova Scotia's endless shoreline. Puffins breed off Cape Breton Island; on sea-bound trips one can spot shearwaters, phalaropes and storm petrels and, with luck, a jaeger or skua as well. It's a treat to see these feeding alongside huge whales.

As in most places, Nova Scotia's birds have a time and a place. A winter birding trip can produce visiting seabirds such as the tiny dovekie, murres and Glaucous and Iceland

**BIRDERS AT
HARTLEN POINT**

gulls. And if you want to spend a quick weekend in winter ogling eagles, you can see scores of bald eagles during the Sheffield Mills Eagle Watch in the Annapolis Valley at the end of January.

Spring and early summer birding offers the sounds of warblers. Their sounds are so varied you often wonder what bird you are hearing. The ovenbird, for example, yells "teacher-teacher." Twenty-two species of warblers breed in Nova Scotia, which is filled with woodland roads and both national and provincial parks. The national parks have birding lists and may offer field trips. The *Atlas of Breeding Birds of the Maritimes* by Anthony J. Erskine will help pinpoint where particular birds can be found. Also, in late springtime, a careful walk on a quiet beach might give you a glimpse of the breeding endangered piping plover that Nova Scotians are trying so hard to protect. Late July features more than 20 species of shore birds, which stop in Nova Scotia to fatten up on the way south from their northern breeding grounds. Fall is delightful, when scores of bird species are coming and going, and there's always the chance that one of Nova Scotia's edge-of-the-continent weather surprises can bring a rarity or two or three.

In addition to the actual excitement and anticipation of bird watching, most birders enjoy the homework they must do before a trip. Information about birding in all parts of Nova Scotia is on-line, but if a computer is not yet part of your life, write a letter requesting information to the Nova Scotia Bird Society, c/o Nova Scotia Museum, 1747 Summer Street, Halifax, Nova Scotia, B3H 3A6. The Nova Scotia Bird Society's website (www.chebucto.ns.ca/Recreation/NS-BirdSoc/) offers a range of information, including contacts throughout the province and recommended reading. If you are in Nova Scotia for a Bird Society

meeting, join some local birders. Nova Scotians are very friendly, particularly the binocular-wearing species. The dates and meeting topics are included online, as are upcoming field trips to which visitors are most welcome. Try to let the leader know you are joining the group.

An important part of the society's website is its links to other birding websites. Birders can browse various sites and plan their birding locations. The Cape Sable Island Important Bird Area website, maintained by Grant Milroy, includes wonderful photos of the shorebirds you can expect to see at this location. Ted D'Eon's homepage has great photos and shows his achievements in helping to preserve the endangered roseate tern. The classic *Birds of Nova Scotia* by Robie W. Tufts is also linked to the site.

A visit through cyberspace will offer thousands of websites linked to birding in Nova Scotia. The Birding the Americas website (www.birdingtheamericas.com), maintained by Blake Maybank, includes trip reports from Nova Scotia that will give visiting birders a sense of what they can expect to see. Blake also maintains the Nova Scotia rare bird alert site at http://group.yahoo.com/group/NS-RBA.

There are many bird reference books and field guides available. If you want to keep a handy reference guide in your pocket or on the kitchen counter, try the *Formac Pocketguide to Nova Scotia Birds: Volume 1 — 120 Common Birds* and *Formac Pocketguide to Nova Scotia Birds Volume 2 — 80 Seashore and Water Birds.*

Nova Scotia is a special place for all kinds of birders and birds.

BIRDERS ON THE TRAIL

BOATS AND LIGHTHOUSES

DAVID STEPHENS AND SUSAN RANDLES

FISHING BOAT, PEGGYS COVE

When Europeans first dropped anchor off Nova Scotia, they found that the Mi'kmaq, with their sleek birch-bark canoes, were accomplished seafarers. Over the centuries, almost every coastal hamlet had one or more ship under construction, using the ample supply of local timber and the knowledge and skill of master builders and seamen.

On the shores of Maitland, W. D. Lawrence built what is believed to be the largest wooden sailing ship in Canada. His home is now a museum dedicated to the man and the ship.

BLUENOSE II

The undefeated champion of the Grand Banks fishing schooner fleet was the *Bluenose*. (A distinctive feature of a schooner is that the sails are attached to spars on the two masts rather than hanging from yardarms.) Built entirely of local materials (except for the masts), this sleek vessel was constructed in Lunenburg and launched on March 26, 1921. While the original tragically sank

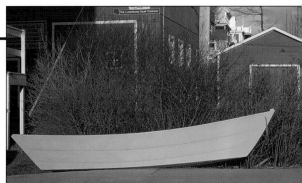

off Haiti in 1946, her memory lives on in the form of *Bluenose II*, a replica that sails each summer out of Halifax and Lunenburg. The Canadian dime bears a likeness of this winner of the International Fishermen's Trophy.

LUNENBURG DORY

Long associated with fishing schooners, the sturdy dory still remains a nostalgic symbol of the fishing industry. At The Dory Shop Museum in Shelburne, the almost forgotten art of dory-making is still practiced.

The development of the Cape Islander, a unique fishing boat with a high bow, wide mid-section, and forward wheelhouse, resulted in a design that even today is still duplicated, although in various modified forms. The Archelaus Smith Museum on Cape Sable Island is a testament to this sturdy workhorse of the inshore fishery.

One of the finest collections of boats and models can be viewed at the Maritime Museum of the Atlantic in Halifax, while the Yarmouth County Museum is reputed to have Canada's largest collection of ship portraits. In Pictou, the ship *Hector* was reconstructed using traditional materials and methods. The Hector Heritage Quay provides insight into the reconstruction and launch process.

LIGHTHOUSES

Without these "signposts of the sea," mariners would have been lost in fog, darkness and stormy seas. The honour of being the first lighthouse in Canada belongs to the circular stone tower built by the French between 1731 and 1734 at Louisbourg. Twice replaced, the present octagonal tower is now part of the Fortress of Louisbourg National Historic Site.

ABOVE: A PEPPERPOT LIGHTHOUSE BELOW: LAUNCH OF *HECTOR*, PICTOU

Originally lit by oil, then kerosene, and finally electricity, several hundred lighthouses have guided ships past the dangers of the sea off Nova Scotia. Many were isolated, and the keepers and their families were often the only inhabitants on desolate islands. Totally automated today, many of the remaining 150 lighthouses and range lights (a pair of towers used to direct

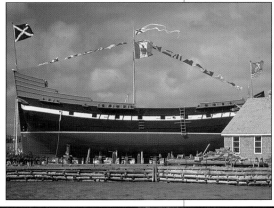

SUNSET AT PEGGYS COVE

vessels into port) are being replaced with modern towers of fibreglass or metal. Others have been replaced by buoys, self-guiding harbour sector lights, or skeleton masts, as modern vessels rely increasingly on satellite navigational systems.

About 80 lights are accessible (with varying degrees of difficulty) on the mainland. Considering that they were erected as aids to navigation and not as attractions for visitors, it is surprising that so many can be easily visited.

A few lights have been incorporated into public or historic parks by local community groups and are open seasonally. One of the most photographed lighthouses in North America is the tall tapering tower at Peggys Cove. First erected in 1868 at the entrance to St. Margarets Bay, the original light was replaced with the present octagonal tower in 1915.

At Burncoat Head on the Bay of Fundy, a lovely little park incorporates a replica of the keeper's house surmounted by a lantern. A similar light is located on the

GEORGES ISLAND, HALIFAX HARBOUR

eastern shore at Port Bickerton, where the community has restored the 1930s home and roof-mounted lantern. Open seasonally to the public and situated beside a modern operational light tower, the lighthouse allows visitors to appreciate the dedicated work of the light keeper. Another roof-mounted light at Gilbert Cove near Digby has also been restored by a local group.

One of the most common designs for lighthouses along our shores is the wooden tapered square or pyramid style commonly referred to as a "pepper shaker." The non-operational light at

CAPE FORCHU

Walton Harbour is open to the public. This restored light is situated in a quiet little park with commanding views of the Bay of Fundy. A similar light graces the waterfront in Annapolis Royal. Moved several times due to constant shoreline erosion, the small Five Islands lighthouse can be seen in a local campground. Another tapered-design light is part of a public park at Abbotts Harbour, near West Pubnico. The little light tower overlooking the Bay of Fundy at Spencers Island is now a heritage property. Famous as the home of the ghost ship *Mary Celeste*, this tiny village is nestled along a gravel beach. At Margaretsville, a viewing platform surrounds the base of its lighthouse. The beauty of Neils Harbour, with its colourful fishing boats and the wharf below its lighthouse, is the subject of many a photograph.

The unique "apple core" tower at Cape Forchu, near Yarmouth, is perhaps out-photographed only by the rock-mounted light at Peggys Cove. Although the Forchu light isn't open to the public, the keeper's house displays artifacts of a bygone era. A replica of the Seal Island light is open seasonally in Barrington, while the lovely setting of the uniquely designed lighthouse at Fort Point in Liverpool makes it a popular attraction. The Cape d'Or light near Advocate Harbour isn't unusual, but its location is dramatic, hugging the edge of a steep cliff. The tower at Cape George, north of Antigonish, is similar in design to

FORT POINT, LIVERPOOL

the one at Peggys Cove, and offers a sweeping view of the Canso Strait.

Its maritime heritage is a strong component of Nova Scotia's culture, and the lighthouses of the province offer visitors and residents alike many rewarding glimpses into the seafaring life of yesterday and today.

The Nova Scotia Lighthouse Preservation Society can be contacted via www.nslps.com.

PLACES

HALIFAX

Halifax has emerged as one of Canada's most attractive cities to visit. It's a relatively small city in an appealing setting, offering a variety of attractions. Halifax is at its best in summer and fall — and fall lasts longer here than in the rest of Canada, with many beautiful days in October and even into November. Spring, on the other hand, often comes late, and there are even years when it doesn't seem to come at all.

The waterfront area has become the most popular place to spend time in the summer. It's a long, vibrant boardwalk along the harbour, with many attractive cafés, bars and restaurants, street entertainment, the Maritime Museum of the Atlantic and the Historic Properties. The city's best bargain, and one kids love, is the ferry trip across the harbour. All this, together with the added thrill of the occasional container ship, navy vessel or cruise ship passing by, appeals to residents and visitors alike. Almost every visitor makes the trip up to the Citadel, a historical attraction with wonderful views of the harbour. The Spring Garden Road area rivals the waterfront for friendly, low-key street life and its variety of shops, bars and restaurants.

Within 40 minutes' drive of downtown there are beautiful ocean beaches at Crystal Crescent and Lawrencetown, fine for warm summer afternoons when small children (and hardy adults) don't mind the relatively cool temperatures of the Atlantic shore. In the evenings, Halifax offers a surprisingly wide range of entertainment options, and that is one of the reasons why most visitors to Nova Scotia make a point of including the city on their itinerary. One caution: in recent years, summer and fall tourism has been on the increase, but accommodation hasn't expanded as quickly as demand. Don't count on being able to find a downtown hotel in summer or fall unless you've booked well in advance. If you don't have

HALIFAX FROM THE HARBOUR

TOWN CRIER

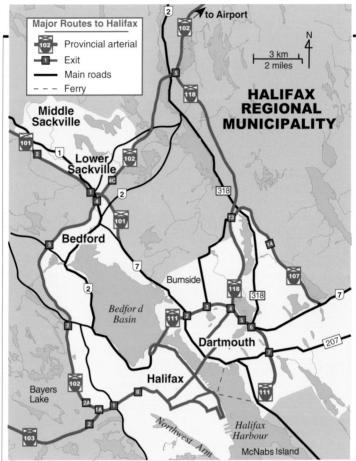

Major Routes to Halifax
- 102 Provincial arterial
- 1 Exit
- —— Main roads
- - - - Ferry

Middle Sackville

Lower Sackville

Bedford

Bayers Lake

Burnside

Bedford Basin

Halifax

Dartmouth

Northwest Arm

Halifax Harbour

McNabs Island

HALIFAX REGIONAL MUNICIPALITY

to Airport

N

3 km
2 miles

time to book much in advance, don't be surprised if you're offered a room in one of the old-fashioned motels along the Bedford Highway, some distance from the downtown. Depending on your preferences, that may not be as appealing as being downtown, but the motels have their own 1950s charm. Halifax also has some excellent inns and B&Bs.

Halifax sits atop a great slab of slate that rises from the harbour. There is precious little topsoil. It was the harbour that attracted the Mi'kmaq for centuries and the British in

MACDONALD BRIDGE

1749. The harbour extends inland about 16 kilometres from its seaward approaches, through the Narrows, spanned by two bridges connecting Halifax and Dartmouth, and into Bedford Basin. Except for an occasional freakish episode, it remains ice-free — a point long stressed by those interested in steering winter traffic the way of Halifax.

Recreational sailors happily coexist with shipping in the

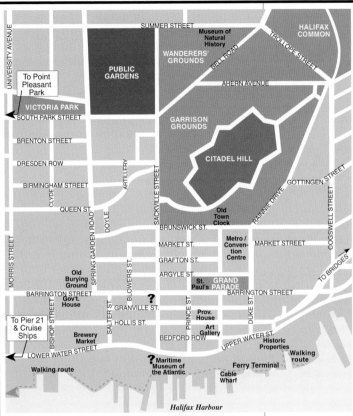

SUMMER STREET

UNIVERSITY AVENUE

Museum of Natural History

HALIFAX COMMON

TROLLOPE STREET

WANDERERS' GROUNDS

BELL ROAD

PUBLIC GARDENS

To Point Pleasant Park

AHERN AVENUE

VICTORIA PARK

SOUTH PARK STREET

GARRISON GROUNDS

BRENTON STREET

CITADEL HILL

DRESDEN ROW

ARTILLERY

BIRMINGHAM STREET

CLYDE

SACKVILLE STREET

GOTTINGEN STREET

QUEEN ST.

SPRING GARDEN ROAD

DOYLE

Old Town Clock

RAINNIE DRIVE

COGSWELL STREET

MORRIS STREET

BRUNSWICK ST.

Metro / Convention Centre

MARKET STREET

MARKET ST.

TO BRIDGES

GRAFTON ST.

Old Burying Ground

BLOWERS ST.

ARGYLE ST.

St. Paul's

GRAND PARADE

BARRINGTON STREET

Gov't. House

SALTER ST.

GRANVILLE ST.

PRINCE ST.

Prov. House

BARRINGTON STREET

DUKE ST.

To Pier 21 & Cruise Ships

BISHOP STREET

HOLLIS ST.

Art Gallery

?

Historic Properties

Brewery Market

BEDFORD ROW

UPPER WATER ST.

Walking route

LOWER WATER STREET

?

Maritime Museum of the Atlantic

Ferry Terminal

Walking route

Cable Wharf

Halifax Harbour

harbour. During the summer months, Bedford Basin is flecked with hundreds of colourful sailboats. The Northwest Arm, on the southwest side of the Halifax peninsula, is also a yachting haven.

Summers in Halifax tend to be mild, with sunny days made fresh by sea breezes. Winters are cool and snowy.

EARLY MORNING FOG IN HALIFAX HARBOUR

Although there are days in January that are cold enough to draw wisps of sea smoke off the harbour, Haligonians are accustomed to spending much of their winters around the freezing point. Nice spring days are cherished because they are few. But autumn — Nova Scotia's finest season — flatters Halifax. Then, the days are crisp and bright, and the city's tree-lined streets blush with colour.

TOP: INTERNATIONAL VISITOR CENTRE, BARRINGTON STREET MIDDLE: MARTELLO TOWER, POINT PLEASANT PARK

Halifax was established in 1749 to counter the military threat posed by the French Fortress of Louisbourg. During the last century, the city's magnificent harbour served as a marshalling area for North Atlantic convoys during two world wars. Halifax's economic fortunes have flowed during conflict and ebbed with peace.

Today, the Citadel in the heart of the city and the historic fortifications at Point Pleasant Park and York Redoubt are celebrated aspects of Halifax's military landscape, but there is also a contemporary military presence to go along with those reminders of the past. Warships regularly ply the harbour and helicopters fly overhead. A substantial number of military personnel are stationed here and sailors from the NATO fleet are regular visitors.

Despite the steady thrum of naval activity, Halifax is no longer primarily a military town. In post-war Halifax, rapid growth in the research, transportation and public service sectors has turned the old garrison town into a vital

NAVY FRIGATE AT THE DOCKYARD

commercial and government centre. This is Atlantic Canada's largest city. The provincial legislature is here, and a substantial federal bureaucracy works out of the city. There is a thriving alternative scene, and the city's five universities, including the Nova Scotia College of Art and Design, provide much of the impetus for it.

PROVINCE HOUSE, HOLLIS STREET

Halifax serves up some startling contrasts. The same city that annually hosts the popular Nova Scotia International Tattoo, with its regimental bands and drill teams, also stages the Halifax Fringe Festival — alternative theatre that scandalizes the city's conservative element. The military is here, but so is Vajradhatu, the headquarters for an international network of Buddhist meditation centres. Burgers and draught beer or bean sprouts and herbal tea — the downtown pubs and bistros cater to a city with multiple personalities.

BELOW: HOLLIS STREET
BOTTOM: GRAND PARADE AND CITY HALL

A walk along Hollis Street, one of the city's oldest, tells some of the story. Government departments and law offices operate cheek by jowl in high-rises that stand along the street's northern end.

You can explore the downtown area by foot, as the heart of the city extends for only a few — but very hilly — blocks.

The Grand Parade, framed by Argyle and Barrington Streets, sits between Citadel Hill and the waterfront. City Hall is situated on the north side and special activities, like the Remembrance Day service and the New Year's Eve party, take place here. On mild nights, people collect at the Grand Parade as they go from bar to bar, and summer days see business people patronizing hot dog vendors in the square.

Completed in 1750, St. Paul's Church still

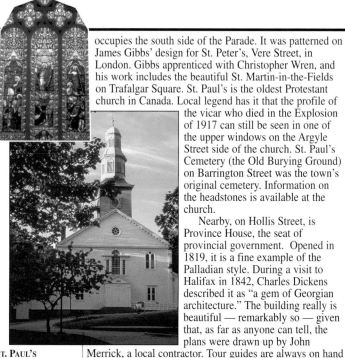

occupies the south side of the Parade. It was patterned on James Gibbs' design for St. Peter's, Vere Street, in London. Gibbs apprenticed with Christopher Wren, and his work includes the beautiful St. Martin-in-the-Fields on Trafalgar Square. St. Paul's is the oldest Protestant church in Canada. Local legend has it that the profile of the vicar who died in the Explosion of 1917 can still be seen in one of the upper windows on the Argyle Street side of the church. St. Paul's Cemetery (the Old Burying Ground) on Barrington Street was the town's original cemetery. Information on the headstones is available at the church.

Nearby, on Hollis Street, is Province House, the seat of provincial government. Opened in 1819, it is a fine example of the Palladian style. During a visit to Halifax in 1842, Charles Dickens described it as "a gem of Georgian architecture." The building really is beautiful — remarkably so — given that, as far as anyone can tell, the plans were drawn up by John Merrick, a local contractor. Tour guides are always on hand to take you through the building's splendid interior. Highlights include the Red Chamber, with its tall windows and ornate plasterwork, where you can see the oak table from the *Beaufort*, the ship that brought Edward Cornwallis to Halifax in June of 1749. The Legislative Library, complete with hanging staircases and a three-sided balcony, is also magnificent.

ST. PAUL'S ANGLICAN CHURCH

OLD TOWN CLOCK (RIGHT)
PROVINCE HOUSE (BELOW)

The city's turn-of-the-century commercial success is reflected in the Barrington and Granville streetscapes. Many of these buildings were of steel beam construction, a new technology that emerged in the wake of the Chicago fire of 1871. The walls of these structures were not load –bearing, so they were often built high with lots of windows and decorative arches. Contemporaries questioned their extravagance, but millionaires like George Wright could afford the best. The Wright Building still stands at 1672-4 Barrington Street. (Wright was one of 33 millionaires to go down with the *Titanic* in 1912.) This area is also the old stomping ground of Anna Leonowens, immortalized in the Rodgers and Hammerstein musical *The King and I*, and several movies, including the film *Anna and the King* starring Jodie Foster. In 1876 Leonowens moved here with her daughter and son-in-law. Soon after, Leonowens was actively involved in establishing libraries, reading clubs and a Shakespeare Club. Today, the Nova Scotia College of Art and Design represents the culmination of Leonowens's interest in the local artistic community. Halifax jewellers and graphic designers — and there are many — share in her legacy.

The Art Gallery of Nova Scotia, a modern facility located in a heritage building on Hollis Street, houses a collection of historic and contemporary art, and an acclaimed folk art collection. Paintings by Nova Scotian artists can be purchased at the Art Sales and Rental Gallery. The work of many of the province's best craftspeople and designers is displayed at the Nova Scotia Centre for Craft and Design on Barrington Street.

Unique Nova Scotian wares can also be found in Barrington Place and the shops at Granville Mall, adjacent to the Delta Barrington Hotel. These open up to a courtyard and feature such stores as Jonathon Bond and Christmas By The Sea.

The International Visitor Centre on Barrington at Sackville holds multi-media displays and videos about Nova Scotia. Here, multilingual travel counsellors help with vacation planning, reservations, car rentals, tickets to events and tours. Next door, the Discovery Centre makes science fun for all ages with interactive displays and experiments.

Continue south on Hollis to the Brewery Market, the former home of Alexander Keith's brewery (Keith's beer, now brewed by Labatt, is still sold in Nova Scotia liquor stores). The brewery

THE BREWERY MARKET, LOWER WATER STREET

is frequently held up as an example of what can be achieved by preservation-minded developers. Its arches and gothic windows provide a comfortable setting for one of Halifax's best restaurants, Da Maurizio's. On Saturday mornings, the Brewery hosts a farmers' market, where local crafts, baked goods and produce are available.

Further south, between Hollis and Barrington streets, Government House is another example of a beautiful Georgian building in the Palladian style. When John Wentworth became Lieutenant-Governor of Nova Scotia in 1792, he sought to upgrade his accommodation. A member of a well-connected family who knew royalty on the most intimate terms, he was probably justified in doing so. The cornerstone of Government House, the Wentworths' new residence, was laid in 1800. It has served as the Lieutenant-Governor's residence ever since. Normally not open to the public, the Lieutenant-Governor continues a long-standing tradition of hosting a New Year's Day levee, when everyone is invited inside for a look (and a glass of sherry).

GOVERNMENT HOUSE, BARRINGTON STREET

Backtracking on Barrington, you come to Spring Garden Road. There are a number of fine boutiques and

craft shops in the Spring Garden Road area. The Halifax Folklore Centre provides the city's best introduction to the traditional music of Nova Scotia. Jennifer's of Nova Scotia sells everything from small souvenirs to the prized works of some of Nova Scotia's best artisans.

Fine foods and wines are available at the Spring Garden Place Market, and at Port of Wines and the Italian Market on Doyle Street. There are also a number of good bookstores and coffee shops along the city's most fashionable street. Nearby, on the other side of the Public Gardens, the Museum of Natural History features the natural wonders of Nova Scotia's land and sea — whales, fossils, dinosaurs, birds, along with a number of other permanent and temporary exhibits.

BARRINGTON STREET (TOP)
VIEW FROM THE CITADEL (MIDDLE)

The Halifax Citadel, a national historic site operated by Parks Canada, is Nova Scotia's most visited attraction. Built between 1828 and 1856, the fortification is the fourth to occupy the hilltop site, with its commanding view of Halifax Harbour.

The present Citadel was built through the semi-divine intervention of the "Iron Duke," Arthur Wellesley. The Duke of Wellington, a strong proponent of

ENTRY TO THE CITADEL(TOP)
THE 78TH HIGHLANDERS (BELOW)
AERIAL VIEW OF CITADEL HILL (BOTTOM)

colonial defenses at a time when opinion was sharply divided, used his prime ministerial authority to push approval for the project through the British Parliament. In his view, a strong fortification was needed to defend against the American threat, which remained palpable in the wake of the War of 1812.

The fort was designed to prevent a land-based attack on the naval dockyard. It was left to the harbour defenses to repel an attack from the sea. Whether the Citadel was a necessary discouragement is open to debate. No attack ever came. The Citadel's smooth-bore cannons were never fired in anger.

During the summer months, Citadel staff re-enact the fort's military routines as they were carried out during the years 1869–71. At that time, the Citadel was manned by soldiers from the 78th Highlanders and the Royal Artillery, along with sailors of the Naval Brigade. Today, students take on these roles, drilling according to instructions laid out in the 1860s manuals, hoisting the signal flags and

standing watch at the sentry posts. The firing of the noon gun is heard throughout downtown Halifax year-round. The signal flags flying above the ramparts once told civilians what ships were in the harbour and where they were docked. They were also used to send messages to the other harbour fortifications. At one time,

it was thought that a series of signalling stations could be used to reach as far as Quebec!

Tour guides help explain the Citadel's rituals and exhibits, adding anecdotes, in French or English, about the fort's colourful past. "The Tides of History," a 40-minute audiovisual presentation, takes visitors on a dramatic tour through Halifax's military history. Visitors to Halifax are encouraged to find time for the Citadel, where they will discover why it held pride of place for much of the city's long life as a garrison town. And the view of downtown Halifax and the harbour is often reward enough to make the steep climb up Citadel Hill.

LITTLE DUTCH CHURCH

The Old Town Clock has marked the time at the base of Citadel Hill since 1803. Unperturbed by such cataclysmic events as the Halifax Explosion in 1917, the clock has undergone restoration to ensure that it will remain, in the words of Joseph Howe, "a good example to all the idle chaps in town."

From the Citadel, looking east and north, you see Halifax's North End, and the area demolished in the explosion. Nearby, there are some fascinating historical buildings.

The Little Dutch (Deutsche) Church was originally built to accommodate German settlers who were brought to Halifax not long after its founding. Across the street is the beautiful St. George's Round Church, largely reconstructed after a disastrous fire several years ago. It is one of Prince Edward's many round-shaped buildings in the city. Several handsome 19th century townhouses still stand along Brunswick Street. Further from the Citadel in the North End is the Hydrostone, known to Canadian town planners as the first example of 20th century urban renewal (and a much better precedent than what came later). By the

ST. GEORGE'S ROUND CHURCH

MacKay bridge is Seaview Park, site of Africville, which was razed by Halifax city hall in the 1960s in a relocation scheme meant to better living conditions for the Black community. The residents were opposed to the plan, a vital community was destroyed and Africville is mourned to this day.

MODEL OF RMS *TITANIC*, MARITIME MUSEUM OF THE ATLANTIC

Along the waterfront are the Historic Properties, a 1970s restoration project that revitalized the downtown core. The Privateers' Warehouse, one of 10 buildings from the Georgian and early Victorian periods, is the most storied. Early in the 19th century, Enos Collins, a wealthy Halifax merchant, used the building to warehouse booty that he seized during legalized privateering raids off the New England coast. Today, these buildings house a variety of shops and services. Handsmith sells lovely crafts made by artisans from across Canada. The Upper Deck Restaurant, overlooking the harbour from the Privateers' Warehouse, prepares some of the city's best seafood dishes. The food court at the properties is certainly unique, offering, among other things, seafood, Italian dishes and a micro-brewery.

Follow the boardwalk along the harbour's edge to Cable Wharf, named for the transatlantic cable ships that once docked here, where more shops and restaurants can be found.

ABOVE: PRIVATEERS' WAREHOUSE
BELOW: MARITIME MUSEUM OF THE ATLANTIC

Nova Scotian Crystal, home of Canada's only mouth-blown, hand-cut crystal, has a window that gives visitors a peek at the glass-blowers at work.

Boats operating from Cable Wharf are available for private charter. If you are interested in deep-sea fishing, make careful inquiries before booking your spot or you may find yourself simply drifting in the harbour off Point Pleasant Park — hardly a deep-sea experience! The *Harbour Queen I* and the *Haligonian III* offer historical commentaries during their harbour cruises. A private ferry will take you to McNabs Island, where grassy trails lead to secluded coves, overgrown forts and rocky beaches.

Further along the boardwalk from Cable Wharf is the Maritime Museum of the Atlantic. The museum houses over 20,000 maritime artifacts and gives a poignant account of the Halifax Explosion of 1917. There are

exhibits on shipwrecks and lifesaving, the *Titanic*, the Navy, steamships and sailing ships. The William Robertson & Son ship chandlery has been restored, and there are lots of boats — about 70 in all.

Since the blockbuster movie *Titanic*, the museum has mounted a permanent display of its fine collection of artifacts from the ship *Titanic*. Halifax's connection to the disaster came about because the city was the nearest large port to the site of the sinking. It was from Halifax that efforts were organized to search for the wreckage and to recover the bodies of the victims. Funerals were organized, and many of the dead lie in graves in Halifax. Crew members on the ships sent out to the wreck site collected memorabilia (a deck chair, for example), and many of these items gradually found their way into the museum's collection.

Items in the exhibit also reflect the work of scientists from the Bedford Institute of Oceanography, who were more recently involved in expeditions to the wreck site, and who conduct research on the deep ocean environment.

Though modest in size, the *Titanic* exhibit is informative and appealing to visitors of all ages. It has become the museum's leading attraction, and is well worth a visit. Note that there is a visitor information centre at Sackville Landing behind the museum.

Continue south and visit Pier 21 on Marginal Road. This was the last immigration shed in Canada and a million immigrants and refugees passed through here to their new country. Now a National Historic Site, multimedia presentations, live performances and genealogical records tell their stories.

One of the easiest and least expensive ways for visitors to get out on the water is to take a trip on the Halifax Harbour ferry. In Dartmouth, Ferry Terminal Park affords outstanding views of the Halifax waterfront. The World Peace Pavilion on the Dartmouth waterfront displays historical rocks and bricks from countries around the world, including pieces of

PIER 21 NATIONAL HISTORIC SITE

HALIFAX HARBOUR FERRY

CHAIN ROCK BATTERY, POINT PLEASANT PARK

the Berlin Wall and the Great Wall of China.

Nearby, you will find one end of the Shubenacadie Canal. Following the old Mi'kmaq canoe route cross-country from the Bay of Fundy, the canal took more than 30 years to build. Shortly after it was completed in 1861, the new Intercolonial Railway made it obsolete. But the canal workings remain a source of fascination. More of the canal, including locks 2 and 3, can be seen at Shubie Canal Park, off Waverley Road.

Up by the MacKay Bridge in Dartmouth, the Bedford Institute of Oceanography is one of the world's largest oceanographic establishments. Models and tours explain to visitors the institute's research of fishery science, oceanography and hydrography.

While in Dartmouth, plan to visit the Black Cultural Centre for Nova Scotia on Main Street (Route 7) at Cherrybrook Road. The history and culture of Black Nova Scotians is preserved here with a library, auditorium and exhibits on life dating back to the 1600s.

The Cole Harbour Heritage Farm is also worth a look. Right in the middle of the suburbs, this 1-hectare farm includes heritage buildings, farm animals, archival materials, gardens and a tea room. Special events are held here throughout the year.

On February 1, 1793, a 22-year conflict began with the French declaration of war against Britain. A year later, Prince Edward, son of George III and, eventually, father to Queen Victoria, arrived to take command of the garrison in Halifax. He set to work strengthening the town's fortifications. Martello towers were all the rage, and Edward built three of them. Two of these, one overlooking the western approaches of the harbour at York Redoubt, and the Prince of Wales Tower in Point Pleasant Park (which Edward named after his favourite brother) are national historic sites. Both locations are worth visiting, for their scenic as well as historical value. York Redoubt is a perfect spot for a picnic, affording a wonderful view of the harbour.

Point Pleasant Park covers 75 wooded hectares in Halifax's South End and is leased by the city from the Crown for a shilling a year. From the park, you can watch ships enter the harbour or see sailboats tack across the

Northwest Arm. A series of walking paths makes Point Pleasant ideal for an afternoon stroll. Along the way, you will pass a number of interesting ruins (see the map in the parking lot at the western entrance). From the Chain Rock Battery, a chain boom once stretched across the water to defend against enemy warships. During the First World War, mines were laid between the Point Pleasant Battery and McNabs Island, leaving a narrow channel lit by searchlights. A steel anti-submarine net was added later. Tall pine trees and beautiful harbour vistas now obscure the park's military past.

Returning from Point Pleasant Park towards the downtown, you pass through Halifax's South End. Here are many of the city's grandest homes and a wonderful collection of unique Victorian townhouses built of wood and painted bright colours.

VICTORIAN CRAFTSMANSHIP

If you drive or walk along Young Avenue (which becomes South Park Street), you can explore the Victorian South End by turning east along any one of the streets that run between Inglis and Spring Garden. Of course, the Victorian streetscape is regularly interrupted by clumsy, unappealing post-1945 construction, including high-rise apartments, but many of the original buildings remain and there are wonderful architectural details to notice in these houses' porches, windows, gables and trim.

For visitors curious about Halifax's royal past, a small park along the Bedford Highway has a wonderfully romantic origin and a beautiful small building to

MUSIC BUILDING,
BEDFORD HIGHWAY

PUBLIC GARDENS

appreciate. Three months after Prince Edward arrived, his beautiful French mistress followed. Governor John Wentworth lent them his country estate along the shores of Bedford Basin. The only building still standing is a round ornamental garden temple that is similar in design to several buildings that had been constructed at Kew

Gardens, Edward's childhood home. Visible from the Bedford Highway, the building is not open to the public, but visitors are welcome to stroll through Hemlock Ravine opposite the rotunda. The pond in the 75-hectare park is heart-shaped and known as Julie's Pond in honour of Edward's mistress. Legend has it that the paths that once meandered through the estate spelled out her name.

PUBLIC GARDENS

Many of Halifax's parks evoke a sense of Victorian times, when Halifax "society" took leisurely strolls through Point Pleasant Park and picnicked on McNabs Island. The Royal Nova Scotia Yacht Squadron held regular regattas. Athletic pursuits were thought to be ennobling. By the 1880s, skating parties were held regularly at the rink in the Exhibition Building. In 1882, the Wanderers' Amateur Athletic Association Club was established to foster the growth of cricket, football and hockey. After a purifying workout on the Wanderers' Grounds, participants could cross Sackville Street and take a relaxing stroll through the Public Gardens.

These formal Victorian gardens are the oldest in North America. Originally owned by a group of prominent Haligonians who constituted the Nova Scotia Horticultural Society, the 7-hectare gardens were opened to the public in 1867. In 1874, the society sold them to the city, which still maintains them. The Public Gardens were to serve a threefold purpose: they would improve the physical and mental health of the working classes, provide material for polite discourse among the more refined and be a source of civic pride for all.

The gardens are outstanding. Pathways wander among beautiful weeping trees, formal flowerbeds and subtropical plantings. They lead across classical bridges, past cast-iron fountains to the elaborate central bandstand. During the summer months, Sunday afternoon concerts are held there. On Saturday afternoons, brides, grooms and attendants can be seen posing for photographers. If you need a break from the demands of travel, the gardens are a fine oasis.

Across the Northwest Arm

THE DINGLE

from Point Pleasant is Sir Sandford Fleming Park, or "the Dingle." Fleming, creator of Standard Time Zones and engineer for the Canadian Pacific Railway, donated the park to Halifax in 1908. The 38-hectare park features the Dingle Tower, a sandy beach, a frog pond and two walking trails.

Connected to the trails in Shubie Park in Dartmouth, the Trans-Canada Trail winds from Sullivans Pond along Lake Banook and Lake MicMac for 7 kilometres. The paths are wide and wheelchair accessible.

Throughout the summer months, Halifax and Dartmouth host a wide range of festivals and events. What follows here is only a small sampling. Dates vary, so call the province's Check-In information line (1-800-565-0000) or consult the *Nova Scotia Doers' and Dreamers' Guide* for details.

ARMDALE YACHT CLUB, NORTHWEST ARM

The Nova Scotia International Tattoo, which draws military bands from around the world, runs for a week each July at the Metro Centre. The International Busker Festival, held in August on the Halifax waterfront and along city

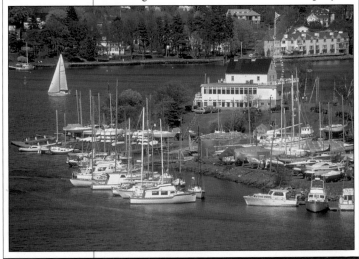

sidewalks, is very popular with both locals and visitors. Children especially enjoy the clowns and jugglers. The Atlantic Jazz Festival is a first-rate event. Held in July, mainstage and late-night concerts make for crowded downtown bars. The annual Africville Reunion brings together former residents of the Halifax suburb that was razed in the 1960s. Visitors are welcomed, and the reunion provides a good opportunity to learn about the Black community of Halifax.

Evenings, dine out at one of the city's fine restaurants. Not surprisingly, seafood is a ubiquitous specialty. Check the dining section of the listings at the back of this book for recommended dining spots.

If you prefer a raucous tavern evening, try the Lower Deck in the Privateers' Warehouse, where Celtic bands are a regular feature. The Economy Shoe Shop on Argyle Street is a mecca for the cultural set. The Midtown Tavern, a Halifax institution, offers sturdy fare in a noisy, friendly atmosphere. The late-night cabarets are for the boldly adventurous — when the sailors are in town, these places are reminders of the seamier side of old Halifax.

AT THE AFRICVILLE REUNION

FIREWORKS OVER THE HARBOUR (INSET) *BLUENOSE II* **IN HALIFAX HARBOUR**

LIGHTHOUSE ROUTE

LIGHTHOUSE AT PEGGYS COVE

Peggys Cove is a 30 to 40 minute drive from Halifax on Route 333. Along the way, at Bayside, the 18-hole Granite Springs golf course welcomes card-carrying members of the Royal Canadian Golf Association and their guests. The course is usually in great shape, with tight fairways and interesting hazards that offer a stiff challenge.

Peggys Cove, with its vivid, pitched-roof houses perched atop a mass of granite overlooking the snug harbour, has been exposed on miles of film and acres of canvas. It has become the postcard profile of an east coast fishing village.

Historian Ian McKay has described what he terms "the invention of Peggys Cove." A fishing village since the early 1800s, Peggys Cove as the principal icon of Nova Scotia tourism did not emerge until the 1920s and 30s. It was born out of the region's economic hard times. With the failure of industry in Nova Scotia came the assertion that quaint fishing villages and rugged seascapes had always been more real — more Nova Scotian — than the illusory progress of the late 19th and early 20th centuries. The

SWISS AIR MEMORIAL

invention of Peggys Cove was part of a developing mythology that idealized the Golden Age of Nova Scotia's seafaring past.

Canadian journalist J. F. B. Livesay was one of the cove's early protagonists. He discovered the village in the 1920s, and his book, *Peggy's Cove*, based on a summer visit in 1943, was published posthumously a year later. Livesay presented an unabashedly romantic view of the

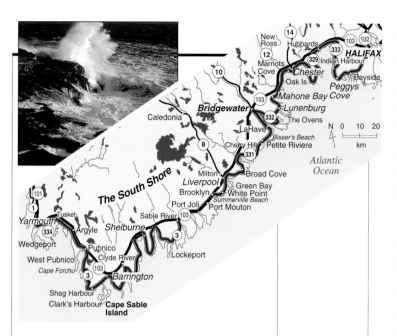

village: "The Cove on that first glance was still quite perfect, nothing to be added and nothing to be taken away, a little pulsing human cosmos set in the uneasy sea." He characterized the unwillingness of a local woman to purchase a washing machine as an emphatic rejection of modernity. As McKay points out, Livesay did not mention that the same woman also owned the only telephone in Peggys Cove, nor did he make any allowance for the discouragement that solid granite might offer someone who was considering additional plumbing!

What Livesay's prose did for Peggys Cove in the 1940s, the photographs of W.R. MacAskill had been doing since 1921. In that year, MacAskill's "Quiet Cove" appeared. Tourist promoters seized the opportunity afforded by MacAskill's beautiful photography. Peggys Cove was close enough to Halifax to offer visitors to the city a chance to encounter the "essential" Nova Scotia — the desolate boundary where land meets sea.

The successful promotion of Peggys Cove has led to a curious irony. You are exhorted to discover the unspoiled beauty of Peggys Cove in the company of tens or even hundreds of other people. A mass of glacier-scarred granite cuts an impressive profile against sky and

WILLIAM DE GARTHE RELIEF SCULPTURE IN PEGGYS COVE

sea, but here you will also find air-conditioned coaches from all over North America. There is a busy restaurant and gift shop (the Sou'wester) and the old lighthouse now serves as a post office.

But something truly elemental is still revealed at Peggys Cove — something about the human spirit in the face of adversity. William DeGarthe, one of many artists who have lived here and drawn inspiration from the rugged beauty of this place, immortalized Peggys Cove with a 30.5-metre sculpture of local fishermen and their families, carved into a huge wall of slate behind his home. If you visit on a day when a stiff onshore breeze sends waves crashing against the rocks (heed the warnings to keep your distance), you will marvel at the pluck of those who choose to live here.

For an impressive landward view of the cove, Peggys Cove Whale and Puffin Tours leaves twice-daily from the government wharf. The tour offers frequent sightings of puffins, dolphins, whales and seals.

Upon leaving Peggys Cove, continue along Route 333 through the picturesque villages that dot the eastern shore of St. Margarets Bay. If you time things right, you may arrive at Candleriggs, in neighbouring Indian Harbour, for a Scottish afternoon tea or a fine evening meal.

Route 333 eventually rejoins Highway 3, which takes you back to Halifax or farther along the South Shore towards Chester and Mahone Bay.

Nova Scotia's South Shore is a storied stretch of shoreline. In colonial times, privateers — American, French and Nova Scotian — plied these waters with letters

CHESTER WATERFRONT

of marque from their governments, licensing them to plunder enemy ships. Later, rum-runners unloaded their illicit cargoes in secluded coves and bays. Tall ships once crowded South Shore harbours. Today, coastal towns like Chester and Mahone Bay have retained the romantic aura of earlier days, and their harbours are still boating havens.

The village of Chester lies across three fingers of a peninsula that overlooks Mahone Bay, a sailor's paradise. Local lore has it that there are

365 islands in Mahone Bay (one for each day of the year). However, 100-odd islands appear on the charts today. The village itself is a New England coastal town that just happened to end up in Nova Scotia.

THE CAPTAIN'S HOUSE (TOP) CHESTER HARBOUR (ABOVE)

Appropriately, Chester's first settlers (it was called Shoreham then) sailed from Boston in 1759. Much of the rest of the Mahone Bay area was colonized by Germans, French and Swiss. Although Chester is also increasingly the haunt of yachtsmen from Halifax, Toronto and beyond, its predominantly Cape Cod-style architecture and the Yankee accents of many of its summer residents still give the town an unmistakable New England flavour.

Despite its New England roots, Chester was unable to avoid the attention of American privateers. It is believed that the Blockhouse,a private dwelling near the government wharf, on the village's Front Harbour, was part of the community's defenses. This was the site of a curious happening in 1782. Apparently, three American privateers were on their way to sack Chester when the commander of the local forces came up with an inspired plan. Since all the local men were away gathering firewood, this chap gathered a brigade of

broom-wielding women from the village to march back and forth on the hill overlooking the harbour with the red linings of their cloaks exposed. The Americans, so the story goes, were fooled into thinking there were British Redcoats guarding Chester and sailed down the coast to take out their frustrations on Lunenburg.

Most Americans came to Chester with friendlier intentions. In 1822, the Reverend John Secombe, a Harvard graduate, sailed to the village from Boston with several friends. His home, now the Captain's House on Central Street, is a Chester landmark and offers fine meals in grand surroundings — Sunday brunch (July–Labour Day) is especially popular with Chesterites.

TOP: CHESTER RACE WEEK
INSET: CHESTER PLAYHOUSE

As the 19th century moved along, a growing number of wealthy Americans discovered Chester. They came to sail, fish and get away from it all. Students from Yale came to Chester to unwind following their studies. And the town's magnificent Front Harbour and Back Harbour provided a scenic refuge for yachtsmen and retired naval brass. American admirals joined their Canadian counterparts, as did bankers, doctors, and oilmen from Boston, Baltimore, and Pittsburgh. Their houses are among Chester's main attractions, especially those along the peninsula at the western boundary of Front Harbour. Chester homes have names like Sea Chest, Wisteria and Lordly.

In the early days of the 20th century, American families would travel by steamer from Boston and Philadelphia to Yarmouth, Halifax or Digby, where they would catch a train or take another boat to Chester. Several gruelling days later, their chauffeurs would arrive with their fancy cars. Of course, this annual pilgrimage changed Chester. Chesterites, who traditionally fished and farmed, began working as guides on the trout and salmon streams, and crewed on splashy sailboats.

Visitors who arrive at Chester by boat will find a range of yachting services without equal in Atlantic

Canada. South Shore Marine, in nearby Marriotts Cove, is the region's largest marina. Not surprisingly, the facility's restaurant, The Galley, specializes in seafood, and window tables provide an unforgettable view of Mahone Bay.

Chester Race Week, held in early August, is the height of the summer social season. Then, the Front and Back harbours are filled with sleek yachts. Some participants race to win; others are happy to be a part of the hoopla. The parade grounds off South Street, site of the Yacht Club, a bandstand, a war memorial and a saltwater swimming pool (the Lido), provide the best vantage point for non-sailors who are interested in viewing the races.

For those who want to get out on the water but lack a boat, cruises and charters are available. There is also a 45-minute ferry trip (pedestrians only) from the government wharf to Big Tancook, the largest island in Mahone Bay, and Little Tancook. The ferry is a great way to enjoy the beauty of the bay. The islands have many lovely walking trails.

Chester offers a number of landward diversions. Just outside the village, an 18-hole golf course is characterized by its short, tight fairways and wonderful views of the ocean and nearby islands. Live theatre and concerts are presented at the newly renovated Chester Playhouse year-round. Those who like to shop should visit the Warp and Woof on Water Street. Nova Scotia's oldest gift shop sells local art and prints, handcrafts and table accessories.

As a special treat and highlight of your Nova Scotia holiday, stay at Chester's magnificent Haddon Hall Resort Inn. Built in 1905 as a summer home, the inn sits atop Haddon Hill and affords unrivaled views of Mahone Bay. Choose from the luxurious suites in the main house or the chalets that are scattered throughout the grounds of the 49-hectare estate.

Leaving Chester and driving towards the nearby town of Mahone Bay, you pass Oak Island (now joined to the mainland by a causeway), reputed to be the hiding place of Captain William Kidd's treasure. Since 1795, when a pit

THREE CHURCHES AT MAHONE BAY

MAHONE BAY

**ABOVE: SUTTLES
AND SEAWINDS
BELOW: WOODEN
BOAT FESTIVAL**

was discovered on the island, fortune-seekers have sought in vain for the booty. And for just as long, people have tried to explain the ingenious method by which the famous pirate is thought to have hidden his treasure in an elaborate network of underground tunnels. The story is well told by Mark Finnan in *Oak Island Secrets*, and by Graham Harris and Les MacPhee in *Oak Island and its Lost Treasure* — both are available in local bookstores and gift shops. The Oak Island Resort and Spa, a recently renovated oceanfront hotel, is a good jumping off point from which to explore the area.

Be sure to take the old road, Route 3, from Chester to Mahone Bay. The road dips and winds its way along the shore until a long, sweeping bend brings one of Nova Scotia's most recognizable landscapes into view. Colourful buildings and wharves, monuments to Mahone Bay's seafaring past, line the waterfront of the town's near-perfect harbour. Sailboats and other pleasure craft are moored offshore. And three fine 19th-century churches — United, Lutheran and Anglican — stand side by side at the head of the harbour.

The area's original inhabitants were Mi'kmaq. The Mushamush River on the edge of town bears the name of an early encampment. The pretty drive to Indian Point is

worth the few minute's detour. The bay was also a haven for French fishermen and pirates. The name Mahone is believed to be derived from the French *mahonne*, a low-lying vessel that kept French pirates hidden from their prey.

The present town was established by "Foreign Protestants" in 1754. A display at the Settlers' Museum, on Main Street, tells their story.

Mahone Bay had its own encounters with American privateers. During the War of 1812, the *Young Teazer* was chased into Mahone Bay by a British warship. One of the privateer's crew was a British deserter. Rather than risk capture, he set fire to the ship's powder magazine; 28 died in the explosion that followed. Today, the Teazer, on Route 3, is an upscale gift shop carrying both fine local crafts and imported goods.

Mahone Bay was once a flourishing shipbuilding centre. Many Main Street businesses now occupy buildings formerly used in the trade. On the second floor of the Settlers Museum, the town's shipbuilding heritage is revealed. It is also visible in the architecture of Mahone Bay. A walking-tour brochure is available at the museum and will steer you towards some of the beautiful Cape Cod, Georgian and Victorian homes that used to belong to local shipbuilders. After the three churches, Mahone Bay Bed & Breakfast, with its lovely wrap-around porch, is probably the most photographed structure in Mahone Bay. It is one of many heritage bed and breakfasts in the area.

In mid-summer, the town holds its Wooden Boat Festival. Inaugurated in 1990, the festival is one of Nova Scotia's best. The quality of craftsmanship of many of the boats displayed at the festival upholds Mahone Bay standards. The newer Great Scarecrow Festival and

LUNENBURG WATERFRONT

Antiques Fair held in early October may have already exceeded the Wooden Boat Festival in popularity.

Fine shops abound — the kind of shops that have given way to malls in so many other places. Birdsall-

ADAMS & KNICKLE, LUNENBURG

Worthington Pottery on Main Street has an international reputation for its distinctive wares made of Nova Scotia clay. Across the road is Amos Pewter, where boats were once built. An interpretive workshop allows visitors to see Greg and Suzanne Amos at work fashioning pewter items — vases, candleholders, goblets, annual Christmas collectible ornaments, earrings, pins and pendants. Still on Main Street, but away from the water, Suttles and Seawinds is one of Mahone Bay's most successful enterprises. Vicki Lynn Bardon is responsible for the explosion of colour that greets you upon entering the store. Inspired by traditional quilts, her line of distinctive clothing has won international acclaim. The jewel-hued quilts in the adjacent quilt barn must be seen. The traditional craft of rug hooking is fostered by two studios exhibiting and selling beautiful rugs, kits and supplies. Mahone Bay is a favourite antiquing destination.

Several local restaurants attain the same high standard as Mahone Bay's shops. The Innlet Café, with a harbour view that includes the three churches, emphasizes stylish seafood dishes in casual surroundings. Mimi's Ocean Grill serves up interesting and unusual dishes on Main Street. For good pub fare and 12 beers on tap (and often Saturday night bands), try the Mug & Anchor. Mahone Bagels serves great coffee and sandwiches with European flair.

Make time for Lunenburg during your visit to Nova Scotia. With the possible exception of Annapolis Royal, Lunenburg is the province's prettiest and most interesting town. Its architectural integrity has been preserved to a

WALTERS BLACKSMITH SHOP

remarkable degree. Lunenburg's "Old Town" — first laid out by the province's chief surveyor in 1753 — has been designated a National Historic District by the Government of Canada and a World Heritage Site by UNESCO. Lunenburg's beautiful harbour, its outstanding architecture, its seafaring tradition, and its proximity to Halifax

have attracted many visitors over the years. Some have stayed. Lunenburg is home to a vital artistic community and has long been at the centre of Nova Scotia's fishing industry. The demand for wooden ships has declined, but waterfront companies continue to outfit and repair local boats.

DORY BUILDING AT LUNENBURG

Lunenburg represents the second attempt made by British authorities to colonize Nova Scotia (Halifax was the first). This site had a number of advantages. It offered the best agricultural land along Nova Scotia's Atlantic coast, some of which was already cleared — though not nearly as much as was promised. There was a fine harbour, the narrow peninsula could be easily defended by a palisade, and the site was close to Halifax and far from the French settlements at Ile-Royale (Cape Breton) and along the Bay of Fundy.

In 1753, a group of German-speaking "Foreign Protestants" (French, German and Swiss) arrived by boat from Halifax. These labourers and farmers had been recruited by British authorities to populate their colony. Surveyor General Charles Morris measured off blocks and streets in a gridiron pattern along the slope overlooking the harbour. The Old Town was a 48-block rectangle with rows of six blocks running parallel to the shore and columns of eight blocks running up the hill. A central core of four blocks was reserved for public purposes.

The settlers overcame the adversities of hostile French and Mi'kmaq in the area, and their endeavours eventually flourished. Surpluses in timber, boards and root vegetables were sent to Halifax. Settlement reached southwest as far as West Berlin, and northeast to Mahone Bay and beyond. Prime land along the banks of the LaHave River drew

FISHERIES MUSEUM OF THE ATLANTIC

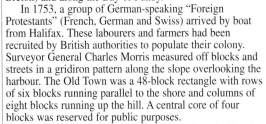

people farther and farther upriver, from Bridgewater to New Germany.

It was inevitable that some of the new settlers would turn to the sea for their livelihoods. Towards the end of the 18th century, the inshore fishery began to flourish. Cod, mackerel, dogfish, salmon, herring and gaspereaux were easily caught from small boats close to shore.

Lunenburg's waterfront still reflects the importance of its shipbuilding industry and the fishery. At the eastern end of Montague Street, Scotia Trawlers has been outfitting and repairing fishing vessels since acquiring the Smith and Rhuland boatyards in 1976. Smith and Rhuland, established in 1900, built both the *Bluenose* (1921) and the *Bluenose II* (1963). Lunenburg shipbuilders were renowned long before the *Bluenose* was launched, but it was this 285-ton racing schooner, never defeated in Nova Scotia waters, that won them international recognition. In addition to the *Bluenose II*, the same shipyard also launched replicas of HMS *Bounty* (1960) and the *Rose*.

The fishery spawned other industries. The buildings of the old Adams & Knickle outfitting company can still be seen. Nearby, Thomas Walters and Sons' blacksmith company, established in 1893, has been the sole survivor of a once-thriving Lunenburg trade.

Farther west on Montague Street, the Fisheries Museum of the Atlantic occupies buildings that were once a part of National Sea Products processing plant (now located at Battery Point). The museum, one of Nova Scotia's best, has many excellent exhibits relating to Lunenburg's fishing and shipbuilding heritage. The aquarium of Atlantic fish is especially popular with children; adults may find the rum-running display more to their taste. An exhibit on the Banks fishery and the Age of Sail includes meticulously crafted models. Various demonstrations take place throughout the summer. Moored alongside the museum's wharf, the *Theresa E. Connor*, a salt-bank schooner, and the *Cape Sable*, a steel-hulled trawler, welcome visitors aboard. You may also find the *Bluenose II* here (she sails out of Halifax and other Nova Scotia port towns as well).

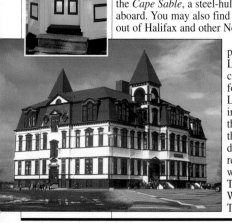

In recent years, careful planning has preserved Lunenburg's architectural character. Before that, good fortune was largely responsible. Lunenburg's failure to industrialize in areas other than the fishery is one explanation for the absence of major fires in the downtown area. And significant redevelopment in the Old Town was averted when the "New Town" was established in 1862. With a few minor exceptions, Old Town remains remarkably similar

in both form and function to Morris's 1753 plan. Public buildings still stand where they did in the settlement's early days. St. John's Anglican Church, built between 1754 and 1763, was the tragic victim of a Halloween fire in 2001. A campaign has been launched to rebuild the church, the heart of Old Town. Lunenburg's courthouse was built in 1775, and is now used by St. John's parish as a church hall. Predictably, the new courthouse, built in 1902, also stands on the Grand Parade in the centre of town.

There are a number of other 18th-century structures. Typically, these are one-storey Cape Cod-style houses or two-storey dwellings in the British Classical tradition. Knaut-Rhuland House Museum (c. 1793), a designated heritage property on Pelham Street, has one of the most intact original Georgian interiors in Nova Scotia.

Nineteenth-century buildings dominate Old Town. Although architecturally conservative, Lunenburgers permitted themselves one extravagance in the latter half of the 19th century: Scottish dormer windows were added to British Classical houses. Over time, these were moved down the slope of the roof until they hung over central doorways. The "Lunenburg Bump" can be quite ostentatious, and probably was a reflection of the town's success in the salt fish trade.

Built just before the turn of the 20th century, the second Lunenburg Academy (the first was destroyed by fire in 1893) is one of the town's architectural gems. It stands outside Old Town, atop Gallows Hill, and the four towers that jut from its Mansard roof are visible for miles. Young Lunenburgers are still educated at the academy.

Lunenburg hosts a series of first-rate festivals during the summer. Its growing reputation as a centre for arts and crafts is reflected in the quality of work displayed at the Lunenburg Craft Festival (mid-July) and the Nova Scotia Folk Art Festival (early August). The Lunenburg Folk Harbour Festival (August) features top North American performers, as well as some from further afield, and attractive waterside venues. For many, the highlight of the summer season is the Lunenburg Fishermen's Reunion and Picnic (August). The fishermen's competitions, including dory racing and scallop shucking, are hotly contested by

OX TEAM AT WORK, ROSS FARM

highly skilled participants. They also are great fun.

The town boasts a number of fine shops and galleries, and across the harbour you can shoot nine holes of golf at the Bluenose Golf and Country Club, while enjoying the spectacular view. There are several good restaurants serving, not surprisingly, lobster and fish dishes, but when you've had your fill of seafood, go to the Lion Inn for a superb rack of lamb.

To the south of Lunenburg, the privately run Ovens Natural Park has a series of coastal caves. A cliff-side hiking trail leads down a concrete stairway to the mouth of Cannon Cave — so named because of the dramatic boom created by the surge of waves into the narrow cavern. Zodiac tours of the caves are available between late June and early September (weather permitting).

Follow the coastline south to the LaHave River, and then go up river to Bridgewater, a thriving town that prides itself as the main street of the South Shore. Bridgewater offers its visitors numerous services and conveniences, including restaurants, accommodations, bustling malls, banks, a regional hospital, museums, recreational facilities and a visitor information centre. Built in 1860, the Wile Carding Mill displays machines that once carded wool for spinning and weaving. The DesBrisay Museum relates the history and development of Lunenburg County through documents, exhibits and artifacts, including a beautiful Mi'kmaq quillwork cradle. Bridgewater hosts its rural neighbours each July at the South Shore Exhibition and International Ox Pull.

LAHAVE RIVER

A pleasant drive down the western banks of the LaHave leads to the dock where a cable ferry provides a transportation link across the river, and on to the Marine Museum on Bell Island. Nearby is the Fort Point Museum, a former lighthouse keeper's house, and site of the Fort Sainte-Marie-de-Grâce National Historic Site, where Isaac

PERKINS HOUSE

de Razilly, the first governor of New France, landed with his settlers in 1632. At Rissers Beach, supervised swimming, picnic areas and change facilities are provided.

More beaches, museums and inviting villages can be found at such shoreline communities as Cherry Hill, Broad Cove, Petite Rivière and Green Bay.

Situated at the estuary of the Mersey River, Liverpool was settled by New England Planters in the 1760s. These settlers were invited to Nova Scotia by Governor Charles Lawrence to take up lands made vacant by the expulsion of the Acadians and to bolster the loyal British population of the province.

Much of Liverpool's colonial past has been popularized in the historical fiction of Thomas Raddall. Raddall was far and away Nova Scotia's best-selling novelist, with millions of copies sold in the United States, Great Britain and Canada. In *His Majesty's Yankees,* he told the powerful story of a fictional Liverpool family caught up in the events surrounding the American Revolution. To give his novel life, Raddall relied heavily on the diaries of an 18th-century Liverpool merchant, Simeon Perkins.

Perkins' diaries give a unique account of colonial Nova Scotia. They describe the dilemma faced by the Planters, who had spent most of their lives as New Englanders, when the American Revolution polarized loyalties. Perkins was among those community leaders who eventually called for armed resistance to the attacks of American privateers.

Today, Perkins House on Main Street is one of Liverpool's chief attractions. Built in 1766, the house was acquired by the Queens County Historical Society in 1936 and is now a part of the Nova Scotia Museum. Like Raddall's novels, Perkins House and the adjacent Queens County Museum tell a romantic story of Liverpool's tumultuous early days. Much is made of privateers — hardly surprising in a town that styles itself as the "Port of the Privateers." Liverpool hosts a Privateer Days

PERKINS HOUSE

LOYALIST DAYS, SHELBURNE

HANK SNOW MUSEUM

celebration at the end of June. The town also stages a summer program of concerts and plays at the beautiful Astor Theatre, once Liverpool's town hall. This is also the venue for the Liverpool International Theatre Festival, a biennial springtime series of high-calibre performances.

Logging has been the backbone of Liverpool's economy almost from the beginning. Some of the lumber was used to build ships, which often took on additional lumber for export to Great Britain.

In the 1920s, the forest industry in Queens County was given a major boost by the decision of Yarmouth-born financier Izaak Walton Killam to build a pulp and paper mill at Brooklyn, on the north side of Liverpool Bay. Completed in 1929, the Mersey Paper Mill got off to a slow start, but soon picked up speed. When Killam died in 1955, he held approximately three-quarters of the company's common stock and his estate was valued at around $200 million. The Killam trusts are still used for university endowments and the construction of public buildings across Canada. Bowater Mersey continues to be the major employer in the Liverpool area.

The Sherman Hines Museum of Photography and Galleries, located in Liverpool's historic town hall, is the only photographic museum east of Montreal. It features artifacts and vintage photographs by the likes of Karsh and MacAskill.

The former Liverpool train station is now the Hank Snow Country Music Centre, honouring the Queens County-born country music legend. The centre has rotating displays and memorabilia from well-known Nova Scotia musicians, interactive exhibits, railway memorabilia, workshops and a gift shop. In August, the Friends of Hank Snow Society hosts a weekend of classic country music at the exhibition grounds in Bridgewater.

Nova Scotia's fourth oldest surviving lighthouse is the centrepiece of Fort Point Lighthouse Park. Once a welcome sight for seafarers entering Liverpool's busy harbour, the lighthouse now

contains an exhibit area with models, interpretative panels and an audiovisual presentation.

South of Liverpool, Route 3 leads to White Point Beach Lodge. A full-service resort, the lodge has wide-ranging facilities, including a playground, pool, nine-hole Canadian PGA-rated golf course, tennis courts, freshwater paddling and, of course, a long stretch of fine, white, sandy beach (warm-water enthusiasts will prefer the pool for swimming). Continue along Route 3 towards some of the province's best beaches. Summerville Beach Park, with its saltwater lagoon, is a great spot for a picnic and swim. The Quarterdeck Beachside Villas & Grill is situated along this white sand beach. The resort offers all the amenities including full kitchen facilities, jacuzzis and fireplaces.

For a more secluded setting, drive on to Carters Beach at Port Mouton. The beach is actually three crescent-shaped stretches of the finest white sand imaginable. It's worth the trouble to ford the small stream that separates the first of these beaches from the last two. Here, you will find magnificent dunes and unmatched views of Port Mouton Bay.

The endangered piping plover has also taken advantage of the relative seclusion of this coastline. Kejimkujik National Park's Seaside Adjunct protects key nesting areas between Port Mouton and Port Joli. Two hiking trails lead to isolated beaches, sections of which are closed from late April to late July, so that nesting birds remain undisturbed. Both hikes offer spectacular coastal views. There are still more wonderful beaches at Lockeport, just off Route 3. Crescent Beach, one of five in the area, is a fully-serviced 1.5-kilometre-long stretch of fine, white sand. It is a short drive from here, up the indraft of Jordan Bay, and across the peninsula to Shelburne.

Shelburne is Nova Scotia's Loyalist town. Drawn by the outstanding harbour, one of the largest in the world, thousands of Loyalists settled along the shores of the Roseway River estuary in 1783. Within a year, nearly 10,000 people were there, making Shelburne the largest town in British North America.

A number of Loyalist-era structures have survived in Shelburne. Ross-Thomson House is operated by the Shelburne Historical Society for the Nova Scotia Museum. Built around 1784, the store was soon occupied by business

FORT POINT LIGHTHOUSE PARK

PIPING PLOVER

LOYALIST DAYS, SHELBURNE

partners and brothers Robert and George Ross (Robert Thomson would become their clerk). The old store has since been refurbished with period furnishings and merchandise. The comfortable, solid building, no doubt the work of a shipbuilder, is impressive in itself.

The Cooper's Inn, also on Dock Street, is one of several waterfront restoration projects that grew out of the visit of the Prince and Princess of Wales to Shelburne in 1983. The former owners received an award from Heritage Trust Nova Scotia for their work on this 18th-century Loyalist home (c. 1785).

South on Dock Street, the Shelburne County Museum tells more of the Loyalist story. For a small fee, the museum will provide a walking tour brochure that points out several other Loyalist buildings in town. Most points of interest are along the waterfront, on or near Dock Street.

Like other fishing communities along the South Shore, Shelburne also has a rich shipbuilding heritage. The town is renowned for its dories. In 1877 Isaac Coffin Crowell, a native of nearby Barrington, invented and patented a metal clip for joining the floor futtocks with those on the sides of the dory. In Lunenburg, dory builders continued (and continue) to use naturally crooked tamarack roots for the job. A debate still rages as to whose method is better, but Crowell's clip allowed Shelburne builders to undersell their Lunenburg competitors. At one time, Shelburne had seven dory shops.

The Shelburne Historical Society operates the Dory Shop Museum, which was a going concern from 1880 to 1970. It demonstrates the building and outfitting of a Shelburne dory and explains the crucial role that these boats played in the fishery. The museum has a dory builder and is well worth visiting.

Between Shelburne and Yarmouth lies Barrington. Just four years after Barrington was founded by Planter families from Cape Cod in 1761, the new township had a New England-style meeting house. Now part of the Nova

Scotia Museum, the unadorned structure that served both religious and secular purposes is Canada's oldest extant nonconformist place of worship.

Nearby, the Barrington Woolen Mill, built in 1884, is also operated by the museum. The mill houses original machinery and includes exhibits on sheep raising and wool processing. The Seal Island Lighthouse Museum was constructed in Barrington to commemorate the light and its keepers, who steered countless sailors past Seal Island's notorious shoals for 160 years. Built in 1830, the lighthouse was automated in 1990. The exhibits relate to lighthouse life. There is a good view of Barrington Bay from the top of the five-storey museum.

Reached by causeway from Barrington Passage, Cape Sable Island in Barrington Bay is also steeped in maritime lore. The island was home to Ephraim Atkinson, who first built the boat that became the workhorse of the North Atlantic lobster fishery. Typically, the Cape Islander is about 12 metres long with a 3- to 4-metre beam. You'll find them in working harbours throughout Atlantic Canada. Learn more about the Cape Islander and this storied fishing community at the Archelaus Smith Museum in Centreville.

At West Pubnico, the oldest Acadian settlement still inhabited by descendants of its founders, historic Acadian Village honours the perseverance and generosity of the Acadian people. Original structures and artifacts donated by local residents were used to create vintage Acadian buildings, including houses, a forge, a barn and a lobster peg mill. Guides in period costume welcome visitors to a reception centre, a restaurant serving traditional Acadian dishes, and an arts and crafts shop.

Take a stroll through the town of Yarmouth and you'll be struck by the houses. On the slope rising up from the ferry terminal are lavish 19th-century homes — Georgian, Gothic and Italianate, among others. Some have costly frills, like the one on Parade Street, not far from the Yarmouth County Museum, which is trimmed with wooden rope and comes complete with portholes.

Fish-processing plants along the waterfront attest to a fairly healthy fishery (a rarity in Nova Scotia these days) and the town is well serviced, but there are few clues as to where the extravagant wealth

ALONG THE CLYDE RIVER
BOTTOM: DORY SHOP MUSEUM, SHELBURNE

BARRINGTON MEETING HOUSE

YARMOUTH COUNTY MUSEUM

came from that built these homes. That is because Yarmouth's century was the 19th — first as Nova Scotia's most prosperous "wood, wind and sail" community, and then as a thriving industrial centre. The County Museum is a good place to begin a tour of the town. Here, there are many paintings of the fleet, commissioned by Yarmouth captains in ports like New York, Belfast and Hong Kong.

During the middle of the 19th century, Yarmouth families like the Killams and Lovitts, who traced their roots back to the New England Planters who first settled Yarmouth in the 1760s, became powerful shipping magnates. Their ships, flush with lumber and salt fish, made for the West Indies. There, they laded rum, sugar and molasses bound for Boston, then returned to Yarmouth with manufactured goods. They reinvested the profits in shipping. For a time, Yarmouth boasted the largest per capita concentration of registered shipping tonnage in the world.

By the 1860s, huge ships were being built for the international bulk trade. Yarmouth's wealthiest families entered into partnerships to finance their construction. All along the French Shore — the string of Acadian communities between Yarmouth and Digby — shipyards were kept busy.

The Killam Brothers Building, part of the County Museum and located along the waterfront, attests to the wealth of the ship owners. Look for the hand-worn grooves in the cash tray of the huge, stand-up chestnut desk.

And then, so the story usually goes, sail was replaced by steam, and it was over. The worldwide slump in trade in 1873 is often cited as the turning point. The golden age of wooden ships and iron men had passed. Yarmouth's mercantile class was left to languish in the face of progress.

But that's not what really happened. A visit to Yarmouth's excellent Firefighters Museum on Main Street provides some insight into the real story. Among the exhibits is a horse-drawn hose reel that was built in Yarmouth by the Burrill-Johnson Iron Company in 1891.

The threat of fire was real because Yarmouth industry boomed until the turn of the century. In addition to the Burrill-Johnson foundry, which had been expanded during the 1880s to supply more products to national and international markets, the Yarmouth Duck and Yarn Company was started in 1883. It was one of several cotton mills established in the Maritimes to take advantage of the federal government's National Policy. That policy, implemented in 1878, sought to stimulate the Canadian

manufacturing sector by slapping tariffs on foreign manufactured goods, while allowing certain raw materials, including cotton, to enter the country duty-free. So, Yarmouth merchants did not suddenly abandon shipping in a fit of panic. Rather, they scaled back operations in light of the advent of steam and sought to take advantage of the new technologies by investing in land-based manufacturing. The National Policy provided the economic stimulus, and the newly completed Western Counties Railway linked Yarmouth to the national market.

But regional manufacturers could not compete with their central Canadian counterparts. The transfer of local capital to larger Ontario and Quebec interests was a problem experienced in all of Nova Scotia's industrial towns. Yarmouth's decline was as dramatic as its rise. By 1900 little industry was left. The cotton mill was still around, but was soon controlled by outsiders.

Today, there are some wistful reminders of Yarmouth's heyday. But there is a bright side to the story. The town still thrives as the service centre for southwestern Nova Scotia and a key entry point for the province. The MS *Scotia Prince*, a combination cruise ship and car liner, connects Yarmouth to Portland, Maine. Bay Ferries operates a speedy car ferry, the *Cat*, from Bar Harbor, Maine to Yarmouth.

CAT FERRY IN YARMOUTH HARBOUR

The Yarmouth Arts Centre (Th'YARC) stages a variety of entertainment, including summer theatre, in its 380-seat theatre on Parade Street. Dory races are a highlight of Seafest, a week-long community festival held each July.

For the most part, Yarmouth offers hotel/motel-style accommodation, but there are notable exceptions. Murray Manor (c. 1820) is a beautifully restored heritage property with lovely gardens and tasteful rooms. Harbour's Edge Bed & Breakfast is a heritage property with a view of the harbour. The Manor Inn, in nearby Hebron, features all the amenities (dining room, pub, tennis courts and more) on about 4 hectares of attractively landscaped waterfrontage.

If you are looking for a good meal in a hurry, visit Harris's Quick and Tasty, a Yarmouth institution since the 1960s. The simple diner-style fare, including fishcakes and lobster sandwiches, will not disappoint.

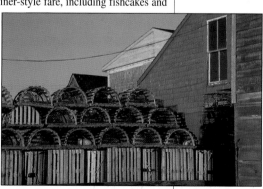

Yarmouth's lobster fishery still flourishes. Take a drive out to the lighthouse at Cape Forchu between the spring and fall lobster seasons and you'll see thousands of traps piled along the roadside.

113

EVANGELINE TRAIL

CAPE BLOMIDON

The Annapolis Valley is an area of peaceful beauty. The North and South Mountain ranges provide shelter from heavy winds and Fundy fog. The valley is blessed with more sunshine than anywhere else in Nova Scotia. The fertile soil has been farmed since the Acadians settled the land early in the 17th century. Stately elms and beautiful willows (an Acadian favourite) impart a sense of timelessness to the valley. Is it any wonder that you can find a village named Paradise here?

The Annapolis Valley is an ideal setting for a tragic romance. And history obliged with a suitable cast of characters, the Acadians — French farmers who were Nova Scotia's earliest European settlers. Unable to maintain their neutrality in the struggle between France and Britain for supremacy in the New World, the peaceful Acadians were expelled in 1755 for refusing to take an unconditional oath of loyalty to the British Crown — their lands, houses and livestock were all confiscated. All that was needed was for someone to write their story.

GRAND PRÉ

Henry Wadsworth Longfellow's epic poem *Evangeline* was published in Boston in 1847. It was immensely popular, running through five editions in its first year. Other publications followed, which further aroused the curiosity of New Englanders in the "Land of Evangeline." A rail link between Halifax and Yarmouth, completed in 1891, provided a convenient way of getting here. The

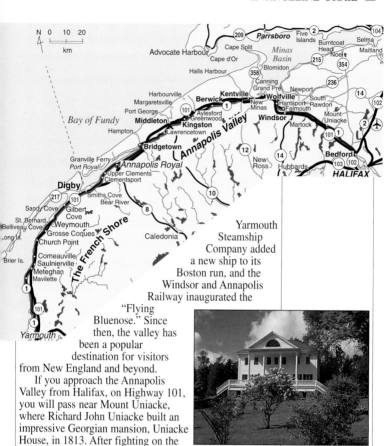

UNIACKE HOUSE

Yarmouth Steamship Company added a new ship to its Boston run, and the Windsor and Annapolis Railway inaugurated the "Flying Bluenose." Since then, the valley has been a popular destination for visitors from New England and beyond.

If you approach the Annapolis Valley from Halifax, on Highway 101, you will pass near Mount Uniacke, where Richard John Uniacke built an impressive Georgian mansion, Uniacke House, in 1813. After fighting on the rebel side of the American Revolution, Uniacke bounced back nicely, becoming one of Nova Scotia's wealthiest and most influential men. As Attorney General and Advocate General to the Admiralty Court during the War of 1812, he made a fortune — a chunk of which went into building his country home. The Uniacke Estate Museum Park is now part of the Nova Scotia Museum, and features many original furnishings and Uniacke family portraits. Many kilometres of walking and hiking trails have been developed throughout the landscaped grounds and natural woodlands.

As you continue your journey toward Windsor, the lush valley landscape makes a dramatic appearance. Spread out before you are the rich farmlands that skirt the Avon River. If the tide is out, the river is an expanse of red mud flats. The Tidal View Farm in Newport offers one of the best views of the tide coming in. Remnants of Acadian dykes are here, although it is impossible to distinguish the originals from later reconstructions.

Windsor is a service centre for Hants County farmers. The town was also home to Thomas Chandler Haliburton, the Nova Scotian humourist who created the character Sam Slick, the Yankee clockmaker with the acerbic wit. Haliburton House, a provincial museum, features Victorian furnishings and an attractive 10-hectare estate. Shand House, another provincial museum, is a state-of-the-art

Victorian home with all of the modern conveniences of the time. Windsor is the home of Howard Dill, the farmer who developed the "Atlantic Giant" pumpkin that has produced pumpkins weighing more than 500 kilograms. Visitors flock to the Dill farm on College Road, particularly in late summer and early fall, to marvel at the monster vegetables.

The Dill farm is also the site of Long Pond, where residents are convinced that students at King's College School played the first-ever game of hockey. Downtown, the Windsor Hockey Heritage Centre tells the story of how Canada's great sport began.

Close by, at Falmouth, the Saint Famille Winery, which provides tours, and the well-kept greens and fairways of the Avon Valley golf course, both attest to the fine Annapolis Valley weather.

Hantsport, once a prosperous shipbuilding centre, is now home to a busy pulp and paper products plant, and serves as a depot for the export of gypsum. As you travel west, fields and orchards appear, reminders that agriculture has always been the mainstay of the area. During harvest season, roadside stands do a brisk business as locals and visitors load up with fresh fruit and vegetables.

SAINT-FAMILLE WINERY, FALMOUTH

In late May, the Annapolis Valley is in full bloom — orchards and orchards of apple trees are laden with delicate pink and white blossoms. Since the 1930s, valley residents have celebrated the start of the growing season with an Apple Blossom Festival.

Before the mid-19th century, there was not much of an apple industry in the area. Poor roads and contrary winds made the shipment of perishable goods a dubious enterprise. Railways and steamships changed all that. By the 1880s, apples from the Annapolis Valley were being regularly shipped to Great Britain. In 1905, the Nova Scotia Fruit Growers' Association convinced the federal government to locate an experimental farm in Kentville. Valley farmers successfully lobbied rail and shipping interests for favourable rates that strengthened their position in the British market. For their part, the British co-operated by gobbling down more apples than any other people

in the world. By the 1930s, Britain regularly consumed three-quarters of Nova Scotia's commercial crop. When that market suddenly dried up with the outbreak of war, the problem was thought to be temporary. It was not. A sluggish post-war economy

forced Britons to severely limit the number of pounds that they could convert for purchases made in dollars, and apples were a high priority. Currency restrictions were eventually relaxed, but the British market for Annapolis Valley apples never recovered. Now, much of the crop is bought by multi-national corporations for processing; relatively few apples are grown for export.

But there are plenty of apples for the local market. In early fall, roadside stands brim with apples — Cortland, MacIntosh, Gravenstein, Delicious and more. Visitors with their own favourite apple recipes can spend an afternoon at one of the valley's many U-pick orchards.

Between Windsor and Wolfville is the Grand Pré National Historic Site. Hundreds of Acadians were deported from the area in 1755, and the village of Grand Pré became the setting for Longfellow's *Evangeline*. The grounds of the historic site are beautiful, with gardens and winding paths shaded by old willow trees. A memorial church built in 1922 houses an exhibit, and a new interpretive centre explains the history of the expulsion. Bilingual tours are provided. There is also a thriving winery (the first in Nova Scotia) in the village of Grand Pré.

Today, an increasing number of valley residents live in towns, most of which are service centres for the agricultural hinterland. Wolfville is the cultural and academic centre of the Annapolis Valley. Acadia University, established as Acadia College in 1838, is situated on one of Canada's prettiest campuses. A 2.4-

ACADIA UNIVERSITY, WOLFVILLE

GRAND PRÉ

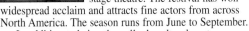

hectare native botanical garden is part of the university's new K.C. Irving Environmental Sciences Research Centre.

Not surprisingly, when organizers (including Christopher Plummer) were looking for a home for their new classical theatre festival, they chose Wolfville. Inaugurated in 1995, the Atlantic Theatre Festival stages top-quality traditional performances in a beautifully renovated, 500-seat, thrust-stage theatre. The festival has won widespread acclaim and attracts fine actors from across North America. The season runs from June to September.

In addition to being the valley's cultural centre, Wolfville is also one of its prettiest towns. Beautiful Victorian homes line elm-shaded streets. The visitor information centre at Willow Park, on Main Street, will provide you with a brochure for the Heritage Home Walking Tour.

Several of Wolfville's grandest homes are now among the province's best hostelries. The Blomidon Inn features 26 rooms in a lavish 1877 mansion. The entrance and public spaces are especially impressive, as are the Blomidon's best rooms. The Tattingstone Inn is a special place — you'll find four-poster beds and marble-tiled bathrooms, but also a swimming pool and tennis court. There is a carriage house and a cottage for honeymooners. Victoria's Historic Inn and Carriage House Bed & Breakfast (1893) is another registered heritage property. The main house includes three honeymoon suites, complete with jacuzzis.

Wolfville offers fine dining as well. Two of the inns mentioned have excellent dining rooms, and two more restaurants — the Tempest and Acton's, where a popular lunch buffet features fresh Valley produce and Fundy seafood — make dining out in Wolfville a pleasure.

There are a number of interesting shops in town. Box of Delights is a good general bookstore with the valley's best selection of local titles. Treasures is a quirky gift shop where you will find out-of-the-ordinary gardening supplies and Victorian housewares alongside local jewellery and crafts.

Wolfville's Robie Tufts Nature Centre provides summer visitors with a rare spectacle. From May to late August, chimney swifts gather here for a startlingly acrobatic descent down a chimney. (Tufts's bird books are available at most Nova Scotia bookstores.)

Randall House, another grand Wolfville home, features a collection of historical materials

relating to the Planters — New Englanders invited to Nova Scotia to settle the lands left vacant by the Expulsion of 1755 — who settled Mud Creek before it became Wolfville. Across the street, a path leads to a series of dykes that are ideal for walking and offer great views of the town and surrounding countryside.

NEW ENGLAND PLANTER HOUSE, NEAR WOLFVILLE

In an area renowned for its agriculture, it may surprise you to learn that many of Wolfville's elegant homes, including the Blomidon Inn, were built with wealth earned from the shipping trades. Nearby Kingsport, Hantsport and Port Williams were all important shipping centres. After 1928, some independent growers shipped local apples directly from Port Williams. Three kilometres away, at Starrs Point, Prescott House was built in 1815 by Charles Prescott, a businessman and horticulturist who introduced several varieties of apples, including the Gravenstein, to Nova Scotia. The house is filled with period furnishings, and the perennial garden and grounds are especially attractive. Today, visitors can enjoy a sunny early fall afternoon picking their fill of apples at U-picks in Starrs Point and many other locations throughout the valley.

Back at Port Williams, Route 358 continues north across Acadian dykes, through Canning, then on to a look-off. From high atop Cape Blomidon, you can survey the Minas Basin and six river valleys. In autumn, the view is made even more beautiful by the fall foliage that spreads out beneath you.

At the end of Route 358, hikers can carry on to the end of Cape Split (the continuation of Cape Blomidon) along a 13-kilometre marked trail that yields spectacular views of

TIDE RIPS AT CAPE SPLIT

CAPE BLOMIDON

the Bay of Fundy. Further along Route 358 is Blomidon Provincial Park, which has many hiking trails offering amazing views of the Minas Basin and opportunities for rockhounding for the amethysts and agates that are constantly being exposed along the cliffs and beaches by the massive Fundy tides.

Kentville services the richest farming area in the valley and has been a long-time leader in the apple industry. The Agriculture Canada Research Station assists fruit growers with an ongoing program of scientific research. Blair House is an on-site museum with exhibits relating to the history of the apple industry and the research station's involvement in it. Guided tours of the station are available by prior arrangement during the summer months. In town, the Old Kings Courthouse Heritage Museum on Cornwallis Street devotes much of its space to the social history of the area — especially to the arrival of the New England Planters in the 1760s. A good walking tour brochure is available from the visitor information centre. The tour lasts about three hours and will take you past several outstanding heritage homes.

Back towards Wolfville, the Ken-Wo Golf Club is one of the valley's best courses. The sheltered fairways are well maintained, and the casual atmosphere makes green-feers feel more than welcome.

Villages and towns run into one another as you continue west through the valley along Route 1. Road-weary travellers can choose from the many rural bed and breakfasts in places like Berwick, Middleton and Lawrencetown. Fairfield Farm Inn and Falcourt Inn in the Middleton area are gracious old establishments. At Aylesford, families will enjoy the Oaklawn Farm Zoo, which features over 100 species of mammals and birds. The 18-hole Paragon golf course at Kingston is usually less crowded than other courses in the valley, and is almost always drier (a nuisance at the height of summer, but a blessing at other times). Its wide-open fairways make it a forgiving course for novices. A short side trip over North Mountain takes visitors to picturesque fishing villages hugging

OAKLAWN FARM ZOO

the shores of the Bay of Fundy. At places like Halls Harbour, Harbourville, Margaretsville or Hampton, fishing boats dramatically demonstrate the rise and fall of the tides, as they alternately ride high at their moorings or sit on the mud flats awaiting the next high tide. Stop for fresh lobster at the pound in Halls Harbour. If you have time, take a detour through Bridgetown and see for yourself why it is billed as "the prettiest little town in Nova Scotia." A self-guided walking tour highlights Bridgetown's heritage homes and history. Bridgetown was the setting for Ernest Buckler's *The Mountain and the Valley*, probably the best work of fiction to come out of Nova Scotia.

LOW TIDE, BAY OF FUNDY

The communities along the shores of the Annapolis Basin are a treasure trove of history. All Nova Scotia school children know the story of the arrival of Sieur de Monts and Samuel de Champlain to Port Royal at the beginning of the 17th century. They also learn how a second Port Royal, established on the opposite shore of the basin in 1635, became Annapolis Royal in 1710 and served as the seat of British colonial government in Nova Scotia until Halifax was established in 1749. Here was the first successful European settlement in what is now Canada — and the genesis of British rule in Nova Scotia.

THE HABITATION AT PORT ROYAL

Off Route 1, about 10 kilometres

EVERYDAY WORK AT PORT ROYAL

southwest of Granville Ferry, is the reconstructed Port Royal Habitation. Close to here, de Monts and Champlain established a fur-trading post in 1605. The reconstruction is based on Champlain's sketch of the site. Like Normandy farms of that time, buildings form a rectangle around a central courtyard.

A good deal is known about the French stay at Port Royal through the writings of Champlain, Marc Lescarbot and Father Pierre Biard. Lescarbot, a disenchanted lawyer with literary aspirations and an ebullient personality, wrote extensively about his year at the habitation. His frivolous Neptune pageant, now celebrated as Canada's first theatrical presentation, was played out along the shores of Port Royal in November 1606. Even Champlain, no great fan of Lescarbot, was entertained.

The winter that followed was a relatively mild one, made even more bearable by Champlain's *Ordre de Bon Temps* (Order of Good Cheer). Champlain sought to ward off the ravages of scurvy by promoting feasting and fellowship among the order's members.

In 1607, de Monts' fears were realized when his monopoly was revoked; the habitation was abandoned until 1610. Father Biard, a Jesuit priest, arrived the following year. His frequent clashes with the Biencourts, the father and son who now ran the habitation, and the difficulties he encountered in his mission work with the Mi'kmaq, were well suited to Biard's acid pen. When Port Royal was sacked by a group of Virginians led by Samuel Argall in 1613, Biard may well have breathed a sigh of relief had he not been wrongfully accused of complicity in the raid by the younger Biencourt. (To learn more about the Port Royal

PORT ROYAL

years, Elizabeth Jones provides a lively narrative history of the period in *Gentlemen and Jesuits*.)

The present-day habitation evokes Canada's first European settlement. Costumed interpreters, employed as 17th-century artisans, go about their tasks. Visitors can imagine Marc Lescarbot scribbling away in his reconstructed dwelling. Other buildings at the site, which include the Governor's House, the Priest's Dwelling, the Chapel, the Blacksmith's Shop and the Trading Room, may well inspire 17th-century reveries.

At Granville Ferry, pause long enough to look across the river at the Annapolis Royal waterfront. On a calm, clear day this is one of Nova Scotia's special views. Also worth a

HISTORIC GARDENS, ANNAPOLIS ROYAL

look is the fine collection of Georgian furniture, ceramics, glass and silver housed at the North Mills Museum in Granville Ferry.

At the Annapolis River Causeway, there is a prototype tidal power installation. An on-site interpretive display shows how the generators work, but the power house itself is underground and off-limits to the public. From here, Route 1 leads directly to Annapolis Royal.

Beautiful Annapolis Royal, on the shores of the Annapolis Basin, is a showcase of heritage restoration. A reconstruction project launched in 1979 spruced up some of the town's fine old buildings, attracting both business and tourists. Before the project, visitors to Annapolis Royal had to leave town to get a good meal. Today, three local restaurants, Newman's, Leo's and The Crooked Floor, have been listed in *Where to Eat in Canada*. All occupy buildings of historic interest. The Adams-Ritchie House, site of Leo's, was built by a New England merchant in 1712.

FORT ANNE, ANNAPOLIS ROYAL

Since 1984, the restored King's Theatre has featured the Annapolis Royal Arts Festival, a September celebration of local, regional and national talent. The same venue hosts a summer theatre festival during July and August. The work of local artists and artisans, many of them recent arrivals to Annapolis Royal, can be seen in waterfront shops and galleries.

In the centre of town, the Fort Anne National Historic Site represents the fourth and last fort built by the French at this location. Governor Subercase's powder magazine (1708) is the only extant building from the French era. The story of the struggle for supremacy between the French and English is told in the museum building, which was

constructed as officers' quarters by the Duke of Kent in 1797. A stroll along the earthworks affords some beautiful views of the Annapolis Basin.

The Annapolis Royal Historic Gardens were opened in August 1981 as part of the heritage restoration project. Abutted by reclaimed marshland and a 20-hectare wildfowl sanctuary, the stunning 4-hectare gardens display much of the area's natural history. Among the more than 200 varieties in the Rose Garden are several that were grown by Acadian settlers in the area in the 17th century (the roses are at their peak from late June until August). Next to the replica of an Acadian cottage, willow and apple trees shade an Acadian potager, or vegetable garden, wherein can be found the makings of an outstanding pot of soup. Other highlights include the Governor's Garden, which was modelled after 18th-century gardens in southern New England, and the carefully ordered Victorian Garden with its 300-year-old elm tree.

Annapolis Royal bustled during the late 18th and 19th centuries. Ships left waterfront wharves loaded with apples, potatoes and lumber, and returned with sugar, molasses and rum from the West Indies. Packet boats from Digby, Saint John and Boston made Annapolis Royal a regular port of call. The town was a popular overnight stop.

Today, the O'Dell Inn Museum, dating from the 1860s, recreates the cosmopolitan atmosphere of a busy 19th-century inn. It catered to well-off travellers, the nicer rooms going for $1.50 a night. The museum also houses collections of Victorian costume and furnishings, artifacts of childhood, as well as the ubiquitous relics of a shipbuilding past.

GARRISON HOUSE INN, ANNAPOLIS ROYAL

Bonnett House, also on Lower St. George Street, is a research centre for local history and genealogy. The centre is open year-round by chance or appointment.

Several other outstanding Georgian and Victorian structures are along or just off St. George Street. The de Gannes-Cosby House, built in 1708, is thought to be the oldest wooden house in Canada. "Stroll Through the Centuries," a brochure put out by the Historical Association of Annapolis Royal, provides an interpretive walking tour of the town. During the summer months (except Sundays), the association offers regular guided tours from its headquarters at the lighthouse on Lower St. George Street.

From Annapolis Royal, Route 1 meanders along the shore of the Annapolis Basin towards Digby. (Alternatively, Highway 101 provides a faster, but less scenic, route.) At Upper Clements, the 10-hectare Upper Clements Park is popular with children. The flume ride, roller coaster and carousel are special favourites, as is the large waterslide. Across the highway, the Upper Clements Wildlife Park offers visitors a chance to see native Nova Scotian animals —

BEAR RIVER IS HOME TO A FLOURISHING ARTISTIC COMMUNITY

lynxes, cougars, porcupines, foxes, ground hogs, skunks, deer and moose — along winding, wooded trails.

To the southwest, Route 1 eventually crosses Bear River into Digby County. The work of Nova Scotia artisans, many from Bear River, is showcased at Flight of Fancy on Main Street. Featured downstairs are striking bird paintings on stone, Mi'kmaq crafts, sculptured hardwood burls, pottery, weaving, jewellery, stained glass and carved birds. The upstairs gallery displays paintings, photographs and sculptures by well-known Nova Scotia artists. Bear River's Cherry Carnival, held in mid-July (blossom time), includes an auction, parade and woodsmen's show. Bear River is stunning in autumn when the hardwood hills on either side of the river are ablaze with colour.

ACROSS THE ANNAPOLIS BASIN TO DIGBY GUT

Back on the main drag is the resort community of Smiths Cove. Outstanding views of the Annapolis Basin and Digby Gut make Smiths Cove a good choice for an overnight stay. The recently renovated Mountain Gap Resort offers waterside accommodation (including cottages) at reasonable prices — especially for families, who will appreciate the resort's beach, swimming pool, tennis court and playground.

From there, it is a short drive to Digby, home of the world's largest scallop fleet. Scallops and Digby chicks (smoked herring) are served in local restaurants. From the deck of the Fundy Restaurant on Water Street, you can enjoy Digby seafood with a view of the boats that caught your meal. Golfers rave about Stanley Thompson's championship course at the Digby Pines Resort. The par-

71, 18-hole course plays through mature stands of spruce and pine while affording some beautiful views of the Annapolis Basin. The hotel, built in 1929, features a Norman-style chateau and 30 cottages strung out along a bluff that rises from the shores of the basin. There are a number of excellent inns and bed and breakfasts in the Digby area. Thistle Down Country Inn has 12 spacious room, views of the scallop fleet and a gracious dining room. A regular ferry service shuttles across the Bay of Fundy between Digby and Saint John, New Brunswick.

Whale- and seabird-watching tours are just some of the reasons to enjoy a drive and two short ferry rides along Digby Neck to Long Island and Brier Island. Along the way there are spectacular panoramas of rocky headlands that have been carved by the powerful Fundy tides. At Tiverton on Long Island, a scenic hiking trail leads to the amazing Balancing Rock. Brier Island Lodge offers food and accommodation as well as breathtaking ocean views.

Between Digby and Yarmouth, along the margin of Baie Ste-Marie (St. Marys Bay), runs a string of Acadian villages. There is no mistaking Nova Scotia's Acadian Shore. Every few kilometres, a steeple soars from one of the magnificent Catholic churches. Colourful houses adorned with curious whirligigs and gizmos line the road at Mavilette or Grosses Coques. Yet for generations after their arrival from France, the original Acadian settlers ignored this area. Most preferred the fertile land of the Annapolis Valley.

The British paid no heed to Acadian preferences in 1755. The Acadians were deported, their houses and barns put to the torch, and the lands they had farmed for 100 years were seized by the Crown. Soon after, the governor

BRIER ISLAND, AT THE ENTRANCE TO ST. MARYS BAY

began granting these lands to new settlers, the so-called Planters, many of whom came from New England and whose loyalty he trusted.

Some Acadians managed to escape deportation. They withdrew to the forests or fled to remote corners of the province, where they lived as refugees. Many died during that first winter, while others were caught and imprisoned at Halifax, Windsor or Annapolis Royal. Still, there was a group of Acadians in Nova Scotia who somehow persevered. When the Treaty of Paris ended the war between France and England in 1763, these people began to look for a home. Others returned from exile. Sadly, the Annapolis Valley was lost to them.

Eventually, Lieutenant-Governor Michael Francklin responded to their plight. Land was surveyed along St. Marys Bay. In 1768 the Township of Clare, named after the Irish county, was created for settlement by the Acadians. The villages of St. Bernard, Belliveau Cove, Grosses Coques, Church Point and Little Brook fall within the boundaries of that original grant. As families grew and others returned from exile, Acadian settlement extended southward to Salmon River. Today, this entire stretch is part of the Municipality of Clare.

Life along the shore was much different from the life the Acadians had known in the Annapolis Valley. They still kept gardens, although the soil was poorer, but the forest

L'Église Saint Bernard

Acadian pride, Clare

L'ÉGLISE SACRE COEUR, SAULNIERVILLE

and the sea were irresistible forces. Acadian farmers became woodsmen, shipbuilders and fishermen — jacks of all trades.

Today, their self-reliance is revealed by a drive along Route 1, sometimes called "the longest main street on earth." Family-run businesses crowd the shore. U. J. Robichaud and Sons run a lumber business at Meteghan Centre. A. F. Theriault and his sons have a shipyard at Meteghan River. Comeau and Deveau are another two French names that you will frequently see. Comeau's Sea Foods in Saulnierville is a huge operation. The Deveaus have a fish operation at Belliveau Cove and an insurance business at Meteghan. Few businesses along the Acadian Shore are run by outsiders.

The Acadian Shore has long served as a centre for Acadian culture in Nova Scotia. Both in terms of size and population density, it is the largest Acadian region in the province. In villages all along Baie Ste-Marie, people gather each July to celebrate their Acadian heritage during the Festival Acadien de Clare. Festivities are fuelled by Acadian music and food. (For a special treat try rappie pie, a savoury casserole of potato and chicken, at the Cape View Restaurant, overlooking Mavillette Beach.) Mavillette, one of several wonderful beaches in the area, has 5 kilometres of magnificent shore.

In 1890, a group of Eudist priests established Collège Sainte-Anne at Church Point. Over the years, Saint-Anne, which became a university in 1977, has made enormous contributions to Acadian culture in Nova Scotia. *Evangéline*, a musical drama based on Longfellow's poem, is staged here during the summer months (English translation is available, and there is one performance a week in English). *Evangéline au bois* is an outdoor evening performance of the play that takes you on a 2-kilometre walk through the woods. The Magasin Campus (campus bookstore) has a wide selection of books on Acadian themes.

A large, fairly homogeneous Acadian population has benefited the people of the Acadian Shore in other ways. The area also has a long tradition of political representation by Acadians, both at the federal and provincial levels. And recent studies have shown that the French spoken in this part of the province has retained more 17th-century features than that spoken elsewhere in Nova Scotia.

But the most visible expressions of the cultural vitality along the shore are the beautiful churches. Acadians pride themselves on their Catholic faith, and parishioners of modest means went to great pains to demonstrate this pride. Hidden behind the graceful exteriors of these churches are surer signs of Acadian faith, workmanship and resourcefulness. Two churches — L'Église Ste-Marie at Church Point and L'Église St-Bernard at St. Bernard — should not be missed.

The plans for Sainte Marie were drawn up in France, but construction of the church was left in the skillful hands of Leo Melanson, a master carpenter from nearby Little Brook. Between 1903 and 1905, he and many others laboured. They must have been in awe of their achievement.

Sainte Marie is the largest wooden church in North America. Its steeple rises 56 metres above the community of 318 people. It is anchored by 36 tonnes of stone ballast to keep it from blowing off in hurricane force winds.

Other things impress. The interior of the church belies its size. A wooden floor softens the stained glass light, lending a warm and comfortable feeling to the entire nave. The "stone" pillars that support the roof are not stone. They are huge tree trunks that have been lathed and covered in plaster. Overhead, the "marble" arches are wooden as well.

The parishioners of St. Bernard were not to be outdone. They hired an architect from Moncton, New Brunswick, who had visited France. He sent down the plans, but the work was left to locals. Between 1910 and 1942, they built a huge stone church that seats over 1,000.

Visitors to the Acadian Shore will receive a warm welcome in French or English. All but a handful of the Acadian population speak both languages. However, it is through French, like their magnificent churches, that the Acadians of Clare express pride in their culture.

The Evangeline Trail continues on to Yarmouth.

FESTIVAL ACADIEN DE CLARE

GLOOSCAP TRAIL

UNUSUAL ROCK FORMATIONS AT CAPE D'OR

Spectacular views of the Bay of Fundy, where the world's highest tides twice daily move 115 billion tonnes of water, await the visitor to the Glooscap Trail. Named for the mythic cultural hero of the Mi'kmaq and other northeastern Native tribes, the Glooscap Trail starts at Amherst, the border point with New Brunswick, and follows the shores of the Bay of Fundy to Windsor.

Along the shores of Cobequid Bay, the tide can rise 2.5 centimetres in a minute, and in some areas the difference between low and high tide has been recorded at 16 metres. The explanation for these extreme tides lies in the bay's funnel shape, which serves as an amplifier. The bulge of water that floods up the Fundy is less than a metre high at the edge of the continental shelf, but at its mouth it meets a slow-moving wave that continually sloshes up and down the bay. This wave, reinforced and pushed by the tide, moves up the bay, where it is squeezed by the rising ocean bottom and the narrowing Fundy shores.

This produces some dramatic effects. Tidal bores occur when a wave of water moves upstream and collides with the current, making it appear as though rivers are flowing

ECONOMY POINT

backwards. Depending on the phase of the moon and other factors such as wind direction, the tidal bore can be either a barely detectable ripple or a wall of water a metre high. Tidal bores can be viewed along a number of rivers in the upper Fundy region, including the Salmon River near Truro (the Palliser Restaurant provides an ideal vantage point and great home-style cooking); the Shubenacadie River at various locations; and from the Maccan and

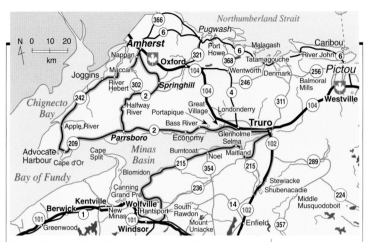

River Hebert bridges. Several companies offer upriver rafting trips on the Shubenacadie. These are safe, but can be very exciting, as the small craft go down river, then return on the crest of the incoming tide.

Join the Glooscap Trail at Amherst, where some truly grand homes, especially along Victoria Street, and the shells of old factories stand as evidence of past industrial glory. The Cumberland County Museum tells some of Amherst's industrial and labour history. Amherst was one of the towns able to take advantage of the steam-based technologies that fueled the new industrialism of the 19th century. Amherst boomed, as textile milling, boot and shoe manufacturing, gas-boiler production and railway car construction drew hundreds of people to the town.

FIRST BAPTIST CHURCH, AMHERST

There is a choice of routes from Amherst to Parrsboro. One can either follow Route 302, the Fundy Shore Scenic Drive, along a sparsely populated section of the Fundy Shore, or Highway 2, to enjoy a stop at Springhill, which remembers the bustle and tragedy of its coal mining history and celebrates the success of its contribution to the continent's entertainment industry. Over the years, more than 400 people have died in local mines. The "Springhill Bump" of 1958, remembered more for the miraculous survival of 18 men who spent a week trapped underground than for the 75 who did not make it, brought an end to large-scale mining in the town. But it did not bring an end to tragedy. In 1975, fire ravaged the town's main street business district. Today, retired miners give underground tours at the Springhill Miners' Museum, where exhibits include

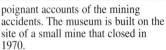

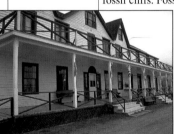

SPRINGHILL MINERS'
MUSEUM

**SPRINGHILL MINERS'
MUSEUM**

poignant accounts of the mining accidents. The museum is built on the site of a small mine that closed in 1970.

The Anne Murray Centre pays tribute to the Springhill-born recording artist and offers a surprisingly candid look at her life — including report cards and baby pictures. Fans of "Canada's Country Sweetheart" should definitely drop in.

Those who choose to take the Fundy Shore Scenic Drive following Route 302 to Apple River will see a part of the province that has long been recognized as a treasure trove of fossil remains. The Fossil Centre at Joggins, an old coal mining town on Chignecto Bay, offers guided tours of the famous fossil cliffs. Fossil finds, usually plant material, date from the time when Nova Scotia's vast coal deposits were formed about 300 million years ago. The cliffs themselves are off-limits, but they erode so quickly that new fossils are always falling to the beach. Children will enjoy the outing, and are almost always assured of finding something. As you search the beach beneath the cliffs, take an occasional peek behind you; you will be surprised to see how quickly the tide is falling — or rising!

**OTTAWA HOUSE,
PARRSBORO**

At Apple River, continue on Route 209, passing Cape Chignecto Provincial Park, Nova Scotia's newest and largest provincial park — 4,000 hectares of coastal wilderness trails, dramatic cliffs and old-growth forest. This is Nova Scotia's premier hiking destination. There is a picnic area overlooking the Bay of Fundy.

The Bay of Fundy, like most large bodies of water, has its share of marine folklore, and one of these stories, the saga of the ghost ship *Mary Celeste*, is recounted at a cairn at Spencers Island. In December 1872, the brigantine was discovered at sea with sails set and everything in order, but no one was on board, or was ever found. It would turn out to be one of the great sea mysteries of all time.

**AGE OF SAIL
HERITAGE CENTRE,
PORT GREVILLE**

Along the stretch of coastline between Advocate and Parrsboro, the scenery rivals the coastal views along Cape Breton's Cabot Trail. Across the Minas Channel, Cape Split and North Mountain loom large on a clear day, and Cape d'Or is just as spectacular. There is a look-off at the Cape d'Or lighthouse (just off Route 209) with an unforgettable view — east toward the Minas Basin, south across the Minas Channel and west to

the Bay of Fundy.

In Parrsboro, the Fundy Geological Museum houses a display on the effects the giant Fundy tides have had on the people and the land. Museum exhibits also detail the geological and fossil history of the area.

Good opportunities for rockhounding are plentiful in the Parrsboro area. The town holds Nova Scotia's Gem and Mineral Show each August. Zeolites — semi-precious stones such as agate and amethyst — are common finds along the beaches and cliffs of the Minas Basin. Eldon George, Parrsboro's most famous rockhound, has a rock shop at the edge of town. In April 1984, George found a rock with some very tiny — and soon to be highly celebrated — dinosaur footprints on its surface.

GLOOSCAP STATUE, PARRSBORO

Parrsboro's Ship's Company Theatre stages innovative productions aboard the MV *Kipawo*, a beached ferry boat that once serviced Parrsboro, Kingsport and Wolfville. The acclaimed company features many plays by Maritime writers during a season that runs from mid-June to Labour Day.

The road from Parrsboro to the TransCanada Highway at Glenholme offers an opportunity to visit several quaint and historic hamlets such as Economy, Bass River, Portapique, Great Village and Londonderry. If you stop at Five Islands Provincial Park, you can see where the legendary Glooscap threw handfuls of sod at Beaver, creating Moose, Diamond, Long, Egg and Pinnacle islands. There are also a number of hiking trails in the park. Five Islands Lighthouse, a "pepper pot" wooden structure, also has a terrific view of the islands. Scenic waterfalls in the region are popular destinations for hikers. A novel opportunity to observe the evolution of nature can be enjoyed at Economy Falls, where a major rock fall changed the appearance of that popular attraction in late 1997.

WENTWORTH FALLS

Truro is the commercial crossroad in the centre of the province and is known as "the Hub of Nova Scotia." Truro is a good stopping place. It has many shops, restaurants and accommodations. It is also a hub for golf, with several good courses in

the area, including the Truro Golf Club, the oldest club in the province. Victoria Park is a surprising 405-hectare oasis in the middle of town with shady walking trails, waterfalls and Jacob's Ladder — about 200 wooden steps that are a challenge for even the fittest legs.

From Truro, there is the option of heading towards Halifax or continuing along the Fundy Shore to Maitland. Route 2 towards Halifax passes the Shubenacadie Wildlife Park, where most of Nova Scotia's native birds and animals can be seen in natural surroundings.

The village of Maitland, located at the mouth of the Shubenacadie River, flourished during the Age of Sail. At one time, 11 shipyards bordered an 11-kilometre stretch of shore near Maitland. Fortunes were made and lavish homes were built. Close to 50 of these have survived, prompting the provincial government to designate Maitland as Nova Scotia's first Heritage Conservation District. A walking tour brochure is available at the local visitor information centre. The Frieze and Roy General Store, established in 1839, displays a number of interesting historical items.

On October 27, 1874, more than 4,000 people gathered in Maitland to see the launching of the *William D. Lawrence*, the largest full-rigged ship ever built in Canada, and named after the man who built it. The village commemorates the event with a Launch Day Festival in September. The *William D. Lawrence* was nearly 2,500 tonnes and turned a handsome profit for her owners. At Lawrence House, designated a National Historic Site in 1965, the signs of wealth are everywhere. English iron-work radiators are topped with Italian marble. At the back of the house, you can see the huge blocks that were used to step the masts of Lawrence's ships. Not surprisingly, William Lawrence, elected to the Nova Scotia Assembly in 1863, strongly opposed Confederation, and fought for the repeal of the Union Act. The Intercolonial Railway, the linchpin of Confederation and a symbol of future prosperity, would not run through Maitland.

Continuing west from Maitland, along coastal Route 215 toward Windsor, one soon begins enjoying the scenic Noel Shore, one of the prettiest spots in the province when the horse chestnuts are in bloom in late June. At Burncoat Head, during the Saxby Tide in 1869, the highest tides in the world were recorded. Gale-force winds helped generate a high tide of 16.5 metres.

SUNRISE TRAIL

The Sunrise Trail follows the North Shore, from Amherst to the Canso Causeway. With its picturesque towns, gentle farmland and seaside views, this route is a recommended alternative to the TransCanada Highway. Several fine beaches and the warm waters of the Northumberland Strait help make it a popular summer holiday destination.

The tourist information centre at the provincial gateway displays information on the Chignecto Ship Railway, the ambitious 19th-century venture that would have transported ships from the Bay of Fundy to the Northumberland Strait by rail. A 4-kilometre walking trail follows the remnants of the railbed to Tidnish Dock Provincial Park.

Not much farther, near Lorneville, is the Amherst Shore Country Inn. The inn offers four rooms and four suites, as well as a rustic seaside cottage and memorable dining. In Port Howe, Chase's Lobster Pound offers fresh

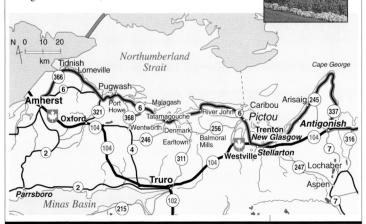

SEAGULL PEWTER, PUGWASH

live and cooked lobsters.

Pugwash, with street signs in both Gaelic and English, is one of several North Shore communities with a rich Scottish heritage. The village holds a Gathering of the Clans Festival in early July.

During the 1950s and 60s, wealthy Cleveland industrialist Cyrus Eaton hosted a number of Thinkers Conferences at his Pugwash estate, to which he invited Western and Soviet intellectuals. Albert Einstein was among the attendees.

Today, Pugwash is home to several silver and pewter manufacturers who ship pewter jewellery, dishes and picture frames to worldwide markets. Seagull Pewter has a large shop on the main road. The Hidden Jewel sells fine silver and gold jewellery from their retail craft outlet. The jewellery is made on-site, and daily tours are offered from June to October. High-quality Maritime handcrafts are also featured at the shop.

Just outside town, serious golfers can enjoy 18 challenging holes on the Northumberland Links. The open, tree-lined fairways are well maintained. Several holes play

along the water, and the views of the strait can be quite a distraction.

The views are just as striking at the Sunrise Beach Golf & Country Club, overlooking Brule Harbour near Tatamagouche. But unlike the Pugwash course, this wide-open, nine-hole round of golf is well suited to beginners.

In addition to a modest fishery, Tatamagouche is a service centre for local dairy farms. Appropriately, Highland cattle are beginning to catch on in the area as well. And the favourable climate sustains some other, more exotic enterprises. The Josts, one of several German families to settle along the North Shore since the Second World War, have a winemaking operation in nearby Malagash. Tours of the vineyards are provided and visitors are invited to sample Jost wines at the on-site retail store. Here, there are some good-quality, inexpensive wines, including some award-winning ones, available for purchase.

Farther along, two restored mills give a glimpse of earlier times. The Balmoral Grist Mill Museum, at Balmoral Mills (Route 256), grinds wheat, oats and buckwheat into flour using 19th-century water-powered milling techniques. The Sutherland Steam Mill, in nearby Denmark (Route 326), began sawing logs into lumber in 1894. Now part of the Nova Scotia Museum, the steam

boilers are fired up Wednesdays to Saturdays from June to mid-October and visitors can watch the mill in operation from 1 to 3 pm. On Route 311 between Balmoral Mills and Denmark is Earltown and Sugar Moon Farm, a year-round Maple Sugar Camp and Pancake House. On the way to Earltown, you may see Nova Scotia's first herd of buffalo grazing by the roadside.

The Northumberland Strait is a choice area for the lobster fishery. The season runs from early May to late June, when communities like River John bustle. The village holds frequent lobster suppers during the season, and visitors are invited to take part.

SCOTTISH DANCERS, PICTOU

The good beaches — such as the one at Caribou, northwest of Pictou — attract cottagers to this shoreline. For a shorter stay, you might choose the Pictou Lodge on Braeshore Road, just east of the town of Pictou and 4 kilometres from the Prince Edward Island ferry. Built in the mid-1920s as an exclusive retreat, the lodge was originally managed by the Canadian National Railway. Its log construction is typical of many CNR resorts, including the Jasper Park Lodge in the Canadian Rockies. The cabins include several dating from the 1920s, plus many more modern units. Ocean views can be spectacular, especially at sunset, from the sun porch bar.

Pictou's Scottish culture, scenic harbour and fine architecture make it the North Shore's most popular destination for visitors. And for those Nova Scotians who take great pride in their Scottish heritage, Pictou is a kind of Plymouth Rock. The *Hector,* which landed Nova Scotia's first Scots on the shores of Pictou Harbour in 1773, has been called the "Scottish Mayflower." For a Nova Scotia Scot, having ancestors aboard the *Hector* accords special status.

BALMORAL GRIST MILL

Today, the showpiece of Pictou's waterfront is the ship *Hector,* at the Hector Heritage Quay. The 33-metre-long full-rigged ship was reconstructed on-site, and as of September 2000, began its career as a floating heritage exhibit. Although no plans for the original *Hector* exist, engineers went to some trouble to ensure that the reconstructed ship closely resembled its predecessor. The story of 18th-century Scottish immigration and the *Hector* voyage is told in the adjacent interpretation centre. The site also includes a carpentry shop, a blacksmith shop and a gift shop. You can also nip into a nearby pub for a wee dram.

During August, the Hector Festival celebrates the arrival of the ship and the town's Scottish heritage, and features Scottish music, dance and food, with Celtic musical performances at the de Coste Centre on Water Street. This venue

also serves as northeastern Nova Scotia's centre for the performing arts throughout the year. New Scotland Days, held in September on the anniversary of the arrival of the *Hector*, features lots of bagpipes, highland dancing and wooden boat-building demonstrations.

Next to the Hector National Exhibit Centre, on Old Haliburton Road, is the restored McCulloch House which was built in 1806 with bricks brought over from Scotland.

Pictou's architecture is another Scottish legacy. Throughout the town you can see 19th-century neoclassical buildings, mostly of stone. Typically, these have gabled walls that extend above the plane of the roof at either end of the house. The Scottish dormer, recognizable by its bay window, is another prominent feature. Fine trim and mouldings lend elegance to houses that would otherwise appear stark. Some Pictou streets, especially those with row houses, could easily run through towns in western Scotland. Walking tours of the town are available Sunday mornings throughout the summer.

The tourist bureau, located at the rotary just outside town, can direct you to the town's historic buildings. Several are open to visitors. The Walker Inn (c. 1865) and the Consulate Inn (c. 1810) are registered heritage properties that offer bed and breakfast-style accommodation in the downtown area. The Customs House B&B offers carefully restored rooms in what was Pictou's Customs House. The Braeside Inn, though built this century, also impresses from its hilltop perch overlooking the harbour. The inn offers fine harbour views from its two large dining rooms (seafood is a specialty) and from several of its 20 guest rooms.

Pictou's architecture and landscape also reflect its historic importance as a shipbuilding centre. The Consulate Inn, so named because it housed the American Consulate during the last half of the 19th century, is one sign of this legacy. The shipyard, where visitors who arrive on the right day may still see a large vessel in dry-dock, is another. The lobster fishery also makes this a working harbour. Here,

and in countless other villages along the strait, fishermen spend May and June mornings setting and unloading traps. Since 1934, the town has celebrated this fishery during the Pictou Lobster Carnival, held in early July. Local boat races, a lobster dinner and concerts featuring the best of Nova Scotia's musical

MELMERBY BEACH, NEAR NEW GLASGOW

talent highlight the festival.

While in town, you can also visit Grohmann Knives, known to outdoor enthusiasts as the manufacturer of the world-renowned D.H. Russell belt knife. Grohmann offers free factory tours (some restrictions apply), and the gift shop often has good buys on seconds. Nearby gift shops and galleries offer a range of crafts from local artisans.

The Pictou Golf Club, overlooking the harbour, is a fairly easy nine-hole course despite all the downhill, uphill, and sidehill lies that you'll encounter. The Jitney Trail, spanning the southern portion of Pictou Harbour, is a scenic 3-kilometre pathway connecting the waterfront to the original landing site of the *Hector*.

Melmerby is the best of several good warm-water beaches in the Pictou area. Take Exit 25 off Highway 104 (the TransCanada) to get to this 2-kilometre stretch of broad, sandy beach. Melmerby is supervised and offers a canteen, shower and change facilities.

Most of the area's heavy industry sprang up in the towns across the harbour, to the southeast of Pictou. Coal mining transformed the landscapes of Westville and Stellarton. Canada's first integrated metalmaking and metalworking complex did the same to New Glasgow and Trenton. These towns, with their long history of industrial activity, have fascinating stories to tell, including the 1992 disaster at the Westray coal mine.

There was nothing exceptional in the rise of the Pictou County coal industry; similar growth was taking place in Cape Breton and Cumberland County. It was the metals industry that relied heavily on the entrepreneurial spirit of the Pictou County elite. When shipbuilding became unprofitable in the 1880s, New Glasgow's wealthy merchant families began looking for somewhere else to put their money. What they founded — the Nova Scotia Steel and Coal Company — changed Pictou County. The populations of New Glasgow and Trenton exploded as people came to work in one of the country's foremost industrial enterprises. During the First World War, "Scotia"

MCCULLOCH HOUSE

employed close to 6,000 miners and steelworkers. Many other Pictou County operations were busy converting Scotia's steel into a wide range of secondary metal products.

But Scotia's story is a familiar one. During the 1920s, increased freight rates, competition from central Canada, and outside ownership led to a rapid decline. Pictou County industry has been

teetering on the brink ever since. There were, however, some hardy survivors. Maritime Steel and Foundries Limited marked its 100th anniversary in 2002. Maritime Steel produces steel castings that are exported around the world. The story of industrial boom and bust is told at the Nova Scotia Museum of Industry, just off the TransCanada Highway at Stellarton. Exhibits include two of the world's oldest steam locomotives. Children, especially, enjoy working on the museum's toy train assembly line. Stellarton is also where the Sobey grocery giant was born, and today is the home of the corporate office of what is now the second largest grocery retailer in Canada.

MUSEUM OF INDUSTRY IN STELLARTON

The community that was to become New Glasgow was settled by Scots in 1784, and by 1809 the town had been named after Glasgow in Scotland and then officially incorporated in 1875. Enterprise and the entrepreneurial spirit were evident even in 1809, when James William Carmichael and George Amos established a trading post. New Glasgow is still true to its roots and, today, is the commercial and service centre for northern Nova Scotia.

The Festival of the Tartans, a celebration of Scottish music and heritage, is held here annually in mid-July. The New Glasgow Music Jubilee featuring East Coast and Canadian talent is held on the Riverfront in early August. Later in August, there is the new Race on the River, the Pictou County Dragon Boat Festival. New Glasgow's Abercrombie Country Club is a challenging 18-hole course that punishes wayward tee shots. It is essential to book tee-times in advance. More golf is within 10 minutes of New Glasgow at Glen Lovat and Linancy Greens.

Antigonish, along the eastern section of the North Shore, is home to St. Francis Xavier University and the Antigonish Highland Games. The games, held in mid-July, include piping, Highland dancing, heavy events and track and field, making for one of Nova Scotia's best Scottish festivals. Festival Antigonish offers live theatre on the university campus throughout the summer months. The Antigonish Golf Club is the North Shore's best 18-hole bet for spur-of-the-moment golf. It is rarely crowded on

AT THE ANTIGONISH HIGHLAND GAMES

summer weekdays and provides a stiff test, playing 6,100 yards from the men's tees.

If you have time to dawdle, take Route 337 north from Antigonish along the western shore of St. Georges Bay. Like many of the roads along the North Shore, this drive takes you off the beaten track. The views from the Cape George Lighthouse grounds are beautiful, and there are more scenic look-offs, good beaches for bird watching and hiking trails along the way.

MARINE DRIVE

The eastern shore, which extends along the Atlantic coast between Halifax and Canso, is rugged and relatively undeveloped. A vast network of wilderness lakes and rivers makes the area a favourite with canoeists and campers. Coastal kayaking is also popular, especially in the area around Tangier. Outdoor enthusiasts can explore the eastern shore beaches, harbours and islands or the inland forests, lakes and rivers.

But to those who choose the eastern shore's Marine Drive as an alternative to the TransCanada Highway for the trip from Halifax to Cape Breton, take heed. You will find some spectacular coastal scenery, but the 400-kilometre drive along winding roads is best spread over two days.

Lawrencetown Beach is just east of Dartmouth. A provincial park, this steep, sandy beach is supervised and has

SURFERS AT LAWRENCETOWN BEACH

141

change and canteen facilities. Lawrencetown is relatively exposed, and large waves make it a favourite with Nova Scotia surfers. Farther along, to the south of Musquodoboit Harbour, is Martinique Beach (the name is tropical, but the crystal-clear water is not). Because of its distance from Halifax, on some summer days you will have this 5-kilometre-long stretch to yourself. The fine sand hardens at the waterline, making Martinique ideal for long walks. Nearby, the Martinique Beach Game Sanctuary is the northernmost wintering ground of the Canada goose. The Salmon River House Country Inn, at Salmon River Bridge, offers six well-appointed guest rooms in an area where accommodations are scarce. On-site outdoor activities include hiking, boating, hunting and fishing. The Fisherman's Life Museum, in neighbouring Jeddore Oyster Pond, recalls the lives of a turn-of-the-century inshore fisherman and his family. The museum interpreters have some wonderful stories to tell.

At Lake Charlotte, the recently developed Memory Lane Heritage Village recalls the more recent past. Go back to the 40s — tour the site on a bicycle or in a 1949 truck.

Clam Harbour Beach comes next. Its fine, white sand is ideal for sandcastles. In mid-August, thousands come here for the Clam Harbour Beach Sandcastle and Sculpture Contest, with group and individual competitions for young and old. Some of the sculptures are extremely intricate. On Route 224 toward Middle Musquodoboit is the Moose River Gold Mines and Area Museum, which describes gold mining history and the famous mine disaster of 1936. Highway 7 continues east through Tangier on its way towards Sherbrooke Village. Tangier is home to Willy Krauch's Danish Smokehouse. Open year-

**TOP: MARTINIQUE
ABOVE:
FISHERMAN'S LIFE
MUSEUM**

**WILLY KRAUCH'S
SMOKEHOUSE**

round, Krauch's wood-smoked salmon, eel and mackerel have won customers from around the world.

Farther along Highway 7, on a peninsula that juts into the Atlantic, is Taylors Head Provincial Park, where there are a number of boardwalks and trails. Both the beach and the views of the ocean are spectacular.

Sherbrooke Village has been restored to appear as it was during the last half of the 19th century. Area residents work at the village dressed in period costumes and take pride in its history. The result is a low-key living museum, where the past rubs shoulders comfortably with the present.

This area along the banks of the St. Marys River has attracted many people over the centuries. The Mi'kmaq were drawn by the large runs of salmon in the river, as were New England fishermen. In 1755, the French established a fur trading post here (Fort Sainte Marie), where they traded with the Mi'kmaq, fished and cultivated the soil until they were driven out by an English force in 1769.

Around 1800, about 50 settlers from the Truro and Pictou areas moved cross-country to establish new homes. The new arrivals took advantage of the area's most valuable resource, timber, and sawmills began producing lumber for small shipbuilding operations. Sherbrooke, so named in 1815 after Sir John Coape Sherbrooke, Lieutenant-Governor of Nova Scotia, exported timber to Great Britain in locally built ships. Families like the Cummingers and the MacDonalds were involved in both ends of the operation, and grew quite wealthy. During the

1860s and 70s, their shipyards turned out several barques in excess of 500 tons for the carrying trade, as well as many smaller boats for the fishery.

The contributions of these families feature prominently in the restored village. The general store was operated by the Cumminger brothers, Samuel and John. You need only

look at the store's elaborate counters to gain some appreciation of their wealth and the woodworking skills associated with shipbuilding. Superior craftsmanship is also apparent at Greenwood Cottage, built by John and Sarah Cumminger in 1871.

The reconstruction of the MacDonald Brothers' water-powered,

SHERBROOKE VILLAGE RECAPTURES LATE-19TH-CENTURY LIFE

up-and-down sawmill is located a few minutes away from the main village, but do not miss it. The sawmill is wonderful. You can feel the power of the water wheel, and see it in the rise and fall of the huge saw blade. All the workings — great belts and pulleys — are exposed.

There is much more. Sherbrooke Village has a blacksmith shop, which has operated continuously since it was built in 1870. The Sherbrooke Drug Store was given most of its stock by the Nova Scotia Pharmaceutical Society and has a wonderful display of turn-of-the-century medicines. Among the many other buildings on-site are a

LIGHTHOUSE AT PORT BICKERTON

Temperance Hall, a boat-building shop, a village potter, a Presbyterian church and a courthouse. Tea and more substantial meals are served at the What Cheer Tea Room.

There is another smokehouse in St. Marys River near Sherbrooke Village.

The provincially run Liscombe Lodge, at nearby Liscomb Mills (about 20 minutes from Sherbrooke Village)

offers first-rate accommodation in the lodge or cottages and chalets in peaceful riverside surroundings with beautiful walking trails.

The lighthouse at Port Bickerton, which protected the region's seafaring folk since the 1920s, has been refurbished to its original decor, and has been re-opened as the Nova Scotia Lighthouse Interpretive Centre. Inside, interpretive panels show the history behind the 166 lights that dot Nova Scotia's coastline. Visitors can also find detailed information on the Sable Island and Sambro lighthouses, along with local history concerning the 16 lights in Guysborough County. Stepping from old to new, there is a CD-ROM in English and German, detailing all of the Guysborough County lights. A new trail leads from the lighthouse to a beautiful sandy beach.

Take the Country Harbour Ferry from here to Guysborough. The ferry has been operating for 25 years and makes regular crossings year-round.

Near the end of a peninsula that juts far out into the Atlantic is the fishing village of Canso, one of Nova Scotia's oldest communities. It was the rugged and beautiful nature of this area that inspired some of the most memorable songs of Stan Rogers. His music and his place in local folklore are celebrated at the Stan Rogers Folk Festival in early July. Other events include the Seafood Festival in July and the Canso Regatta and Tuna Cup in August.

Offshore, Grassy Island is the site of a once-prosperous community of New England fishermen and merchants until 1744, when the fishing station was sacked by a French force from Louisbourg.

In Canso, a Parks Canada visitor centre tells the story through a brief audiovisual presentation and a series of life-size exhibits detailing the interiors of three Grassy Island properties — a tavern, a merchant's house and the home of a military officer. Between June and September, a daily boat service takes visitors to the island, where an interpretive trail links eight designated sites.

CABOT TRAIL

THE CABOT TRAIL, ONE OF THE WORLD'S SPECTACULAR DRIVES

It is a rare thing for a road to become more famous than any of the places it passes through, but that is what has happened with Cape Breton's Cabot Trail. Its hairpin turns, ear-popping climbs and descents and spectacular cliff-side views have been thrilling motorists since the 1930s.

If we take A. S. MacMillan (Minister of Highways during the 1920s) at his word, the decision to undertake the costly and ambitious construction of the Cabot Trail was, quite literally, the result of one man's dream. In August 1924, MacMillan went to Cheticamp to look into the possibility of building a road that would extend northward to the community of Pleasant Bay and beyond. Apparently, the trip along the northwestern shore of Cape

Breton left quite an impression on the minister. He recalls, in a 1952 document reproduced in the June 1992 issue of *Cape Breton's Magazine*, what took place upon his return to Baddeck: "Some time near morning I fell asleep and dreamed about a wonderful development that I could see underway, numerous houses, cottages and tourist homes in the many bays and inlets as well as sail boats and all kinds of pleasure craft, apparently everybody enjoying themselves." MacMillan was inspired and the rest, as he would have wanted it, is history. Today, the 300-kilometre Cabot Trail, named for the famous explorer who reputedly landed on the shores of

Cape North

Meat Cove Bay St. Lawrence

Dingwall

Smelt Brook

Pleasant Bay

New Haven

Neils

Harbour

Cabot Trail

Ingonish

N 0   20

km

Cheticamp

Margaree Harbour

Indian Brook

North East
Margaree

Tarbotvale

Englishtown

162 Sydney
Mines

Broad Cove

Margaree
Forks

Goose Cove

St Ann's

Inverness

North Sydney Sydney

*Cabot
Trail*

223 125

Mabou

*Ceilidh
Trail*

Nyanza

Baddeck

327

Shunacadie

Whycocomagh

Iona

Eskasoni

19

Orangedale

*Bras d'Or
Lake*

Big Pond

105

4

Marble Mountain

Roberta

Fleur-de-Lis Trail

Craigmore

Fourchu

Dundee

St. Peters

104

Port
Hastings

4

104

River
Bourgeois

Ardoise

**Port
Hawkesbury**

206

D'Escousse

344

Arichat

Petit-de-Gras

Atlantic Ocean

Aspy Bay in June 1497, is a loop that takes you along most of the coastline of northwestern Cape Breton. Contrary to MacMillan's vision, much of that coastline remains undeveloped. This, however, is a good thing. Cape Breton has been named the world's most scenic island. Its unspoiled natural beauty has earned it the highest rating for environment/scenery in a recent poll by a prestigious travel magazine. It is also renowned for the friendliness of its people. The Cabot Trail has become not just a scenic drive but a destination offering the best in adventure tourism, golf, accommodation, dining and beaches — not to mention the stunning scenery. Outdoor adventurers will want to take most of their vacation to explore the beautiful wilderness areas in Cape Breton Highlands National Park.

Baddeck is generally considered to be the beginning and end of the Cabot Trail. However, the village was attracting summer visitors long before it earned this distinction. In 1879, Charles Dudley Warner's *Baddeck, and That Sort of Thing* was published. Though not very popular with Cape Bretoners — they were mockingly portrayed as backward and primitive — the book's description of Baddeck's splendid isolation struck a chord with many American readers. Among those was the inventor of the telephone, Alexander Graham Bell. Seeking refuge from the hot summers of Washington, DC, Bell and his wife, Mabel, decided to stop in at Baddeck on their way to Newfoundland for a holiday in 1885. They fell in love with the place. Eight years later, they built their estate, Beinn Bhreagh (Beautiful Mountain) on a headland overlooking the Bras d'Or Lakes. There, Alexander and Mabel spent many happy summers, until his death in 1922.

Today, the Alexander Graham Bell National Historic

**ALEXANDER
GRAHAM BELL
NATIONAL HISTORIC
SITE, BADDECK**

147

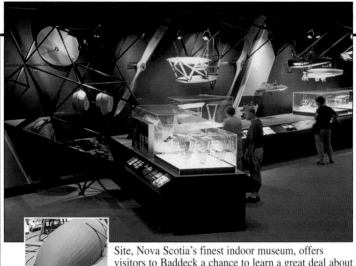

HYDROFOIL HALL AT THE BELL MUSEUM

Site, Nova Scotia's finest indoor museum, offers visitors to Baddeck a chance to learn a great deal about the inventor's life. The site's collection of Bell's artifacts, written materials and personal mementoes is the most comprehensive in the world. Provided you have the time (a complete tour takes several hours), the exhibits give a thorough and intimate account of Bell's life.

Bell was a compulsive inventor. He may have left the Washington heat behind, but Bell brought his passion for invention and experimentation to his summer home. Among his lesser-known efforts were attempts to develop a multi-nippled sheep for Cape Breton farmers, and a device that would relieve the plight of Banks fishermen by converting fog into drinking water. During his last years, the hydrofoil was Bell's special interest. Several models were built and tested in Baddeck.

Baddeck's status as a resort and tourist centre has grown since the Bell era. The friendly bustle of the village makes it a popular stopping place for visitors. Baddeck has a population of approximately 1,000 and about an equivalent number of guest rooms; even so, it is advisable to book early. The Inverary Inn Resort has 125 rooms in five main buildings along with 13 cottages. This full-service resort offers tennis, an indoor pool, canoeing and boat cruises, and a host of other activities. MacNeil House, on the grounds of the Silver Dart Lodge, has six luxurious suites with jacuzzis, fireplaces and kitchen facilities. Other amenities include live entertainment in the dining room, bicycles for the use of guests, and a lakeside beach. For those who prefer quieter surroundings, the Duffus House Inn (c. 1830) features antique furnishings and English gardens in a waterside setting. Telegraph House offers motel-style units or rooms in an old-fashioned inn. (The Bells stayed in Room No. 1 before they built Beinn Bhreagh.) Auberge Giselle's Inn, Broadwater Inn and Lynwood Country Inn also offer fine accommodation. Ask for a room overlooking

the Bras d'Or Lakes. Just before Baddeck at Bucklaw, Castle Moffatt will treat you like royalty.

Baddeck's shops carry a variety of upscale handcrafts and folk art. Fine wool sweaters are sold at Seawinds Chandlery, on the government wharf. Up from the water, Kidston Landing features a wide selection of Nova Scotia crafts, woolens and country clothing. Blue Heron Gifts offers a wide selection of Nova Scotia and Cape Breton books and CDs. The Outdoor Store sells quality outdoor clothing and camping supplies. It's a worthwhile stop for those who plan to spend time in the wilderness areas of Cape Breton Highlands National Park.

BADDECK

Baddeck is full of summertime activity. Since 1904, Baddeck has held its annual regatta in early August. Throughout the summer months, yachts are berthed at the government wharf or at private anchorages along the shores of Baddeck Bay. You can go for a sail on the *Elsie*, an 18-metre yacht built in 1917 for Alexander Graham Bell. Spectacular views and great golf are to be enjoyed at the Thomas McBroom-designed Bell Bay Golf Course.

Some distance inland, near Baddeck Bridge, is Uisage Bahn Falls Provincial Park, one of the prettiest spots in all of Cape Breton. A network of maintained hiking trails leads through hardwood forest to a dramatic gorge and waterfalls. This is a great place for a picnic. (You'll find all the fixings for a delicious lunch at the Highwheeler Café in Baddeck or the Herring Choker Deli & Bakery, a kilometre west of the Cabot Trail entrance at Nyanza.)

When leaving the Baddeck area, you have a choice. You can head for Hunters Mountain and the Margaree Valley, which would take you in a clockwise direction around the Cabot Trail, or you can take the counter-clockwise route along the shores of St. Anns Bay and north to Ingonish.

BEINN BHREAGH, WHERE BELL'S DESCENDANTS STILL SPEND THEIR SUMMERS

The clockwise route takes you away from the salt water and through the beautiful Margaree Valley. The Margaree has been nominated as a Canadian Heritage River. Anglers should not pass it by, especially during August and September. Guides are available for salmon and backwater trout fishing. The Margaree Salmon Museum, near North East Margaree, is one of the best privately run

MARGAREE RIVER

museums in Nova Scotia. If you plan on fishing the river, you should drop in for sure. Fly fishermen will have heard of John Cosseboom. (The Cosseboom fly has fooled many Atlantic salmon.) Cosseboom was an ardent disciple of Izaak Walton (*The Compleat Angler*) and spent many summers on the Margaree. His is one of several stories well told by the museum's wonderful collection of fishing memorabilia.

Nearby, along the mysteriously named Egypt Road, is the Normaway Inn, which has catered to anglers and others since the 1920s. The main lodge and 19 cabins (7 with jacuzzis) are within easy striking distance of some of Nova Scotia's best salmon pools. The dining room offers four-course country gourmet dinners.

NORMAWAY INN IN THE MARGAREE VALLEY

MARGAREE SALMON MUSEUM

The trail follows the Margaree until the river spills into the Gulf of St. Lawrence. There is a small sand beach to the south of Margaree Harbour and a larger sand and gravel beach to the north. The larger beach is part of a narrow sand-spit that serves as a natural breakwater for the colourful fishing boats of Margaree Harbour. From here, the road bends to the northeast towards Cheticamp. At Cap Le Moine, one of several tiny Acadian villages that dot this shore, Joe's Scarecrow Theatre has been giving visitors the willies for a number of years.

Cheticamp is the largest and oldest Acadian village along this shore. Cheticantins take special pride in the large co-operatives that dominate the waterfront. They represent the culmination of a long struggle for independence.

When the Treaty of Paris forced the French to abandon the Gulf of St. Lawrence fishery in 1763, merchants from the English Channel Islands were quick to take their place. Charles Robin, a French Huguenot from the Isle of Jersey, set up his operation at Le Chadye (Cheticamp). He encouraged exiled Acadians who had spent time near the French port of St. Malo (just to the south of Jersey) to

settle in Cheticamp, where they could work for him.

And that's just what they did for more than a century. The Charles Robin Company ruled Cheticamp. It owned boats and fishing gear. Fishermen were paid in provisions from the company store. Indebtedness to the "Jerseys" was a way of life from the time the Acadians first settled Cheticamp in the 1780s until late in the 19th century.

Then Father Pierre Fiset arrived. He devoted himself to the spiritual well-being of the Cheticantins — Cheticamp's beautiful Saint-Pierre Church was built under his direction — but he also took a special interest in the worldly affairs of his parishioners. Determined to loosen the Jerseys' grip on the community, Father Fiset purchased a store in 1883. He traded in fish and livestock, and in 1888 he built a wharf on the harbour. Five years later, Father Fiset bought Cheticamp Island from the Robins. The extent of his involvement in worldly affairs troubled some clergy, but they did not question his motives.

Fiset died in 1909. Six years later, a group of fishermen founded Cheticamp's first sales co-operative. During the 1930s, they were greatly assisted by another Catholic clergyman, Reverend Moses Coady, a professor at St. Francis Xavier University in Antigonish, who was appointed by the government to help Maritime fishermen organize co-operatives. The so-called Antigonish Movement had its greatest successes in Antigonish County and Cape Breton.

DISTINCTIVE ACADIAN ARCHITECTURE (TOP) AND ART (ABOVE)

L'ÉGLISE SAINT-PIERRE, CHETICAMP

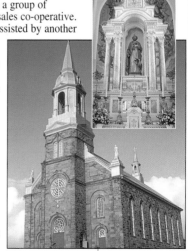

Today, there are seven co-operatives in the Cheticamp area — the most in any Acadian region of Nova Scotia. The Cheticantins jealously guard the management of their own affairs; hardly surprising, given their history.

One of the groups to organize a co-operative in Cheticamp during the

RUG HOOKING IS A MAINSTAY OF THE CHETICAMP ECONOMY

1930s was the rug hookers. Rug hooking is an industry with a peculiar connection to the Bells and Baddeck. Cheticamp women had been hooking rugs from old rags for ages when, in 1922, Lillian Burke, an American friend of the Bells, suggested that they would be able to sell their rugs if they switched from rags to wool and began using softer colours. A cottage industry was born. Burke did well selling Cheticamp rugs in New York until 1936, when Alexandre Boudreau, a leader of the local co-op movement, suggested that the women organize themselves.

Now, the Coopérative Artisanale de Cheticamp Ltée. runs the business. Cheticamp rugs are world famous — especially those of Elizabeth LeFort, whose works can be found at the Vatican, the White House, Buckingham Palace and the Dr. Elizabeth LeFort Gallery & Museum at Les Trois Pignons (The Three Gables) in Cheticamp. Rug hooking is still a cottage industry, but it is no longer quaint. The computerized cash system in the Co-op Artisanale attests to that. Some rugs retail for two thousand dollars. At Le Motif, a local gift shop featuring needlework and folk art, there are some original rag-style rugs for sale. Asked if they were coming back, the woman working at the store replied, "We'll see, if people buy them then they're coming back." Cheticantins are not novices when it comes to the business of art.

There are plenty more rugs (and a wide selection of Cape Breton and Nova Scotian crafts) at Flora's, one of the province's largest craft shops. But Cheticamp area artisans do more than hook rugs. Some of Nova Scotia's most interesting folk art is produced here. You'll see colourful whirligigs and gizmos in shops and front yards throughout the Acadian villages along this coast. One of Canada's best folk artists, Bill Roach, works out of the Sunset Art Gallery in Cheticamp. His whimsical, brightly coloured wood carvings — birds, fish and people among them — are prized by collectors worldwide.

Local artists and artisans draw strength from Cheticamp's rich Acadian culture (Acadian flags are everywhere). Locals still speak French with a 17th-century accent. Cheticantins are justifiably proud of Father Fiset's

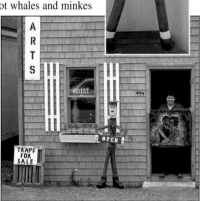

magnificent church. Saint-Pierre, overlooking the village and the bay, anchors the community. Each August, a special mass is held here during the Festival de l'Escaouette, a week-long cultural celebration that brims with Acadian food, song and dance.

The waterfront bustles during summer. Several whale-watching cruises, deep-sea fishing charters and water tours leave from the government wharf and the Quai Mathieu waterfront boardwalk. Pilot whales and minkes are frequently sighted (fin whales less often) and the landward views of Cheticamp and the Cape Breton Highlands are spectacular.

There are a number of restaurants along the water side of Main Street that feature Acadian cuisine. Savoury meat pies and rich seafood chowders are served with thick slices of homemade bread at the Restaurant Acadien in the Co-op Artisanale. Fruit pies are made the traditional way, with flaky biscuit crusts. Several establishments on the waterfront boardwalk have outdoor patios where you can enjoy a drink and watch the sun set behind Cheticamp Island.

A CHETICAMP CRAFT SHOP

If you plan an overnight stay in Cheticamp, book well in advance. For the most part, the village offers motel-style accommodation along its busy Main Street. Laurie's Motor Inn has many guest amenities, including a whale-watching cruise. Across the harbour, the Cheticamp Island Resort features two-bedroom cottages with housekeeping facilities and ocean swimming. The resort offers weekly rates and is ideal for those who plan an extended stay in the Cheticamp area.

Just to the northeast of Cheticamp is the entrance to Cape Breton Highlands National Park. Established in 1936, the park protects about 950 square kilometres of coastline, wooded valleys and barren plateaus. If you plan to hike,

DRAMATIC LANDSCAPES IN THE CAPE BRETON HIGHLANDS

cycle, fish or camp in the park, then stop at the Cheticamp Information Centre for permits and advice. Vehicle permits should be purchased at the centre by anyone intending to use park facilities. Exhibits, including interactive games for children, will introduce you to the park. To get better acquainted, visit the centre's well-stocked bookstore.

Hikers, especially, will find useful resources here. *Walking in the Highlands*, a guide to the park's 26 hiking trails, can be purchased at the centre. So can David Lawley's *Cabot Trail*, an interpretive naturalist's guide to hiking in the area. There are hikes well-suited to a family stroll (like the Lone Shieling Trail near Pleasant Bay) and those with more challenging terrain (the Franey Trail, near Ingonish Beach, ascends 366 metres in only four kilometres). Some offer spectacular coastal scenery (like the Coastal Trail that leaves from Black Brook Beach); others climb to the barren highland plateau (the Lake of Islands Trail, near Ingonish, is a 26-kilometre-long back-country adventure). At the top of the trail, between Cheticamp and Pleasant Bay, is Skyline, the most popular

trail (recently upgraded and wheelchair accessible), which affords spectacular ridgeline views. To truly appreciate the grandeur of the Cape Breton Highlands, park the car and go for a walk.

The 106-kilometre stretch of road between Cheticamp and Ingonish is what made the Cabot Trail famous. Soon after entering the park, the roller coaster ride begins — up French Mountain to a height of 455 metres then down the other side, then another ascent, this time 372 metres to the top of MacKenzie Mountain, and down to Pleasant Bay. Stop at the lookoffs along the way. The view from Fishing Cove Lookoff is breathtaking. On a crystal clear day you might be able to spy the Magdalene Islands to the northwest, across more than 80 kilometres of water.

Pleasant Bay, following a serpentine descent of MacKenzie Mountain (you can imagine the difficulty of a landward approach to this community before the road was built), is a scenic fishing village with a variety of visitor services. Whale-watching cruises leave from the Pleasant Bay wharf, and the Whale Interpretive Centre provides a wealth of background information with models, exhibits and interactive displays. The coastline north of Pleasant Bay is spectacular and pristine (a community of Tibetan Buddhist monks is located here); pilot whales, grey seals and bald eagles are regularly sighted. You'll find plenty of whales and seabirds among the beautiful folk art creations of Reed Timmons, a local lobsterman and gill-netter. His Pleasant Bay studio is also filled with colourful roosters.

From Pleasant Bay, the trail moves inland towards North Mountain. At the mountain's base is the Lone Shieling, a replica of a Scottish crofter's hut. The hut is the result of an outpouring of Scottish sentiment from a rather unlikely source. Donald MacIntosh, a native of Pleasant

PLEASANT BAY

CABOT'S LANDING, NEAR CAPE NORTH

Bay, was a geology professor at Dalhousie University in Halifax. When he died in 1934, he left 40.5 hectares at Pleasant Bay to the Crown. His will expressed the desire that the government use the land for a small park where they would construct a cabin modelled after the Lone Shieling on the Isle of Skye. That is how a Skye crofter's cottage came to be tucked among a stand of 350-year-old sugar maples. While the cottage may leave you scratching your head, the massive trees — some are more than 36 metres tall — along the Lone Shieling hiking trail make the stop worthwhile.

From the top of North Mountain (445 metres), the

Cabot Trail descends into the Aspy River valley, passing some spectacular gorges along the way. At the bottom, a dirt road leads to Beulach Bahn Falls, an ideal spot for a picnic. Nearby, Arts North is a fine craft store that features the functional and decorative pottery of Linda and Dennis Doyon, and the deceptively simple designs of jeweller Johanna Padelt. The work of other local artisans is on display in the loft.

If you have time to explore this remote and awesome part of the Island, there are some very good accommodations in the area, notably Oakwood Manor, a 81-hectare estate at Cape North. Leave the trail here and head still farther north to Cabot's Landing (site of a picnic park and long, sandy beach) and Bay St. Lawrence. To boldly go where few tourists have gone, continue along the shores of Bay St. Lawrence to Capstick and follow the

MEAT COVE, AT CAPE BRETON'S NORTHERN TIP

winding dirt road to Meat Cove, a drive you'll not soon forget! For a landward view of the wild beauty of Cape Breton's northern tip, take a bird- and whale-watching boat tour from either Bay St. Lawrence or Dingwall, on Aspy Bay. At Dingwall, Markland Coastal Resort is a luxurious base from which to hike, bike, canoe, kayak, whale- or seabird-watch and return to a gourmet meal.

Back in the village of Cape North, the Cabot Trail bends to

the southeast, towards Ingonish. Many prefer the alternative coastal route, which takes you through the fishing villages of Smelt Brook, White Point, New Haven and Neils Harbour. For an up-close view of the rugged scenery along this exposed shoreline, you can rent mountain bikes at the Sea Spray Cycle Centre in Smelt Brook. The Doyons, who also operate Arts North, display their pottery in a small studio here. At the end of the village of White Point, there is a hiking trail that gives spectacular views of the Aspy Ridge. At Neils Harbour, the Chowder House restaurant makes good use of the village's active fishery in its thick, seafood chowders. You can see the fishing fleet from the restaurant, and walk down to the edge of the North Atlantic after your meal.

From Neils Harbour, the trail heads south towards Ingonish. On a hot day, stop at Black Brook Beach along the way. The water is reasonably warm and there are usually great waves for body surfing (the left side of the beach is less rocky).

The Ingonish area is the resort centre on the Cabot Trail's eastern shore. The beaches are wonderful. The challenging Highlands Links Golf Course was recently rated by *Golf Magazine* as the best course in Canada, and the 69th worldwide. The Middle Head hiking trail runs the length of the narrow peninsula that separates South Bay Ingonish from North Bay Ingonish. Cliff-side views, including an offshore colony of nesting terns at the trail's end, are ample reward for a relatively easy hike. This same promontory is also the site of the provincially owned Keltic Lodge. Other accommodations in the Ingonish area are more modestly priced, but some visitors are willing to pay a premium for the lodge's commanding view of Ingonish Beach and South Bay. There is a fine dining room at the Keltic, which features fresh seafood and local produce, elegantly presented. There is ample opportunity to survey

NEILS HARBOUR IS ONE OF SEVERAL SCENIC FISHING VILLAGES ALONG THIS SHORE

KELTIC LODGE

GAELIC COLLEGE OF CELTIC ARTS AND CRAFTS, SOUTH GUT ST. ANNS (ABOVE)

the waters of South Bay Ingonish. Whale-watching cruises leave from the ports of Ingonish Beach, North Ingonish and Ingonish Ferry. Minke and pilot whales are frequently sighted and the coastline is pocked with sea caves and unusual rock formations. While most whale cruises use converted fishing vessels, Sea Visions, which runs out of Ingonish Ferry, allows you to hear as well as see the Atlantic from the 11-metre sailing vessel *Resplendent*.

After Ingonish, the Cabot Trail snakes its way up and down Cape Smokey — steel yourself for yet another spectacular look-off before heading south on the home stretch. In Indian Brook, you can see the creations of one of Cape Breton's best artisans at Leather Works. John Roberts got his start doing historic leather-work when someone from Louisbourg approached him to do reproductions for the fortress. Leather buckets and less antiquated leather goods — belts, wallets, work aprons and bags — are handmade on the premises.

At the Barachois River Bridge, the road forks. Route 312 takes you to Englishtown via a short ferry ride across St. Anns Harbour. (While waiting for the ferry, you can visit Sea Shanty Antique and Crafts, where the quilts — old and new — are of special interest.) Englishtown was home to Angus MacAskill, Cape Breton's famous 2.4-metre, 193-kilogram giant.

From the Barachois River Bridge, the Cabot Trail twists its way toward South Gut St. Anns. Beginning at Tarbotvale, the road passes by several interesting craft shops. Wild Things features the wood turnings and carvings of Claire Ryder and Juan Prieto. Unique gifts and clothing (including period costume) are displayed in Sew Inclined. Shape Shift and Goose Cove Pottery sells beautiful stoneware and porcelain pottery.

The Gaelic College of Celtic Arts and Crafts teaches traditional Highland music, dance and craft on the shores of South Gut St. Anns. The Gaelic language is also taught during the six-week summer session. The Gaelic Mod, a week-long festival of Celtic culture, is held here each August.

The Bras d'Or Lakes form Cape Breton's 1,165-square-kilometre inland sea. Two narrow channels — Great Bras d'Or and St. Andrews — and a canal at St. Peter's link this sailors' mecca to the North Atlantic. Numerous islands, harbours, coves and saltwater ponds provide shelter from ocean storms, and the region is virtually fog-free.

Its favourable climate, abundant wildlife and outstanding natural beauty have long drawn people to the shores of the Bras d'Or. The Mi'kmaq have been here for centuries. Today, there are four reserves in the area, including the largest in the province at Eskasoni.

The Bras d'Or Lakes Scenic Drive is a signed series of

DUNDEE RESORT

roads skirting almost the entire coastline of the Bras d'Or. It can be accessed at a number of different points. Setting out from Baddeck, head south on the TransCanada Highway. Wagmatcook Reserve, just past Nyanza, has a Culture and Heritage Centre that demonstrates and interprets Mi'kmaq culture and history from early times to the present. It also has a native crafts shop. Further along at Whycocomagh, the Googoo family has been running the Negemow basket shop for more than 30 years. (Before that, baskets were sold door-to-door.) The craftsmanship is exceptional; so is the smell of sweet grass. Follow the signs with the eagle along the south coast, passing through Orangedale, where the railway station immortalized in the song "Orangedale Station" is now a museum. Continue on the Marble Mountain Road through coves and inlets that are the habitat of many shorebirds and bald eagles.

Perhaps the best view of the Bras d'Or is from Marble Mountain, overlooking West Bay. A steep trail to the abandoned quarry (750 men once mined this hillside) starts from the main road, directly across from a small lookoff and picnic area. Interesting old workings provide a good excuse to stop and catch your breath on the way up. The view from the top — islet-studded West Bay and the wide open waters of the Bras d'Or — will stay with you long after you descend the mountain. Back at the look-off on the main road, a steep path leads downhill to a beach of crushed marble sand. The water is ice-cold (several spring-fed brooks flow down the hillside) and crystal clear.

The Dundee Resort is at the head of West Bay. The resort's 60 hotel rooms and 39 cottages are spread out over 223 hectares. Dundee has all the amenities, including an 18-hole championship golf course. The course was built on a steep slope overlooking the bay, making for great views and difficult golf. The resort also has a large marina where you can arrange a cruise on the Bras d'Or.

At Roberta, not far from Dundee, Kayak Cape Breton offers guided sea-kayaking trips on the Bras d'Or and along the Atlantic Coast. The sheltered waters of the Bras d'Or are ideal for beginners

Continuing along the scenic south shore of the lake brings you to St. Peter's, a good-sized community with all services. You can picnic beside St. Peters Canal, a National Historic Site, while watching ships and pleasure craft pass through the old locks from the Atlantic to the Bras d'Or Lakes. At MacIsaac Kiltmakers, you can order a custom kilt or or see how one is made.

At Chapel Island Reserve, one of the oldest Mi'kmaq

ATLANTIC PUFFINS
ARE AMONG THE
THOUSANDS OF SEA
BIRDS THAT
COLONIZE THE "BIRD
ISLANDS"

settlements in the province, daily re-enactments of a 16th-century encampment feature traditional dancing, drumming and storytelling.

Big Pond is the home of Cape Breton singer Rita MacNeil. Many of her awards and records are on display at Rita's Tea Room, in a converted one-room schoolhouse. You may well see Rita here or at the Big Pond Festival, a week-long celebration of folk music held each July.

Continue through the charming village of East Bay, and the Eskasoni First Nations Reserve, to the Grand Narrows Bridge. Across the bridge is Iona, site of the Nova Scotia Museum's Highland Village.

Bras d'Or also attracted European settlers — mostly Scots, like the MacNeils from the Hebridean Island of Barra, who came to Iona towards the end of the 18th century. In 1956, Iona was chosen by the Association of Scottish Societies as the site for a proposed village that would depict the evolution of Scottish settlement in this part of Nova Scotia. Overlooking the Barra Strait, the Nova Scotia Highland Village tells its story through a series of 10 structures, beginning with a Hebridean Black House and ending with an early 20th-century home. Interpreters are used to hearing complaints about the steep climb that a tour of the village requires, but once they see the view, most visitors come around.

From Iona you have two choices. You can take a car ferry at Little Narrows back to Highway 105, on which you can return to Baddeck or go to the Canso Causeway. Or, if you want to complete the drive around the northern loop of the Bras d'Or, recross the Grand Narrows bridge and follow Route 223.

At the Atlantic entrance to the Great Bras d'Or Channel there are two islands, Ciboux and Hertford. Each summer the "Bird Islands" host Nova Scotia's largest colony of breeding sea birds — razorbills, guillemots, gulls, kittiwakes, cormorants and the feature attraction — Atlantic puffins. Bird Island Tours operates out of Big Bras d'Or. The two-and-a-half hour boat trip trims the shores of both islands and the Van Schaiks, long-time operators of the tour, provide a lively and informative narrative.

PASTORAL
LANDSCAPE ALONG
THE CEILIDH TRAIL

Those who have travelled from the Canso Causeway to Baddeck via the TransCanada Highway, and driven the Cabot Trail in a counter-clockwise direction, might carry on through the Margaree Valley towards Margaree Forks and back to the 105. Or, if you are returning to the Canso Causeway, you might consider taking the alternative Route 19 (the Ceilidh Trail) at Margaree Forks. The Ceilidh Trail, as its name suggests, is the musical heartland of Cape Breton. It passes through villages like

Judique and Mabou that have produced Celtic music luminaries John Allan Cameron, Natalie MacMaster, the Rankins, Celtic "bad boy" Ashley MacIsaac and many others. The western shore's strong Scottish identity is preserved in its music, schools and institutions. Mabou offers Gaelic at its school — but not to attract tourists. *Am Braighe* is the village's Gaelic newspaper. The series of summer ceilidhs held along the shore at Broad Cove, Mabou and Judique draw great crowds from the local population as well as visitors.

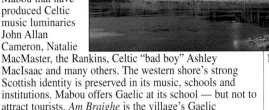

MABOU HARBOUR

The Ceilidh Trail rivals the Cabot Trail for beautiful (if more pastoral) views — especially between Inverness and Mabou, and along the Colindale Road, between Mabou and Port Hood. And there is great saltwater swimming at Inverness, Mabou and Port Hood beaches. (The water of the Northumberland Strait is comfortably warm during summer.)

Inverness is the largest community on the Ceilidh Trail and provides all services. The Inverness Miners' Museum presents the coal mining history of the area. Local arts and crafts are available here and at the Inverness County Centre for the Arts.

The Glenora Inn & Distillery Resort offers nine comfortable rooms in a unique complex. Glenora is North America's only distiller of single malt whisky. Tours are provided and the single malt, Kenloch, is on sale in the gift shop. Inland from Glenville, amidst the rolling hills of the Mabou Highlands, is Lake Ainslie. The 53-kilometre, fairly level, route around the lake is a popular cycling trail. The Cape Mabou hiking trails provide panoramic views of the highlands and seascapes.

The Duncreigan Country Inn, overlooking Mabou Harbour, has eight spacious guest rooms with bay windows. The menu at the inn's excellent dining room includes seafood and local lamb seasoned with garden-fresh herbs. An on-site gift shop features the work of Maritime artists and artisans. Other accommodations in the area include cottages and bed and breakfasts. The Mull Café and Deli, operated by the Mullendores of The Duncreigan, offers informal, family-oriented dining with the same quality you'd find at the inn. The Red Shoe Pub, housed in an extensively renovated, 130-year-old Mabou storefront, presents traditional music three nights a week with a fiddler's matinee on Sundays.

Port Hood marks one end of the Mabou Highlands, which stretch to Inverness and Lake Ainslie. There are a number of warm-water beaches around Port Hood. Judique is another staunchly Scottish community, whose musical traditions are preserved and promoted at the Celtic Music Interpretive Centre.

If the Cabot Trail is your destination, it may be well worth your while to plan on making the journey one way, either up or back, along the richly scenic and cultural Ceilidh Trail.

FLEUR-DE-LIS AND MARCONI TRAILS

KING'S BASTION
BARRACKS,
FORTRESS OF
LOUISBOURG
NATIONAL
HISTORIC SITE

The eastern edge of Cape Breton Island has a French flavour. Starting at Port Hawkesbury, near the Canso Causeway, the Fleur-de-Lis Trail follows the rugged coastline through picturesque Acadian villages. Fishing has been a way of life along this coast since Basque and Portuguese fishermen sought shelter here in the early 1500s. In little coves and harbours you will see colourful houses, lovely wooden churches and wharves stacked with nets and traps dotting the shoreline. You will hear French spoken and taste Acadian cuisine along the way. At the magnificent Fortress of Louisbourg National Historic Site, the Fleur-de-Lis Trail meets the Marconi Trail, which carries on to Glace Bay, linking three sites of Guglielmo Marconi's historic wireless

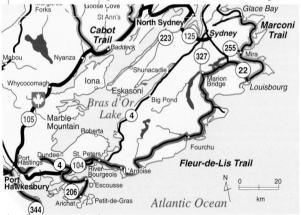

transmissions.

At Louisdale, cross the Lennox Passage Bridge to the cluster of islands that make up lovely Isle Madame. Here, you will find old fishing villages. Arichat was a busy seaport in the mid-18th century and throughout the time of tall ships. Le Noir Forge museum, on the waterfront, is a restored French stone blacksmith shop. There are several accommodations in Arichat. L'Auberge Acadienne has eight rooms in the inn, nine motel units and a dining room. Vollmer's Island Paradise on nearby Janvrin Island offers seven fully equipped cottages and a small — but very good — dining room. You must book a day or two in advance, as all the meals are made from scratch. Petit-de-Grat is the oldest fishing settlement in the area. Nearby, Little Anse is a picturesque spot favoured by photographers. A hiking trail leads to a view of the lighthouse that guards the entrance to the Strait of Canso. With its many little coves, bays and inlets, this area is well-suited to exploring by sea kayak. Cycling is also a good way to see Isle Madame. Bicycle and kayak rentals are available in D'Escousse, another pretty fishing village settled in the 1700s. Rejoining Route 4 on the mainland, you will pass through scenic River Bourgeois to historic St. Peter's. The trail follows Route 247 to L'Ardoise. The excellent sandy beach at nearby Point Michaud is a good place to stop for a picnic. Continue on Route 327 to Marion Bridge, "down on the Mira," the river of the famous song, which is also famous for fishing. Nearby, Two Rivers Wildlife Park displays many native Nova Scotian animals in a natural setting overlooking the Mira and Salmon rivers.

A trip to Louisbourg, where the reconstructed Fortress of Louisbourg National Historic Site brings history to life, provides one of the province's most rewarding experiences.

Tourism has replaced the fishery as the economic mainstay of the modern town, which is situated at the sheltered northern end of the harbour.

The Louisbourg lighthouse is adjacent to the ruins of Canada's first lighthouse, which dates back to 1734. Visitors can enjoy a stroll along the harbourfront boardwalk, and nearby are Louisbourg Market Square, shops, museums, a ship chandlery, accommodations and a post office.

Visitors can take in live theatre and concerts at Louisbourg Playhouse during the summer and fall, and in August, the Louisbourg CrabFest celebrates the bounty of the sea. The S&L Railway Museum houses the visitor information centre, along with

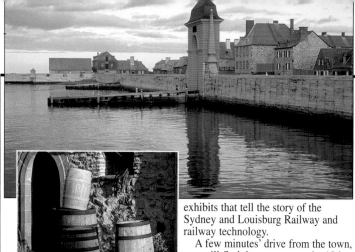

THE QUAY,
FORTRESS OF
LOUISBOURG
NATIONAL
HISTORIC SITE

exhibits that tell the story of the Sydney and Louisburg Railway and railway technology.

A few minutes' drive from the town, you will find the entrance to the 18th-century fortress and the gateway to a living museum.

By the Treaty of Utrecht in 1713, the French agreed to leave their fishing station at Placentia, in Newfoundland, and give up Acadia (which included present-day mainland Nova Scotia) to the British. In exchange, France was allowed to hold on to the islands in the Gulf of St. Lawrence. Ile-Royale (Cape Breton) would emerge as the most important of these, and within a short time, the French had established the Fortress of Louisbourg on its southeastern shore. There, they were soon landing 13,600,000 kilograms of cod a year, worth two to three times the value of the fur trade at Quebec and Montreal. They also had an imposing fortress that lay between the British colonies of Newfoundland and Nova Scotia and, in the fishery, a ready-made training ground for their navy. It is no wonder that the French said of the bargain that they had received an ingot of gold for a bar of silver.

As an entrepôt — a clearinghouse for commodities from France, New France, New England and the West Indies — Louisbourg flourished. Outbound ships, their holds brimming with cod, would return to Louisbourg laden with West Indian rum and sugar, cloths from Carcassonne and the wines of Provence. Enticed by such rich cargoes, wealthy New England merchants supplied wood products and foodstuffs in exchange for them. To a

lesser extent, traders from Nova Scotia and Quebec did the same. Atlantic trade filled Louisbourg's harbour and quickened its waterfront. The quay was a lively place. Scores of shallops (small boats) manoeuvred between large traders so that fishermen could bring their codfish to shore, where they would soon be drying on flakes. Sailors on leave crowded into the inns and taverns that lined the south side of the quay — and Louisbourg fathers made sure their daughters were

accounted for. Commercial necessity overcame the difficulty of haggling with someone who spoke a different language. Goods flowed back and forth between ship and shore.

By 1760 it was over — the town deserted, the fortress destroyed. Louisbourg's commercial promise had been fulfilled, but its military promise had not.

Twice in its short history, Louisbourg fell. When France declared war on Britain in 1744, Louisbourg's commander went on the offensive in the New World, and the British outpost at Canso was captured. A campaign against Annapolis Royal was less successful, but reprisals seemed unlikely. Louisbourg was too well defended and the British seemed unwilling to expend much effort against it.

An attack did come in 1745 — from an unexpected quarter. William Shirley, Governor of Massachusetts, succeeded in raising a force of 4,000 New England militiamen for the purpose. Shirley was strongly supported by wealthy merchants, and the proposed campaign was, in part, a reflection of their desire to take over control of the rich Louisbourg fishery. The militia, under the leadership of General Pepperell, and with the help of a British naval squadron from the West Indies, succeeded in taking the fortress after a 46-day siege.

During the intense negotiations that followed the end of the war in 1748, the British sacrificed Louisbourg in order to hold on to some of their European gains. The following year, Louisbourg was returned to the French. New Englanders were outraged.

In 1756, when war broke out again, the British strategy was to attack France through its colonies and foreign trade. Louisbourg was an obvious target. The town endured several blockades until 1758, when an irresistible combination of British land and sea power overwhelmed the fortress. The French surrendered Louisbourg in July. Two years later, rather than run the risk that Louisbourg would be returned to the French in future negotiations, British engineers were ordered to blow up the fortifications.

The town barely survived. A few people settled in the sheltered northern end of the harbour. Daily, fishermen

CHAPEL IN THE CITADEL (BOTTOM)

made the melancholy trip out of the harbour, past the Royal Battery, around Careening Point, to gaze upon the desolation of the fortress on their way to the fishing grounds.

The reconstruction of Fortress Louisbourg began in 1963 as a creative response to severe unemployment in Cape Breton's coal mines. More than 150 out-of-work coal miners were employed in the project as stonemasons, labourers and carpenters. Researchers had found the original drawings for the military buildings in Paris. Archaeological and graphic evidence was used to reconstruct civilian buildings. The entire effort was characterized by a meticulous devotion to Louisbourg's past.

Proof of this devotion abounds. Buildings sit on their original foundations. Dormer windows jut from gabled roofs, as they did in Poitou, Saintonge and Brittany in the 18th century. Plank siding and a clutter of chimneys speak to an ongoing struggle with cold and damp. Everywhere, timber, sod, stone, mortar and mud have been used to resurrect one quarter of the original town — over 50 buildings in all.

Details help convince. The sculptured trophies atop the Dauphin Gate were quarried from the same French limestone as the originals. In the Carrerot property, mortar laced with glass in the south cellar was used to keep out rats.

Louisbourg's authenticity goes beyond architecture. Bread is baked in the Royal Bakery; savoury dishes simmer in the Engineer's House. The Governor's Apartments are appointed according to Governor Jean-Baptiste-Louis Le Prevost Duquesnel's inventory. They are comfortable and luxurious, well suited to sipping fine Bordeaux. This is a marked contrast to the Hotel de la Marine — a sturdy tavern run by a fisherman where rum and sapinette (spruce beer) flowed freely.

Finally, there are the people. Parks Canada has endeavoured to recreate a moment in the summer of 1744,

and the players know their roles. And, whether by design or not, they seem to fit them. The woman who plays the 18th-century harpsichord in the Ordonnateur's Property does not look out of place. Neither do the soldiers who bear precise reproductions of

1734 French-made flintlock muskets. The man carting firewood to houses along the quay looks just right. Children roll hoops through the streets.

Plan on taking an entire day to fully appreciate Fortress Louisbourg. Ask questions of those who work there. Their answers do more than just inform — they lend flavour to this 18th-century French garrison town.

WENTWORTH PARK, SYDNEY

Should you choose to stay overnight in the town of Louisbourg, there are many accommodations available. The Louisbourg Harbour Inn is a century-old sea captain's house with balconies overlooking the fortress and the harbour. Five of the inn's eight rooms have jacuzzis. Close to the fortress entrance, the Cranberry Cove Inn is another restored turn-of-the-century home. It, too, combines antique furnishings and other traditional touches with modern conveniences like gas fireplaces and jacuzzis. Point of View Suites, at the Louisbourg gates, offers views of the fortress and the ocean from its 13 luxury suites as well as nightly lobster and crab dinners. Fortress Inn Louisbourg has a licensed restaurant. There is also an RV park near the fortress.

The former city of Sydney, now the hub of Cape Breton Regional Municipality, has long prided itself on being the "industrial heart of Cape Breton." Founded in 1785 by Col. J. F. W. DesBarres, Sydney was first settled by Loyalists from New York State, who were followed by immigrants from the Scottish Highlands. The construction early in this century of the Dominion Steel and Coal Company steel plant (now Sydney Steel) took full advantage of the large protected harbour and provided the mainstay of the city's economy for nearly 100 years.

Wentworth Park, a narrow green area near the city centre, with duck ponds, walking paths, picnic areas and a bandstand, is a favourite respite for residents and tourists. Cossit House, built in 1787 on Charlotte Street, is the city's oldest, and now is a provincial museum. Nearby are St. Patrick's Church, the oldest Catholic Church in Cape Breton, Jost Heritage House and the Cape Breton Centre for Heritage and Science. Action Week, during the first week in August, is the time to celebrate Sydney's heritage. Centre 200 is the venue for sports and culture events throughout the year.

GOWRIE HOUSE, SYDNEY MINES

In other parts of this area there are still places that reveal the pride and prosperity that were such a part of the island's past. The Gowrie House in Sydney Mines was

**GOWRIE HOUSE,
SYDNEY MINES**

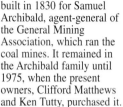

built in 1830 for Samuel Archibald, agent-general of the General Mining Association, which ran the coal mines. It remained in the Archibald family until 1975, when the present owners, Clifford Matthews and Ken Tutty, purchased it. For an overnight stay in metropolitan Cape Breton, there is no better spot. Guest rooms and common areas have since been furnished with beautiful things — Staffordshire figurines, Chippendale chairs and more. A four-course dinner is served each evening; reservations are a must. Visitors to and from Newfoundland find the Gowrie House especially convenient, as it is only minutes away from the ferry terminal in North Sydney.

In Glace Bay, the Savoy Theatre on Union Street is another reminder of a time when Cape Breton industry boomed and the population of coal-mining towns exploded. Built in 1901, the theatre quickly became the venue for a host of cultural activities that Glace Bay residents demanded and could easily support. When the entire Union Street block burned to the ground in 1927, Glace Bay's prosperity was on the wane, but still sufficient enough to quickly rebuild the Savoy — this time with ornamental touches that include the iron rococo chandeliers that hang from the ceiling today. The 761-seat theatre stages theatrical and musical productions throughout the year and is considered one of the finest performance venues in the Atlantic region.

**MINERS' MUSEUM,
GLACE BAY**

At the edge of town, a national historic site commemorates Guglielmo Marconi's experiments with wireless communication. After he received the first trans-Atlantic signal at St. John's, Newfoundland, in 1901, several Canadian communities courted Marconi. He chose to conduct his experiments in Glace Bay. In December 1902, Marconi successfully transmitted signals from here to Poldhu, Cornwall. His story is well told at the museum.

Visitors to Glace Bay should also take an underground tour at the Miners' Museum. Retired coal miners tell of

the dangerous and gritty life below the surface, and of the men who died in explosions, cave-ins, floods and even in union clashes with company police. The Men of the Deeps, a choir of Cape Breton coal miners, which has gained worldwide recognition, performs weekly at the museum during the summer.

CONTENTS

✳ denotes a location recognized by
the publisher for its high quality.

GETTING THERE

BY LAND

The TransCanada Highway enters Nova Scotia from New Brunswick. Visitors from the United States must pass through Canada Customs check-points before entering the country.

Greyhound from New York (1-800-231-2222) and *Voyageur* from Montreal (613-238-5900) connect with SMT bus lines in New Brunswick (506-458-6000). SMT connects with Acadian Lines (902-454-9321), which offers bus service to most Nova Scotia destinations from Amherst.

VIA Rail Canada (1-800-561-3952) provides train service to Halifax via Montreal.

BY SEA

There are several options for car-ferry trips to Nova Scotia.

Portland, Maine, to Yarmouth, Nova Scotia

Daily service by MS *Scotia Prince* from early May through October. Reservations required. In Canada: Box 609, Yarmouth, NS, B5A 4B6. In the USA: Prince of Fundy Cruises Limited, Box 4216, Station A, Portland, Maine, 04101. In USA and Canada call toll-free 1-800-341-7540; in Maine, 1-800-482-0955; www.scotiaprince.com.

Bar Harbor, Maine, to Yarmouth, Nova Scotia

Service from May to October aboard the *Cat*. Contact: Bay Ferries Ltd, PO Box 634, Charlottetown, PEI, C1A 7L3. In USA and Canada call toll-free 1-888-249-7245; www.catferry.com.

Saint John, New Brunswick, to Digby, Nova Scotia

Daily service across the Bay of Fundy aboard the MV *Princess of Acadia*; additional service during peak season. Bay Ferries Ltd, PO Box 634, Charlottetown, PEI, C1A 7L3; In USA and Canada call toll-free 1-888-249-7245; www.nfl-bay.com.

Prince Edward Island to Nova Scotia

Daily service between May 1 and December 20 from Wood Islands, PEI, to Caribou, NS. Northumberland Ferries, Box 634, Charlottetown, PEI, C1A 7L3; 1-800-565-0201 in NS or PEI; elsewhere 902-566-3838. No reservations.

The 12.9-kilometre Confederation Bridge joins Borden-Carleton, Prince Edward Island, and Cape Jourimain, New Brunswick, near the Nova Scotia border.

Newfoundland to North Sydney, Nova Scotia

Daily service from Port-Aux-Basques to North Sydney (additional service during peak). Monday, Wednesday and Friday service from Argentia to North Sydney, mid-June through mid-September only. Marine Atlantic/Reservations, 355 Purves St, North Sydney, NS, B2A 3V2. In the USA and Canada, 1-800-341-7981; www.marine-atlantic.ca.

BY AIR

Air Canada (1-888-247-2262; www.aircanada.ca) provides daily flights to Nova Scotia from most Canadian cities. Air Tango (1-800-315-1390) is a subsidiary of Air Canada, offering low-cost flights to Nova Scotia from St John's, NF, and select destinations in Central and Western Canada.

Air Canada, in partnership with United Airlines, services destinations in the United States and worldwide through all major US airports.

Several airlines offer regularly scheduled flights between Halifax and a number of European destinations (ask about charters as well).

Most air traffic to Nova Scotia touches down at the Halifax International Airport, with connecting flights to Yarmouth and Sydney. Car rentals may be arranged at all three airports.

Airbus offers a shuttle service approximately every hour to major downtown hotels. One way fare is $12, round trip is $20. The Halifax airport is located about 40 kilometres northeast of the city, and the 30- to 40-minute cab ride to downtown Halifax costs about $41; limousine service is about $43.

TRAVEL ESSENTIALS

MONEY

American currency can be exchanged at any bank in Nova Scotia at the prevailing rate. There are also currency exchange booths at the visitor information centre in Yarmouth and at the Halifax International Airport. Units of currency are similar to those of the United States, except for Canadian two-dollar and the one-dollar coins.

Traveller's cheques, major US credit cards and debit cards are accepted throughout Nova Scotia, although you may require cash in some rural areas. Traveller's cheques in Canadian funds can be purchased in the US. Cheques issued by Visa, American Express and Thomas Cook are widely recognized.

American visitors may also use bank or credit cards to make cash withdrawals from automated teller machines that are tied into international networks such as Cirrus, Interac and Plus. These can be found in larger centres throughout the province.

PASSPORTS

Passports and visas are not required for American visitors, although some proof of citizenship or residency might be (a birth certificate or Alien Registration Card will serve). At the border, expect to be asked where you live, why you are coming to Canada, and for how long.

Citizens of other countries should check with the nearest Canadian embassy or High Commission regarding entry requirements (www.cic.gc.ca).

CUSTOMS

Arriving

Visitors to Canada may bring certain duty-free items into the country as part of their personal baggage. These items must be declared to Customs upon arrival and may include up to 200 cigarettes, 50 cigars, 200 grams of manufactured tobacco and 200 tobacco sticks. Visitors are also permitted 1.14 litres (40 oz.) of liquor or 1.5 litres (52 oz.) of wine, or 8.5 litres (24 12-ounce cans or bottles) of beer.

Gift items — excluding tobacco and alcohol products — for Canadian residents that do not exceed $60 are also duty-free. Packages should be marked "Gift" and the value indicated.

Boats, trailers, sporting equipment, cameras and similar big-ticket items may enter Canada free of duty. However, Canada Customs may require a refundable deposit to ensure that these goods are not sold for profit. It might be better to register such items with customs officials in your own country, so that when you re-enter you have evidence that they were not bought in Canada.

Some items are strictly controlled in Canada. Firearms are prohibited, with the exception of rifles and shotguns for hunting purposes. Regulations for temporarily importing firearms or for borrowing firearms while in Canada have changed within the past couple of years. For detailed current information contact the Canadian Firearms Centre at 1-800-731-4000; www.cfc.gc.ca.

Plant material will be examined at the border (www.inspection.gc.ca). Veterinarian's certificates are required for all pets.

For further information on Canadian customs regulations, contact Canada Customs and Revenue Agency, (Canada) 1-800-461-9999; www.ccra-adrc.gc.ca.

Departing

To find out about US customs regulations and what other restrictions and exemptions apply, contact your local customs office or the US Customs Service, Box 7407, Washington, DC, 20044; 202-927-2095; www.customs.gov/travel/travel.htm. Ask for a copy of *Know Before You Go*.

Travellers from other countries should also check on customs regulations before leaving home.

TAXES

Harmonized Sales Tax (HST)

Most goods and services sold in Nova Scotia are subject to the Harmonized Sales Tax, a 15 percent federal/provincial tax that may be either included in or added to the price.

Out-of-country visitors are eligible

for rebates of the HST paid on short-term accommodations, and also on goods purchased for use outside Canada, if removed from Canada within 60 days of purchase. Rebate forms are available from visitor information centres, Revenue Canada offices, Canada Customs ports and many hotels and inns.

GUIDES

The *Nova Scotia Doers' and Dreamers' Guide* is an indispensable aid to visitors. To obtain a copy call toll-free 1-800-565-0000 or see www.novascotia.com. The guide is also available at visitor information centres throughout Nova Scotia.

GETTING ACQUAINTED

TIME ZONE

Nova Scotia falls within the Atlantic Time Zone, which is one hour later than the Eastern Time Zone. Daylight Saving Time, when the clocks are advanced one hour, is in effect from early April until late October.

CLIMATE

Nova Scotia's climate is influenced by the sea. Summers are cooler and winters milder than in central Canada. Average daily maximum temperatures for Halifax:

Jan.	1°C	33°F
Feb.	1°C	33°F
Mar.	4°C	39°F
Apr.	9°C	48°F
May	14°C	58°F
June	19°C	67°F
July	23°C	73°F
Aug.	24°C	74°F
Sept.	19°C	67°F
Oct.	14°C	58°F
Nov.	9°C	48°F
Dec.	3°C	37°F

GETTING AROUND

BUS TOURS

Seasonal bus tours of the province are available through a number of tour operators, including Cabana Tours, Halifax (455-8111), Atlantic Tours GrayLine, Halifax (423-6242), and Nova Tours, Halifax (429-3702). Several tour operators will arrange customized itineraries for groups.

BY CAR

Nova Scotia highway maps are available at visitor information centres throughout the province. Highways are generally well maintained. Gasoline prices are approximately 75-90 cents per litre (about $2.50 per US gal). Speed limits vary depending on the type of highway, with the 100-level controlled access highways having the highest limit, 110 km/hr (65 mph). The speed limit is 50 km/hr (30 mph) in cities and towns. In Nova Scotia, seat belt use is compulsory for driver and passengers.

A valid United States driver's license is also valid in Nova Scotia. Evidence of the car's registration is required (a car rental contract will also serve). US motorists may obtain a Non-Resident Inter-Province Motor Vehicle Liability Insurance Card through their own insurance companies as evidence of financial responsibility within Canada.

Car Rentals

All major car rental agencies are represented in Nova Scotia. Representatives at the Halifax International Airport are listed below:
Avis:
In the US and Canada: 1-800-879-2847
Budget:
In the US and Canada: 1-800-268-8900
Hertz:
In the US: 1-800-654-3131
In Canada: 1-800-263-0600
Thrifty:
In the US and Canada: 1-800-367-2277
Tilden (affiliated with National Rent-a-Car in the US):
In the US: 1-800-227-7368
In Canada: 1-800-387-4747
Consult the Yellow Pages of local telephone directories for local agencies that may offer lower rates.

LODGING

For a complete listing of accommodations in the province, including campgrounds, consult the *Nova Scotia Doers' and Dreamers' Guide* (see Travel Essentials).

Hostellers should contact Hostelling International-Nova Scotia, 1253 Barrington St, Halifax, Nova Scotia, B3J 1Y2; (902) 422-3863. Visitors who are interested in bed and breakfast-style accommodation in Nova Scotia can consult *Atlantic Canada Bed & Breakfasts*, a comprehensive listing of B&Bs published by Formac and updated frequently. Other resources available at local bookstores include an illustrated guide to Nova Scotia's most distinctive inns — Elaine Elliot and Virginia Lee's *Maritime Flavours* (5th ed., Formac Publishing, 2002).

Many establishments are members of Nova Scotia's Check In Reservation and Information Service (see Travel Essentials). Membership is indicated by a check mark in the *Nova Scotia Doers, and Dreamers, Guide*. In general, the accommodations listed below are the best of their kind in Nova Scotia. Most have distinguishing features that will enhance your stay.

Approximate prices are indicated, based on the average cost, at time of publication, for two persons staying in a double room (excluding taxes): $ = under $70; $$ = $70-$100; $$$ = more than $100.

The area code for all of Nova Scotia is (902).

HALIFAX

- Cambridge Suites Hotel, 1583 Brunswick St, Halifax, B3J 3P5; 1-888-417-8483; www.cambridgesuiteshotel.com. At the foot of Citadel Hill in downtown Halifax. Suites with fridge and microwave, guest laundry, exercise room. Complimentary continental breakfast. Open year-round. $$$

- Citadel Halifax Hotel, 1960 Brunswick St, Halifax, B3J 2G7; 1-800-565-7162; www.citadelhalifax.com. A couple of blocks from the clock tower and in the downtown area. Complimentary continental breakfast. All amenities. Open year-round. $$/$$$

- Delta Barrington, 1875 Barrington St, Halifax, B3J 3L6; 1-800-268-1133; www.deltahotels.com. Close to the Historic Properties and most attractions. Adjoins Barrington Place Mall, restaurants and pubs. Open year-round. $$$

- Delta Halifax, 1990 Barrington St, Halifax, B3J 1P2; 1-800-268-1133; www.deltahotels.com. Top-floor restaurant with sweeping view of the city and harbour. All amenities. Adjoins Scotia Square shopping mall. Open year-round. $$$

- Four Points, 1496 Hollis St, Halifax, NS, B3J 3Z1; 1-866-444-9494. Central to downtown. All amenities. Indoor parking. Open year-round. $$$

- Halliburton House Inn, 5184 Morris St, Halifax, B3J 1B3; 420-0658; www.halliburton.ns.ca. Small, elegant hotel. Registered Heritage Property incorporating three 19th-century townhouses in downtown Halifax. Open year-round. $$$

- Inn on the Lake, Box 29, Waverley, B0N 2S0; 1-800-463-6465; www.innonthelake.com. Two hectares of parkland with private freshwater beach and outdoor pool, courtesy shuttle to airport (10 minutes away). Open year-round. $$$

- Pepperberry Bed & Breakfast, 2688 Dutch Village Rd, Halifax, B3L 4E4; 1-877-246-3244; www.pepperberryinn.com. Park-like setting near Armdale Rotary. Heritage property decorated with artistic panache. Full breakfast. Open year-round. $$$

- Lord Nelson Hotel and Suites, 1515 South Park St, Halifax, B3J 2L2; 1-800-565-2020; www.lordnelsonhotel.com. Newly renovated historic hotel adjacent to Public Gardens and shopping. Dining room, fitness centre, business services. Open year-round. $$$

- Prince George Hotel, 1725 Market St, Halifax, B3J 3N9; 1-800-565-1567; www.princegeorgehotel.com. Central downtown location with all the amenities. Open year-round. $$$

- Casino Nova Scotia Hotel, 1919 Upper Water St, Halifax, B3J 3J5; 1-866-425-4329; www.casinonovascotiahotel.com. Luxury accommodation on the Halifax waterfront (ask for a room on the harbour side). Indoor pool, sauna, whirlpool. Adjoins a casino with slot machines and table games.

Adjacent to the Historic Properties. Open year-round. $$$
- Westin Nova Scotian, 1181 Hollis St, Halifax, B3H 2P6; 1-800-228-3000; 1-877-993-7846; www.westin.ns.ca. Comfortable rooms, short walk south of downtown at old train station. Indoor pool, sauna, tennis court. Open year-round. $$$

LIGHTHOUSE ROUTE
Chester and Mahone Bay
- Bayview Pines Country Inn, 678 Oakland Rd, Indian Point, Mahone Bay, B0J 2E0; 624-9970; www.bayviewpines.ns.ca. An 8.5-hectare property with hilltop view of Mahone Bay; century-old farmhouse and converted barn with stylish furnishings. Open year-round. $$
*Haddon Hall Resort Inn, 67 Haddon Hill Road, Box 640, Chester, B0J 1J0; 275-3577; www.haddonhallinn.com. Spectacular country estate with panoramic ocean view. Luxury suites and chalets. Gourmet dining. Open May-Oct. $$$
- Mahone Bay Bed & Breakfast, 558 Main St, Mahone Bay, B0J 2E0; 1-866-239-6252; www.bbcanada.com/4078.html. Restored 1860 stately home; antiques, art, wraparound porch, all amenities. $$/$$$
- Maritime Painted Salt Box, 433 Main St, Box 68, Mahone Bay, B0J 2E0; 624-1544; www.paintedsaltbox.com. Restored heritage cape. Excellent food, antiques, art and flower gardens. Open year-round. $$$
- Oak Island Resort and Spa, Box 6, Western Shore, B0J 3M0; 1-800-565-5075; www.oakislandinn.com. Recently renovated oceanfront hotel. All-inclusive packages include horseback riding, golfing, sailing, and whale-watching. Open year-round. $$/$$$
- Red Barn Cottages, Clearland, RR3, Mahone Bay, B0J 2E0; 624-0800; www.redbarncottages.com. Fully equipped family-oriented housekeeping cottages on old farm property 1.5 km from Mahone Bay. Air conditioning, pool, large barn with pool table, games, videos. Open May1-Oct 31. $$/$$$

Lunenburg
- Bluenose Lodge, Falkland Ave & Dufferin St, Box 399, Lunenburg, B0J 2C0; 1-800-565-8851; www.home.ca.inter.net/~bluenose. Restored 1863 inn. Nine guest rooms, breakfast included. Licensed dining room during summer season. Open year-round. $$
- Boscawen Inn, 150 Cumberland St, Box 1343, Lunenburg, B0J 2C0; 1-800-354-5009; www3.ns.sympatico.ca/boscawen. Victorian mansion in the heart of old Lunenburg. One-of-a-kind rooms; upscale and casual dining rooms. Open year-round. $$/$$$
- Lunenburg Arms, 94 Pelham St, Box 1378, Lunenburg, B0J 2C0; 1-800-679-4950; www.lunenburgarms.com. A 27-room hotel in Old Town with harbour views and all amenities. Complimentary breakfast. Open year-round. $$$
- Lunenburg Inn, 26 Dufferin St, Box 1407, Lunenburg, B0J 2C0; 1-800-565-3963; www.lunenburginn.com. An 1893 heritage inn with sun deck and covered verandah, complimentary full breakfast. Open April to October. $$$
- Ovens Natural Park Oceanview Cabins, Box 38, Riverport, B0J 2W0; 766-4621; www.ovenspark.com. Two-bedroom rustic cabins, some with fireplace. Pool, nature trails and sea caves. Pan for gold on the gravel beach. Open May 15 to October 15. $/$$/$$$
- Schoolhouse by the Sea & Beach House, 963 Kingsburg Beach Rd, Kingsburg, B0J 2X0; 766-4670; www.novascotiavacationrentals.info. A 160-year-old former schoolhouse and new beach house. Schoolhouse sleeps nine, beach house sleeps eight. Open year-round. $$/$$$

Liverpool and Shelburne
- Cooper's Inn, 36 Dock St, Box 959, Shelburne, B0T 1W0; 1-800-688-2011; www3.ns.sympatico.ca/coopers. Loyalist home built around 1785. Six guest rooms in main building and adjoining cooperage, with views of Shelburne Harbour. Open April to October. $$/$$$

- Quarterdeck Beachside Villas & Grill, Summerville Beach, Box 70, Port Mouton, B0T 1T0; 1-800-565-1119; www.quarterdeck.ns.ca. Beachside resort with all the amenities including jacuzzis, fireplaces and kitchen facilities. Open year-round. $$$
* White Point Beach Resort, White Point Beach, B0T 1G0; 1-800-565-5068; www.whitepoint.com. Resort with extensive recreational facilities, including golf, tennis, boating, swimming pools and kilometre-long white sand beach. Cottage accommodation available. Summer dinner theatre. Open year-round. $$$
- Whitman Inn, RR 2, Caledonia, B0T 1B0; 1-800-830-3855; www.whitmaninn.com. Close to Kejimkujik National Park, Route 8, Kempt. Turn-of-the-century homestead with indoor pool and sauna. Park-related recreational packages for canoeing, bicycling and cross-country skiing. Open year-round. $/$$/$$$

Yarmouth
- Manor Inn Lakeside, Route 1, Box 56, Hebron, B0W 1X0; 1-888-626-6746; www.manorinn.com. Inn, coach house and adjacent motel set on 3.6 hectares of landscaped grounds on Doctors Lake. Breakfast included; evening dining available every night. Open year-round. $$/$$$
- Murray Manor, 225 Main St, Yarmouth, B5A 1C6; 1-877-742-9629; www.murraymanor.com. Three large rooms in c. 1820 Gothic-style home. Full breakfast. Open year-round. $
- Rodd Grand Yarmouth, 417 Main St, Box 220, Yarmouth, B5A 4B2; 1-800-565-RODD; www.rodd-hotels.ca. Full-service modern hotel with indoor pool. Open year-round. $$$

EVANGELINE TRAIL
Wolfville to Middleton
- Blomidon Inn, 195 Main St, Wolfville, B4P 1C3; 1-800-565-2291; www.blomidon.ns.ca. Sea captain's mansion from the grand shipbuilding era of the 1880s. Open year-round. $$/$$$

- By the Dock of the Bay Cottages, Haddock Alley, Margaretsville, B0S 1N0; 1-800-407-2856; www.cottagesnovascotia.com. Two- and 3-bedroom housekeeping cottages very near water's edge amidst gorgeous gardens. Open mid-May-October. $$$
- Fairfield Farm Inn, 10 Main St, Box 1287, Middleton, B0S 1P0; 1-800-237-9896; www.fairfieldfarminn.com. Working fruit and vegetable farm. Five rooms in century-old farmhouse; trout fishing on site. Open year-round (by reservation only November to May). $$
- Tattingstone Inn, 620 Main St, Wolfville, B4P 1E8; 1-800-565-7696; www.tattingstone.ns.ca. Tastefully decorated inn and carriage house with tennis court, outdoor pool, library and music room. Elegant dinners. Open year-round. $$$
- Victoria's Historic Inn and Carriage House B&B, 600 Main St, Wolfville, B4P 1E8; 1-800-556-5744; www.victoriashistoricinn.com. Picturesque 1893 Registered Heritage Property. Luxury suites with jacuzzi whirlpool bath; full hot breakfast. Open year-round. $$$

Digby, Annapolis Royal
- Bread and Roses Inn, 82 Victoria St, Box 177, Annapolis Royal, B0S 1A0; 1-888-899-0551; www.breadandroses.ns.ca. Restored Queen Anne Revival mansion with many unique architectural details, antique furnishings. Homemade breakfast included. Open year-round. $$
- Brier Island Lodge & Restaurant, Box 1197, Westport, Brier Island, B0V 1H0; 1-800-662-8355; www.brierisland.com. Modern rooms with ocean view, excellent opportunities for whale- and bird-watching. Open April 1 to October 31. $$/$$$
- Garrison House Inn, 350 Saint George St, Box 108, Annapolis Royal, B0S 1A0; 1-866-532-5750; www.garrisonhouse.ca. Small inn, overlooking Fort Anne, built in 1854; fine dining. Open April 1 to December 31. $/$$

- Milford House, RR 4, Annapolis Royal, B0S 1A0; 1-877-532-5751; www.milfordhouse.ca. On Route 8 at South Milford. Secluded historic lodge amidst 243 wooded hectares between Annapolis Royal and Kejimkujik National Park. Twenty-seven lakeshore cabins with fireplaces. Country breakfasts and dinners in the main lodge (MAP). Open mid-June to mid-October. $$$

- Mountain Gap Inn, Box 504, Digby, B0V 1A0; 1-800-565-5020; www.mountaingap.ns.ca. At Smith's Cove. Resort complex with beach, pool, tennis, and other outdoor recreation. Large garden and grounds. Open May 1 to October 31. $$/$$$

* The Pines Resort, Shore Rd, Box 70, Digby, B0V 1A0; 1-877-375-6343; www.signatureresorts.com. Full-scale luxury resort with championship golf course and all other amenities. Hotel rooms and suites plus thirty cottages with stone fireplaces. Open May to mid-October. $$$

- Thistle Down Country Inn, 98 Montague Row, Box 508, Digby, B0V 1A0; 1-800-565-8081; www.thistledown.ns.ca/theinn. Edwardian inn on the water's edge. Twelve comfortable rooms (six harbourside), dinner for guests. $$$

- Queen Anne Inn, 494 Upper Saint George St, Box 218, Annapolis Royal, B0S 1A0; 532-7850; www.queenanneinn.ns.ca. Registered Heritage Property. Breakfast in elegant dining room. Open April 15-October 31. $$

GLOOSCAP TRAIL

- The Cobequid Inn, RR 1, Maitland, B0N 1T0; 1-877-742-4225; www.bbcanada.com/cobequidinn. Restored 1828 farmhouse with three guest rooms. Near Tidal Bore rafting. Open April 1 to October 31. $/$$

- Four Seasons Retreat, 320 Cove Rd, RR1, Economy, B0M 1J0; 1-888-373-0339; www.fourseasonsretreat.ns.ca. Six beautiful housekeeping cottages on the cliffs overlooking Minas Basin. Near skiing and hiking trails. Open year-round. $$/$$$

- Gillespie House Bed & Breakfast, 358 Main St, Parrsboro, B0M 1S0; 1-877-901-3196; www.gillespiehouseinn.com. An 1890 Victorian farmhouse with antiques, fireplaces, down duvets. Lovely gardens and lawns. Near Fundy hiking, rockhounding. Open May1-October 31. $$/$$$

- The John Stanfield Inn, 437 Prince St, Truro, B2N 1E6; 1-800-561-7666; www.johnstanfieldinn.com. Impressive Queen Anne-style mansion, beautiful woodwork, period furnishings, modern amenities; fine dining. Open year-round. $$$

- The Palliser, Box 821, Truro, B2N 5G6; 893-8951; palliser@auracom.com. Highway 102 at Exit 14. Comfortable motel-style accommodation, with good view of tidal bore on the Salmon River (viewing area lighted in evening). Complimentary buffet breakfast; dining room serves all meals. Open May to October. $

SUNRISE TRAIL

* Amherst Shore Country Inn, RR 2, Amherst, B4H 3X9; 1-800-661-2724; www.ascinn.ns.ca. Route 366 at Lorneville. Small inn with lovely ocean view and renowned dining room. Open May to October, weekends November to April. $$$

- Braeside Inn, 126 Front St, Box 1810, Pictou, B0K 1H0; 1-800-613-7701; www.braesideinn.com. Eighteen air-conditioned rooms, dining with harbour view. Open year-round. $/$$

- Consulate Inn, 157 Water St, Pictou, B0K 1H0; 1-800-424-8283; www.pictou.nsis.com/consulateinn. Bed and breakfast-style accommodation in a restored c. 1810 property overlooking Pictou harbour. Open year-round. $/$$/$$$

* Pictou Lodge Resort, Box 1539, Pictou, B0K 1H0; 1-888-662-7484; www.maritimeinns.com; Braeshore Road. Rustic 1920s resort with modern amenities. Standard hotel accommodation or multiple-bedroom log cottages with huge stone fireplaces and screened-in sunporches. Open mid-May to mid-October. $$$

- Scottish Pines Log Cottages, 2979 Gulf Shore Rd, RR 4 Pugwash,

B0K 1L0; 243-3366; scottishpines.cottagelink.com. Eight fully equipped oceanfront housekeeping log cottages. Beach, playground, near golf. Open May to October. $$$

- Train Station Inn, 21 Station Rd, Tatamagouche, B0K 1V0; 1-888-724-5233; www.trainstation.ns.ca. Three guest rooms in restored century-old train station plus seven guest cabooses reflect railways' past. All modern amenities. Open year-round. $$/$$$

MARINE DRIVE

- DesBarres Manor Country Inn, 90 Church St, Guysborough, B0H 1N0; 1-877-818-7891; www.desbarresmanor.com. Eight large, well-appointed rooms in elegant mansion. Fine dining. Open May-October. $$/$$$
- *Liscombe Lodge, Liscomb Mills, B0J 2A0; 1-877-375-6343; www.signatureresorts.com. Full-service resort featuring sport fishing packages (guides available), boat rentals and marina. Hotel and cottage-style accommodations, some overlooking the beautiful Liscomb River. Fine dining. Open mid-May to October. $$$
- Marquis of Dufferin Seaside Inn, RR 1, Port Dufferin, B0J 2R0; 654-2696; www.marquisofdufferinmotel.com; Route 7. Eight units with ocean view (six more in motel annex). Sport fishing, boating, sun lounge and deck in lodge. Open mid-May to October 31 $/$$/$$$
- Salmon River House Country Inn, 9931 Highway 7, Salmon River Bridge, B0J 1P0; 1-800-565-3353; www.salmonriverhouse.com. Seven well-appointed guest rooms along with on-site hiking, boating, hunting and fishing. Licensed dining. Open April 15 to December 31. $$/$$$

CABOT TRAIL AND CEILIDH TRAIL

- Castle Moffett, Hwy 105, Bucklaw; Box 678, Baddeck, B0E 1B0; 1-888-756-9070; www.castlemoffett.com. Luxury suites with king or queen canopy or four-poster beds, fireplaces, views

of Bras d'Or Lakes, fine dining. Open May-October. $$$
- Cheticamp Island Resort, RR 1, Cheticamp, B0E 1H0; 849-6444; www.nsonline.com/islandresort. Two-bedroom housekeeping cottages on Cheticamp Island. Ocean swimming. Daily and weekly rates. Open May-November (off-season by arrangement). $$$
- Duffus House Inn, 108 Water St, Box 427, Baddeck, B0E 1B0; 295-2172; www.baddeck.com/duffushouse. Circa 1830 home with antique furnishings. B&B. Private wharf, saltwater swimming. Open June 1 to mid-October. No smoking, no pets. $$$
- Duncreigan Country Inn, Box 59, Mabou, B0E 1X0; 1-800-840-2207; www.auracom.com/~mulldci. Four spacious guest rooms with antique furnishings in Main Inn and four large rooms in adjacent Spring House. Fine dining. Open year-round. $$$
- Dundee Resort & Golf Club, RR 2, West Bay, B0E 3K0; 1-800-565-1774; www.dundeeresort.com. Golf with outstanding views of the Bras d'Or. Marina and boat rentals, indoor and outdoor pools. 60 hotel rooms, 38 one- and two-bedroom cottages. Open May-October. $$$
- Four Mile Beach Inn, Aspy Bay; Box 3, Cape North, B0C 1G0; 1-888-503-5551; www.fourmilebeachinn.com. Views of Aspy Bay and mountains, near beach; five rooms and two efficiency units. Open June to mid-October; $$
- Haus Treuburg, 175 Main St, Box 92, Port Hood, B0E 2W0; 787-2116; www.auracom.com./~treuburg. Guest house and cottages close to warm saltwater swimming. Complimentary German-style breakfast at guest house. Licensed restaurant. Open year-round. $/$$
- Inverary Inn and Resort, Shore Rd, Box 190, Baddeck, B0E 1B0; 1-800-565-5660; www.capebretonresorts.com/inverary.asp. Licensed dining room and pub, indoor and outdoor pools, complimentary boat tours and other resort facilities. Open year-round. $$$

* Keltic Lodge, Middle Head Peninsula, Ingonish Beach, B0C 1L0; 1-800-565-0444; www.signatureresorts.com. Full-scale luxury resort with championship golf course (many say the best in Nova Scotia). Choose from the main lodge, White Birch Inn or cottages. Outdoor pool, hiking trails. Open May 24 - October. $$$

• Laurie's Motor Inn, 15456 Laurie Rd, Box 1, Cheticamp, B0E 1H0; 1-800-959-4253; www.lauries.com. Fifty-five motel units, bicycle rentals, whale cruises arranged. Open April-October. $$/$$$

• MacNeil House, Shore Rd, Box 399, Baddeck, B0E 1B0; 1-888-662-7484; www.maritimeinns.com. Luxury suites with all the amenities. Swimming pool or saltwater swimming in the Bras d'Or. Eco-tourism and other packages available. Open mid-May to mid-October. $$$

* Markland Coastal Resort, Dingwall, B0C 1G0; 1-800-872-6084; www.marklandresort.com. Secluded coastal resort with log cabins, outdoor pool, beachfront and dining. Open June-October. $$$

* Normaway Inn, 691 Egypt Rd, Box 101, Margaree Valley, B0E 2C0; 1-800-565-9463; www.normaway.com. Relaxing old-style resort (four of the cabins have jacuzzis). Cottages with wood stoves. Excellent salmon and trout fishing nearby. Open mid-June to mid-October. $$$

• Telegraph House, Chebucto St, Box 8, Baddeck, B0E 1B0; 295-1100; www.baddeck.com/telegraph. On Baddeck's main street. Choose from motel-style units or rooms in the old-fashioned inn. Room No. 1 was Alexander Graham Bell's before he built Beinn Bhreagh. Open year-round. $/$$/$$$

FLEUR-DE-LIS AND MARCONI TRAILS AND METRO CAPE BRETON

• Cambridge Suites Hotel, 380 Esplanade, Sydney, B1P 1B1; 1-800-565-9466; www.centennialhotels.com/cambridge. On Sydney waterfront. Suite accommodation with housekeeping facilities. Rooftop spa pool and exercise facilities. Complimentary breakfast. Open year-round. $$$

• Cranberry Cove Inn, 12 Wolfe St, Louisbourg, B1C 2J2; 1-800-929-0222; www.louisbourg.com/cranberrycove. Seven guest rooms (some with jacuzzis) in a fully renovated turn-of-the-century home. Licensed dining. Open mid-May to October (off-season by arrangement). $$$

• Flat Calm Country Inn, 3281 Hwy 320, D'Escousse, B0E 1K0; 1-877-923-3464; www.flatcalm.ca. On Isle Madame; three rooms, two suites, licensed dining room, pub; kayaking. Open year-round. $$/$$$

* Gowrie House Country Inn, 840 Shore Rd, Sydney Mines, B1V 1A6; 1-800-372-1115; www.gowriehouse.com. Beautifully furnished 1830 home with elegant antique-filled guest rooms. Garden House has four suites with all modern amenities. Exceptional dining. Open April-December. $$$

• Louisbourg Harbour Inn, 9 Lower Warren St, Louisbourg, B1C 1G6; 1-888-888-8466; www.louisbourg.com/louisbourgharbourinn. Eight well-appointed guest rooms in a century-old captain's house overlooking Louisbourg Harbour. Open June-October. $$$

• Point of View Suites, 15 Commercial St Ext, Louisbourg, B1C 2J4; 1-888-374-8439; www.louisbourgpointofview.com. Eighteen oceanfront suites near the gates of Fortress Louisbourg; balconies and decks overlooking fortress and ocean. Open May-October $$$

DINING

Nova Scotia cuisine is a delight. Tastefully and imaginatively prepared seafood, fresh Annapolis Valley produce and Pictou County lamb are among the many specialities of Nova Scotia restaurants. Local wines are inexpensive and surprisingly good.

Where to Eat in Canada (Oberon Press) is updated annually and includes many of the province's finer restaurants. *Maritime Flavours* (5th ed., Formac Publishing, 2002) is an illustrated guide to the best and most distinctive dining establishments in the Maritime provinces, accompanied by a selection of their favourite recipes.

Approximate prices are indicated, based on the average cost, at time of publication, of dinner for two including wine (where available), taxes and gratuity: $ = under $45; $$ = $45-$80; $$$ = over $80.

The area code for all of Nova Scotia is 902.

HALIFAX

- Anatolia, 1518 Dresden Row, Halifax; 492-4568. Turkish cuisine. Try the sampler. Open Mon-Sat noon-2:30 pm, 5-10 pm. $$
- * Bish, Bishop's Landing, 1475 Lower Water St, Halifax; 425-7993; original appetizers, local seafood and rack of lamb; good wine list. Open Mon-Fri 11:30-2 pm, Sat 5:30-10 pm. $$$
- The Cellar, 5677 Brenton Place, Halifax, 492-4412. Big helpings and first-class cooking features salads, pasta and pizza. Open Mon-Thurs 11 am-10 pm, Fri to 11pm, Sat 4 to 11pm, Sun 4-10 pm. $
- * The Chickenburger, 1531 Bedford Highway, Bedford. A landmark since the 1940s. Still has a juke box (although now it plays compact discs). Chicken burgers and real, old-fashioned milkshakes are the staples. Open 9 am-1 am daily. $
- Cheelin, Brewery Market, 1496 Lower Water St, Halifax; 422-2252. The best Chinese food in Halifax. Open Tues-Sun for dinner 5-10 pm, lunch Mon-Sat 11:30-2 pm.
- * Da Maurizio, 1496 Lower Water St, Halifax; 423-0859. Elegant Italian dining in the restored Brewery Market complex. Open Mon-Fri for lunch and dinner to 10 pm, Saturday dinner only. Closed Sunday. $$$
- Fiasco, 1463 Brenton St, Halifax; 429-3499. Stylish, relaxing décor complements Fiasco's inventive, Continental-inspired cuisine. Open Mon-Fri for lunch and dinner, Sat dinner only. $$
- Fid, 1569 Dresden Row, Halifax; 422-9162. Small, creative, perfect menu. Thai food a speciality. Open

daily for dinner 5:30-10 pm, lunch Wed-Fri 11:30-2 pm, closed Mondays. $$$
- Halliburton House Inn, 5184 Morris St, Halifax; 420-0658; www.halliburton.ns.ca. Specialities include fresh Atlantic seafood and wild game entrées. Light fare and cocktails in the outdoor garden café. Open daily 5-9 pm. $$$
- Hamachi House, 5190 Morris St, Halifax; 425-7711. Japanese-style steakhouse with interesting seafood dishes as well. Open Mon-Wed 11:30 am-11 pm, Thurs-Sat 11:30 am-12 am, Sun 3:30 pm-10 pm. $$
- Il Mercato, 5475 Spring Garden Rd, Halifax; 422-2866. Casual northern Italian dining with great desserts. Busy and friendly. Open Mon-Sat 11am to 11pm. $$
- Inn-on-the-Lake, Fall River, Box 29, Waverley; 861-3480; www.innonthelake.com. Located on beautiful Lake Thomas, meals are served in the dining room, on the terrace or by the gazebo bar in the park. Open daily from 7am. $$$
- Kinh-Do, 1284 Barrington St, Halifax; 425-8555. Inexpensive, authentic Vietnamese cuisine. Open daily 11:30 am-9:30 pm. $
- La Perla, 71 Alderney Dr, Dartmouth; 469-3241. Distinctive northern Italian cuisine, a minute's walk from the Halifax-Dartmouth ferry terminal. Open daily for dinner 5-10 pm, lunch on weekdays only. $$$
- MacAskill's, 88 Alderney Dr, Dartmouth; 466-3100. Best view of Halifax Harbour and the cityscape. Located in the ferry terminal on the Dartmouth waterfront. Open daily for dinner 5-10 pm, May-October; closed Sunday off-season; lunch Mon-Fri 11:30-2 pm. $$$
- McKelvie's, 1680 Lower Water St, Halifax; 421-6161. Imaginative preparation of fresh seafood, also an on-site bakery — sample the homemade bannock before your meal. Open daily June-Sept 11:30 am-10:30 pm (4-9:30 pm, dinner only, on Sunday in off-season). $$$
- Maple Bistro and Wine Bar, 1813 Granville St, Halifax; 425-9100; www.maplerestaurant.com. Imaginative dishes using fresh local ingredients. Open daily for dinner

5:30-10 pm; lunch Mon-Fri 11:30-2:30 pm. $$$

- Opa! 1565 Argyle St, Halifax; 492-7999. Atmospheric taverna featuring grilled seafood and traditional Greek favourites. Open Mon-Sat 11 am-11 pm, Sun 4 pm-11 pm. $$
- Press Gang, 5218 Prince St, Halifax; 423-8816. Fine dining in an intimate yet theatrical setting. Popular both with locals and visiting celebrities. Open daily for dinner. Reservations recommended. $$$
- Ryan Duffy's Steak and Seafood, 5640 Spring Garden Rd, Halifax; 421-1116. The city's best steaks, cut to the size you want, and Caesar salads made at your table. The bar and grill is a less formal (and less expensive) alternative to the dining room. Open daily 5:30 - 10 pm, Saturday to 11 pm; lunch Mon-Fri 11:30-2 pm. $$$
- Satisfaction Feast Vegetarian Restaurant, 1581 Grafton St, Halifax; 422-3540. Delicious and inexpensive vegetarian fare, especially the soups and breads. There is a bakery on-site; breads, muffins and bagels can be purchased for take-out. Open Mon and Tues 11:30 am-8 pm, Wed to 4 pm, Thurs-Sat to 9 pm. No smoking, no liquor. $
- *Sweet Basil Bistro, 1866 Upper Water St., Halifax; 425-2133. Fine presentation and service. Great for lunch. Open daily 11:30 am-10 pm. $$
- Upper Deck Waterfront Fishery and Grill, Privateers' Warehouse, Historic Properties, Halifax; 422-1289. Fine seafood dining in an historic waterfront building. Open daily for dinner to 10 pm. $$$

LIGHTHOUSE ROUTE
Peggys Cove

- Candleriggs, Indian Harbour; 823-2722. Traditional Scottish dishes and contemporary fare. Also a fine craft shop adjacent to the restaurant. Open daily 8 am-10 pm (weekends only, noon to sunset, January to mid-April). $$
- Sou'wester, Peggys Cove; 823-2561. Excellent chowders, tasty lobster and traditional Nova Scotia desserts like gingerbread and blueberry cake. Open daily 8 am-10 pm (November-April until 6 pm or sunset). $$

Chester and Mahone Bay

- Captain's House, 35 Central St, Chester; 275-3501. In the 1822 home of New Englander Rev. John Secombe. Open May to October. $$$
- The Galley, Marriotts Cove, near Chester; 275-4700. A relaxed setting with views of Mahone Bay and the yachts at South Shore Marine. Menu features chowders, summer salads and seafood. Open daily 11:30 am-9 pm, March to October. Reservations recommended. $$
- Haddon Hall Inn, 67 Haddon Hill Rd, Chester; 275-3577. A 1905 historic home on almost 50 hectares. Open 6:30-8:30 pm, mid-June to Thanksgiving. $$$
- Innlet Cafe, Keddy's Landing, Mahone Bay; 624-6363. Refreshing seafood-garnished salads or more substantial dishes for dinner. Try the front terrace on a warm evening, with a view of the water and Mahone Bay's three churches. Open daily 11:30 am-8:30 pm. $$
- Julien's, 43 Queen St, Chester; 275-2324. A French pâtisserie featuring croissants, crêpes, soups and salads. Open daily 8 am-6 pm. Shorter hours and closed Monday during off-season. No liquor. $
- Mahone Bagels and Coffee and Noble House, 538 Main St, Mahone Bay; 624-0001. Brunches, sandwiches and great coffee. Open year-round, daily 7 am-8 pm. $
- Mimi's Ocean Grill, 662 Main St, Mahone Bay; 624-1342. Fresh market and ocean cooking. Wide selection of homemade desserts. Unusually good children's menu. Open daily for lunch and dinner, April to October. $$
- Old Settler's Place Steakhouse & Restaurant, 16 Orchard St, Mahone Bay; 624-0046. Maritime and international cuisine. Open Tues-Sun 11:30 am-2 pm, 5-9 pm, May-December. $$$
- Seaside Shanty, Highway 3, Chester Basin; 275-2246. Big helpings of fresh seafood. Open

daily 11:30 am-10 pm. Shorter hours during off-season. $$

Lunenburg

- Arbor View Inn, 216 Dufferin St, Lunenburg; 1-800-890-6650; www.arborviewinn.ns.ca. Candlelit dining at a tranquil, tree-lined estate close to downtown attractions. Open Tues-Sun for dinner. $$
- Boscawen Inn, 150 Cumberland St., Lunenburg; 634-3325. A restored Victorian mansion specializing in fresh local seafood. Afternoon tea in the drawing rooms. Open for breakfast and dinner daily, Easter–December 31. $$$
- Hillcroft Café and Guest House, 53 Montague St, Lunenburg; 634-8031; www.bbcanada.com/1369.html. Restored 1850's house in downtown Lunenburg featuring seafood and vegetarian cuisine. Open daily for dinner. $$
- LaHave Bakery, LaHave; 688-2908. Home baking using clear spring water and locally grown, fresh-milled grains. Sandwiches made to order. Open Mon to Fri 9 am-5:30 pm, weekends 9 am-7 pm. Longer hours during season. No liquor. $
- Lion Inn, 33 Cornwallis St, Lunenburg; 634-8988. Intimate fine dining in a casual atmosphere. Seafood dishes and a great rack of lamb. Open year-round, Mon-Sat 5:30-9 pm; November-May, Thurs-Sat.
- Magnolia's Grill, 128 Montague St, Lunenburg; 634-3287. Bustling atmosphere, tasty and innovative dishes, and lots to look at on the walls while you wait. Key lime pie for dessert. Open Mon-Sat for lunch and dinner, April to late October. $$

Liverpool and Shelburne

- Charlotte Lane Café and Crafts, 13 Charlotte Lane, Shelburne; 875-3314; www.destination-ns.com/lighthouse/charlottelane. Relaxed dining, meals prepared by award-winning chef in a heritage property. Open May-December,

Tues-Sat 11:30 am-8 pm. $$
- Quarterdeck Beachside Villas and Grill, Summerville Centre; 683-2998; www.quarterdeck.ns.ca. Bright restaurant with view of white sand beaches, serving good food. Open daily 10 am-10 pm, May-October. $$
- Seawatch Restaurant, White Point Beach Resort, White Point. 354-2711; www.whitepoint.com. Informal dining room, suitable for children, serves steak and seafood. Open daily 7 am-9 pm. $$

Yarmouth

- Harris's Quick and Tasty, 5 kilometres from Yarmouth ferry on Route 1; 742-3467. Seafood and delicious homemade desserts in a friendly diner atmosphere. Open daily 11 am- 9 pm (10 pm in summer), mid-March to mid-December. $
- Little Lebanon, 100 Main St, Yarmouth; 742-1042. Offers Lebanese and vegetarian meals. Open Mon-Fri 11:30 am-8 pm; Saturday 4-8 pm. Closed Sunday. License pending. $$
- Ye Olde Argyler Lodge, 52 Ye Olde Argyler Rd, Lower Argyle; 643-2500; www.argyler.com. Nova Scotia seafood served in a beautiful oceanfront setting. Open daily 5 pm to 10 pm, mid-May to mid-Oct. $$

EVANGELINE TRAIL

- ✳ Acton's Grill and Café, 406 Main St, Wolfville; 542-7525. Elegant summer lunches, chilled soups, an interesting buffet and open-air patio. One of Nova Scotia's very best restaurants. Open daily for lunch and dinner. $$$
- Austria Dolfgasthaus, Granville Ferry; 532-7300. Right on the water. Delicious pumpkin soup and assorted schnitzels. Open daily 5-10 pm. Closed Mon-Thurs in winter. $
- Blomidon Inn, 195 Main St, Wolfville; 542-2291; www.blomidon.ns.ca. Dine in an elegant restored sea captain's mansion, built in 1877. Open year-round daily for lunch and dinner 11:30 am-2 pm and 5-9:30 pm. $$$
- Brier Island Lodge, Westport, Brier Island; 839-2300;

www.brierisland.com. Acadian dishes and lots of seafood, from fish cakes to Solomon Gundy. Open 7-10 am and 5-9:30 pm daily, June-October. $$

- Café Christophe, Hwy 1, Grosses Coques; 837-5817. Acadian cooking — chicken fricot, rappie pie — served in a homey atmosphere. Open Tues-Sun for breakfast, lunch and dinner. $

- The Cape View, Mavilette Beach; 645-2519. Acadian Rappie Pie a speciality. Open daily 7:30 am-10 pm, early March to late October. $$

- The Crooked Floor, 8 Victoria St, Annapolis Royal; 532-7602. Café serves bagels, scones and lighter fare using local fresh fruits, vegetables, locally made sausage. Open daily 9:30 am-5 pm, May-September; June-August to 7:30 pm, Friday and Saturday only in off-season. $

- Evangeline Café, Evangeline Motel, 11668 Hwy 1, Grand Pré; 542-2703; www.evangeline.ns.ca. Fabulous Valley fruit pies. Open daily to 7 pm, early May to late October. No liquor. $

- Falcourt Inn, 8979 Hwy 201, Nictaux; 825-3399. A restored fishing lodge with an exceptional view, specializing in seafood, and featuring creative beef and chicken dishes. Open year-round, 5-9 pm daily. $$

- Garrison House Inn, 350 Saint George St, Annapolis Royal; 532-5750; www.come.to/garrison. Understated entrées with fresh and simple vegetable accompaniments. Save room for dessert – the strawberry rhubarb pie is wonderful! Open for dinner 5:30-9 pm, May-October. $$

- Leo's Café, Saint George St, Annapolis Royal; 532-7424. Tasty soups and sandwiches. Don't expect a quick lunch in mid-summer; it's apt to be crowded. Open daily 11:30 am-6 pm, mid-March to late December. Licensed for beer and wine only. $

- The Lobster Pound, Halls Harbour; 679-5299. Only lobster, but some of the best to be had anywhere. Take it away to cook yourself, or take it to the boiling shack. Open noon-7 pm, mid-May to October; July and August 11:30- 8:30. $

- Newman's Restaurant, 218 Saint George St, Annapolis Royal; 532-5502. A lively menu combining fresh fruit, fresh herbs and fresh seafood. Open Tues-Sun, noon to 8:30 pm, early April to late October. Open Mondays in peak season. $$$

∗ Pines Resort Hotel, Shore Rd, Digby; 245-2511; www.signatureresorts.com. Specializing in local fish and seafood, in the luxurious surroundings of the Pines Resort Hotel. One of Nova Scotia's best restaurants. Open daily for breakfast 7-10 am, restaurant lunch noon-2 pm, dinner 6-9 pm, May to December. Don't miss Sunday brunch, mid-June to September. $$$

- Restaurant Le Caveau at Domaine de Grand Pré, Hwy 1, Grand Pré; 542-7177; www.grandprewines.ns.ca. Northern European cuisine served in an attractive vineyard setting. Open Mon-Sat 11:30 am-2 pm, 5:30-9 pm, Sun 5-8pm. No smoking. Reservations recommended. $$$

- Tattingstone Inn, 434 Main St, Wolfville; 542-7696; www.tattingstone.ns.ca. A beautifully appointed country inn, with all the touches that make a memorable gourmet dining experience. Open for dinner 5:30-9:30 pm. No smoking. Reservations recommended. $$$

- The Tempest Restaurant, 117 Front St, Wolfville; 542-0588. Fine dining, world cuisine, ethnic lunches, fusion dinners and French accents. Open Tues-Sun noon-2:30, 5:30-9:30 pm. $$$

GLOOSCAP TRAIL

- The Bake Shop, Hwy 209, Advocate Harbour; 392-2330. Splendid pies – fresh fruit in summer, apple and cream pies in the winter. Open Mon-Sat 8 am-5 pm. $

- David A's Café, 125 Victoria St E, Amherst; 661-0760. Good soups, salads, lobster rolls; desserts include old-fashioned white cake with boiled icing. Open Mon-Wed 11 am-3 pm, Thurs-Sat 11-3, 5:30-8

pm; Closed Sunday. $$
- Palliser Restaurant, Exit 14 off Hwy 102, Truro; 893-8951. Traditional boiled lobster, poached salmon or roast chicken dinners. The dining room, overlooking the Salmon River, offers twice-daily views of the tidal bore. Open daily 7:30 am-8:30 pm, May-October. $$

SUNRISE TRAIL

* Amherst Shore Country Inn, Hwy 366, Lorneville; 661-4800; www.ascinn.ns.ca. A different four-course gourmet meal each night. Open daily 7:30 pm by appointment, May to mid-October. Reservations a must. $$$
- Braeside Inn, 126 Front St, Pictou; 485-5046. Fresh Nova Scotia seafood and prime rib of beef. Hillside view of Pictou Harbour. Open daily 6-8:30 pm by reservation. $$
- Consulate Inn, 157 Water St, Pictou; 485-4554; www.consulateinn.com. Specialties include fresh Atlantic seafood. Open daily for dinner, May-October. $$
- Des Barres Manor County Inn, 90 Church St, Guysborough; 533-2099; www.desbarresmanor.com. Fresh local produce, seafood and lamb. Open daily at 7 pm by appointment only. $$
- Gabrieau's Bistro, 350 Main St, Antigonish; 863-1925. Innovative appetizers, light pasta and exceptional desserts. Open Mon-Thurs, 8 am-9:30 pm, Fri and Sat to 10 pm. $$
- Jubilee Cottage Country Inn, Hwy 6, Wallace; 257-2432; www.bbcanada.com/jubileecottage. Local grain-fed chicken, Pictou County lamb, Atlantic salmon, Digby scallops and home-grown herbs. Open daily at 7 pm May-October by reservation only. No smoking. $$
- Mill Room, Balmoral Hotel, Hwy 6, Tatamagouche; 657-2000. German specialities including sausages, sauerkraut, and pickled herring. Open daily 8 am-8 pm May-October. $$
- Pictou Lodge Resort, Braeshore Rd, Pictou; 485-4322; www.maritimeinns.com. A

spectacular oceanfront property, operating as a resort since the 1920s. Open May-October, hours vary seasonally. $$$
- Piper's Landing, Highway 376, Lyons Brook; 485-1200. Fresh and tasty seafoods are complemented by salads and sweets for dessert. Open year-round, Mon.-Thurs. 11 am-2:30 pm, 4:30-9 pm; Fri.-Sun. 11 am-9 pm. $$

MARINE DRIVE

- Golden Coast Seafood Restaurant, Oyster Pond; 889-2386. Family restaurant, children's menu, fish and chips, homemade desserts. Open year-round daily 11 am-7 pm, June-Sept until 9 pm.
* Liscombe Lodge, Hwy 7, Liscomb Mills; 779-2307; www.signatureresorts.com. A relaxed resort setting and casual dining room with an accomplished kitchen. Planked salmon is a speciality — watch it being cooked on the outdoor open fire. Open daily for breakfast, lunch and dinner, May-October. $$$
- Marquis of Dufferin, Hwy 7, Port Dufferin; 654-2696. An 1859 heritage property. Seafood, including smoked salmon from Willie Krauch's smokehouse in nearby Tangier. Open daily 7:30 am-9:30 am, 5:45-8 pm, May-October. Reservations required. $$
- Salmon River House, Hwy 7, Head of Jeddore; 889-3353; www.highway7.com. Fresh boiled lobster and steaks on the verandah overlooking the Salmon River. Open daily for breakfast and dinner (by reservation only from November to April). $$
- Sea Wind Landing Country Inn, 1 Wharf Rd, Charlos Cove; 525-2108; www.seawind.ns.ca. Picnic lunches available to guests. Open to the public for dinner by reservation only, May 1 to October 30. $$
- Willy's Bakery & Sunflower Café, East Petpeswick Rd, Musquodoboit Harbour; 889-2424. Homemade German ice cream, cinnamon buns, lunches, light fare. Open daily mid-May to mid-Oct, 8 am until dark; off-season weekends only 11am-5 pm. $

CABOT TRAIL AND CEILIDH TRAIL

- Acadien, 15067 Main St, Cheticamp; 224-3207. Authentic Acadian specialities including tourtière, chowders and fish cakes. Open daily, early May to late October. Hours vary depending on time of year. High season (late June to late September): 7 am-9 pm. $$
- Castle Rock Country Inn, Cabot Trail, Ingonish Ferry; 1-888-884-7625; www.ingonish.com/castlerock. Seasonal cookery featuring local ingredients in a spectacular location overlooking Ingonish Bay. Open daily for breakfast and dinner. $$
- Chanterelle Country Inn, Cabot Trail, St. Anns Bay; 1-866-277-0577; www.chanterelleinn.com. Cuisine based on organically-grown ingredients in an attractively-appointed setting. Open for dinner by reservation from May 15-October 31. $$
- Duncreigan Country Inn, Mabou; 945-2207; www.auracom.com/~mulldci. High-quality country dining in a tranquil setting. Open for dinner by reservation only, mid-June to mid-October, closed Mondays. $$$
- Haus Treuburg, Highway 19, Port Hood; 787-2166. German-style breakfast for guests. Try the fish for dinner. Open daily 7 pm, April-October, by reservation only. $$$
- Herring Choker Deli, on the TransCanada Highway between Baddeck and Whycocomagh; 295-2275. Speciality and natural food items. Treats from the Indian Bay Bakery. Open daily, year-round. $
- The Highwheeler Café, Chebucto St, Baddeck; 295-3006. The perfect place to stock up for a picnic — deli sandwiches, cookies, cakes, fruit and pasta salads. Open daily 7:30 am-6 pm, longer hours in summer (closed Sunday in off-season). $
- Inverary Inn and Resort, Shore Rd, Baddeck; 295-3500; www.inveraryresort.com. Flora's dining room offers a full-scale menu, with Scottish touches like smoked salmon and bannock. Lakeside Café on the waterfront is more casual, and features seafood appetizers and entrées. Open daily, May-November. Café open from 11 am in summer months only. $$$
- *Keltic Lodge, Middle Head Peninsula, Ingonish Beach; 285-2880; www.signatureresorts.com. Fine formal dining in the Purple Thistle dining room, one of Nova Scotia's best restaurants. Five-course evening meal, menu changes daily. Open daily for breakfast, lunch and dinner (to 9 pm), June to mid-October. $$$
- Markland Coastal Resort, Dingwall; 383-2246; www.marklandresort.com. Fresh lamb and local seafood, with a beautiful view of Aspy Bay from the oceanside deck. Enjoy a walk on the beach before dinner. Open 7:30-10:30 am and 6-9 pm, mid-June to mid-October. $$$
- The Mull Café, 11630 Cabot Trail, Mabou; 945-2244. Casual and quick, hearty deli sandwiches with take-out available. Open daily 11 am to 7 pm, Friday and Saturday to 8 pm, summer to 9 pm. $/$$
- Normaway Inn, Egypt Rd, Margaree Valley; 248-2987; www.normaway.com. Beautifully situated in the Margaree Valley. Four-course country gourmet meals with attentive but unobtrusive service. Open for breakfast and dinner mid-June to mid-October. $$$
- Rita's Tea Room, Big Pond; 828-2667. Baked goods and Rita's Tea Room Blend Tea. Rita MacNeil's awards and photographs are on display. Open daily 9 am-7 pm, June to mid-October. $
- Telegraph House, Chebucto St, Baddeck; 295-9988. Traditional dinners and generous helpings — poached salmon with egg sauce, roast turkey, meat loaf. One of the best breakfasts in Nova Scotia; be sure to sample the oatcakes. Open year-round daily for breakfast, lunch and dinner (to 8:30 pm). $$
- Tin Pan Galley, Salty Mariner's Motel, 23475 Cabot Trail, Pleasant Bay; 224-1400. Cajun shrimp with tomatoes, red and green peppers and onions the favourite. Open daily 5:30-9 pm, May-October. $$
- Vollmer's Island Paradise, Janvrin Island; 226-1507. Make

reservations a day ahead for fish or meat. No smoking. Open daily 7 pm by appointment only. $$

FLEUR-DE-LIS AND MARCONI TRAILS AND METRO CAPE BRETON

- Isle Royale Dining Room, Coastal Inn Louisbourg, 7464 Main St, Louisbourg; 733-2844. Reliable fresh seafood and roasts. Open daily for breakfast, lunch and dinner, June-October. $$
- *Gowrie House, 139 Shore Rd, Sydney Mines; 544-1050; www.gowriehouse.com. Antique-filled country inn, beautiful grounds and gardens. Fine meals are prepared from the freshest Nova Scotia ingredients. One of the province's best dining experiences. Open daily, one sitting at 7:30 pm, April-October. Reservations essential. Dinner for residents only rest of the year. Bring your own wine. $$$

ATTRACTIONS

The *Nova Scotia Doers' and Dreamers' Guide* (see Travel Essentials) provides exhaustive listings of the province's attractions. Guided walking tours or brochures for self-guided tours are available for many Nova Scotia communities (make inquiries at the closest visitor information centre). Here we provide a selective listing of many of the points of interest. The area code for all of Nova Scotia is 902.

HALIFAX

- Anna Leonowens Gallery, 1891 Granville St, Halifax; 494-8223; www.nscad.ns.ca/~gallery (Nova Scotia College of Art and Design)
- Art Gallery of Nova Scotia, 1723 Hollis St., Halifax; 424-7542; www.agns.ns.ca
- Bedford Institute of Oceanography, located near Dartmouth end of MacKay Bridge; 426-4306; www.bio.gc.ca
- Black Cultural Centre for Nova Scotia, 1149 Main St, Route 7 at Cherrybrook Rd, Dartmouth; 1-800-465-0767; www.bccns.com.
- *Bluenose II*, at the wharf by the Maritime Museum of the Atlantic when in Halifax; 1-800-763-1963; www.bluenose2.ns.ca
- Brewery Market, Hollis and Lower Water St, Halifax
- Cathedral Church of All Saints, 1320 Tower Rd, Halifax; 423-6002
- Discovery Centre, 1593 Barrington St, Halifax; 492-4422; www.discoverycentre.ns.ca
- Fort McNab National Historic Site, McNabs Island; information, 426-5080
- Government House, 1451 Barrington St, Halifax. Lieutenant-governor's residence since early 1800s.
- Grand Parade, between Barrington and Argyle St, Halifax
- Halifax Citadel National Historic Site, overlooking downtown Halifax (you can't miss it); 426-5080; www.parkscanada.gc.ca
- Halifax Public Gardens, Spring Garden Rd at South Park St, Halifax
- Halifax Regional Library, 5381 Spring Garden Rd, Halifax; 490-5700; www.halifax.library.ns.ca
- Historic Quaker Whalers' House, 57-59 Ochterloney St, Dartmouth; 464-2253; www.dartmouthheritagemuseum.ns.ca
- Hemlock Ravine Park, Kent Ave, off Bedford Highway
- Historic Properties, on the Halifax waterfront; 429-0530
- HMCS *Sackville*: Canada's Naval Memorial, at the wharf of the Maritime Museum, Halifax; 429-2132; www.hmcssackville-cnmt.ns.ca
- Little Dutch (Deutch) Church, Brunswick St. at Gerrish, Halifax; 423-1059, ext 8250
- Maritime Command Museum, Admiralty House, 2725 Gottingen St, Halifax; 427-0550
- Maritime Museum of the Atlantic, 1675 Lower Water St, Halifax; 424-7490; www.museum.gov.ns.ca/mma
- Museum of Natural History, 1747 Summer St, Halifax; 424-7353; www.museum.gov.ns.ca/mnh
- Nova Scotia Centre for Craft and Design, 1683 Barrington St, Halifax; 424-4062; www.craft-design.gov.ns.ca
- Old Town Clock, at the base of the

Citadel. Halifax's most famous landmark.
- Old Burying Ground and Welsford-Parker Monument, Barrington St. (across from Government House), Halifax; 429-2240
- Pier 21, 1055 Marginal Rd, Halifax; 425-7770; www.pier21.ns.ca
- Prince of Wales Tower National Historic Site, Point Pleasant Park, Halifax; 426-5080; www.parkscanada.gc.ca
- Province House, 1726 Hollis St, Halifax; 424-4661; www.gov.ns.ca/legislature
- Dartmouth Heritage Museum, 100 Wyse Rd, Dartmouth; 464-2300; www.dartmouthheritagemuseum.ns.ca
- St. George's Round Church, Brunswick St. at Cornwallis, Halifax; 423-1059
- St. Paul's Anglican Church, at the Grand Parade, Halifax; 429-2240; www.stpaulshalifax.org
- Sir Sanford Fleming Park (the Dingle), Dingle Rd, off Purcells Cove Rd on Northwest Arm, Halifax
- Shearwater Aviation Museum, at CFB Shearwater; 460-1083; www.shearwateraviationmuseum.ns.ca
- Shubenacadie Canal, 54 Locks Rd, off Waverley Rd, Rte 318, Dartmouth
- York Redoubt National Historic Site, off Purcells Cove Rd, Halifax; 426-5080; www.parkscanada.gc.ca

LIGHTHOUSE ROUTE
Peggys Cove
- Village of Peggys Cove and lighthouse
- William E. deGarthe Memorial Monument, Peggys Cove

Chester and Mahone Bay
- Amos Pewter, interpretive workshop, 589 Main St, Mahone Bay; 1-800-565-3369; www.amospewter.com.
- Mahone Bay Settlers' Museum, 578 Main St, Mahone Bay; 624-6263; www3.ns.sympatico.ca/mbsm
- Ross Farm Living Museum of Agriculture, New Ross (on Hwy 12, inland from Chester Basin); 689-2210; www.museum.gov.ns.ca/rfm

- St. James Anglican Church, Edgewater Rd (Hwy 3), Mahone Bay

Bridgewater and Lunenburg
- Captain Angus J. Walters House Museum, 37 Tannery Rd, Lunenburg; 634-2010
- DesBrisay Museum, 130 Jubilee Rd, Bridgewater; 543-4033; www.town.bridgewater.ns.ca/museum.htm
- Fisheries Museum of the Atlantic, Montague St (on the water), Lunenburg; 634-4794; www.museum.gov.ns.ca/fma
- Lunenburg Art Gallery, Pelham St, Lunenburg
- Lunenburg Academy, atop Gallows Hill, Lunenburg
- Knaut-Rhuland House Museum, 125 Pelham St, Lunenburg; 634-3498
- Wile Carding Mill, 242 Victoria Rd, Bridgewater; 543-8233; www.museum.gov.ns.ca/wcm

Liverpool and Shelburne
- Archelaus Smith Museum, Route 330, Centreville, Cape Sable Island (across the causeway); 745-3361
- Argyle Township Courthouse & Gaol, 8168 Hwy 3, Tusket; 648-2493
- The Dory Shop Museum, Dock St, Shelburne; 875-3219; www.museum.gov.ns.ca/dory
- Hank Snow Country Music Centre, 148 Bristol Avenue, Liverpool; 354-4675; www.hanksnow.com.
- Perkins House Museum, 105 Main St, Liverpool; 354-4058; www.museum.gov.ns.ca/peh
- Queens County Museum, 109 Main St, Liverpool; 354-4058; www.queensmuseum.netfirms.com.
- Ross-Thompson House and Store Museum, 9 Charlotte Lane, Shelburne; 875-3141; www.museum.gov.ns.ca/rth
- Shelburne County Museum, 8 Maiden Lane, Shelburne; 875-3219; www.historicshelburne.com.
- Sherman Hines Museum of Photography & Galleries, 219 Main St, Liverpool; 354-2667; www.shermanhinesphotographymuseum.com.

Barrington
- Barrington Woolen Mill, 2368 Hwy 3, Barrington; 637-2185; www.museum.gov.ns.ca/bwm
- The Old Meeting House, 2048 Hwy 3, Barrington; 637-2185; www.museum.gov.ns.ca/omh
- Seal Island Light Museum, Hwy 3, Barrington; 637-2185

Yarmouth
- Firefighters Museum of Nova Scotia, 451 Main St, Yarmouth; 742-5525; www.museum.gov.ns.ca/fm
- Killam Brothers Shipping Office, 90 Water St, at the foot of Central St on the waterfront; 742-5539
- Yarmouth Light, Rte 304, Cape Fourchu Scenic Drive; 742-1433
- Yarmouth County Museum and Archives, 22 Collins St, Yarmouth; 742-5539; yarmouthcountymuseum.ednet.ns.ca

EVANGELINE TRAIL
Windsor to Wolfville
- Churchill House, Marine Memorial Museum, Hantsport; 684-9527
- Fort Edward National Historic Site, near Exit 6 on Hwy 101, Windsor; 798-4706
- Grand Pré National Historic Site, 542-3631; www.grand-pre.com.
- Haliburton House, 414 Clifton Ave, Windsor; 798-2915; www.museum.gov.ns.ca/hh
- Prescott House, 1633 Starrs Pt. Rd (off Rte 358) Starrs Point (near Wolfville); 542-3984; www.museum.gov.ns.ca/prh
- Randall House Historical Museum, 171 Main St, Wolfville; 542-9775; www.cnet.windsor.ns.ca/Museum/Randall
- Shand House, 389 Avon St, Windsor; 798-8213; www.museum.gov.ns.ca/sh
- Uniacke Estate Museum Park, 758 Main Rd, Mount Uniacke; 866-2560; www.museum.gov.ns.ca/uemp

Kentville to Middleton
- Annapolis Valley Macdonald Museum, 21 School St, Middleton; 825-6116
- Kentville Agricultural Centre and Blair House, Rte 1, Kentville; 679-5333
- Oaklawn Farm Zoo, Hwy 101, Exit 16, Aylesford; 847-9790
- Old Kings Courthouse Museum, 37 Cornwallis St, Kentville; 678-6237

Digby and Annapolis Royal
- Admiral Digby Museum, 95 Montague Row, Digby; 245-6322; www3.ns.sympatico.ca/admuseum
- Annapolis Royal Historic Gardens, Upper Saint George St, Annapolis Royal; 532-7018; www.historicgardens.com.
- Annapolis Royal Tidal Power Project, at the Annapolis River Causeway
- Fort Anne National Historic Site, Saint George St, Annapolis Royal; 532-2321; www.parkscanada.gc.ca/fortanne
- North Hills Museum, 5065 Granville Rd, Granville Ferry; 532-7754; www.museum.gov.ns.ca/nhm
- O'Dell House Museum, 136 Lower Saint George St, Annapolis Royal; 532-7754
- Old St. Edward's Loyalist Church Museum, 34 Old Post Rd (off Rte 1), Clementsport; 532-0917 or 245-2263
- Port Royal National Historic Site (the Habitation), Rte 1 to Granville Ferry, 12 kilometres southwest at Port Royal; 532-2898; www.parkscanada.gc.ca/portroyal
- Upper Clements Park, 2931 Hwy 1, 6 kilometres west of Annapolis Royal; 1-888-248-4567; www.upperclementspark.com.
- Upper Clements Wildlife Park, Hwy 1, 6 kilometres west of Annapolis Royal; 532-5924; www3.ns.sympatico.ca/ucwlp

Acadian Shore
- Acadian Centre Archives, Université Sainte Anne, Pointe de l'Église; 769-2114; www.ustanne.ednet.ns.ca/acadien
- L'Église Saint-Bernard (Church of Saint Bernard), Rte 1, St. Bernard; 837-5687; www.clarenovascotia.com.
- L'Église Sainte-Marie (Church of Saint Mary), Pointe de l'Église; 769-2832

GLOOSCAP TRAIL
- Anne Murray Centre, 36 Main St, Springhill; 597-8614; www.annemurray.com.

- Cumberland County Museum, 150 Church St, Amherst; 667-2561; www.creda.net/~ccmuseum
- Fundy Geological Museum, 162 Two Islands Rd, Parrsboro; 254-3814; www.museum.gov.ns.ca/fgm
- Joggins Fossil Centre, Main St, Joggins; 251-2727, 251-2618 (off-season)
- Lawrence House, 8660 Hwy 215, Maitland; 261-2628; www.museum.gov.ns.ca/lh
- Ottawa House Museum by-the-Sea, 3 kilometres from Parrsboro
- Parrsboro Rock and Mineral Shop and Museum, 39 Whitehall Rd, Parrsboro; 254-2981
- Shubenacadie Provincial Wildlife Park, near Exit 11 on Hwy 102, Shubenacadie; 758-2040 or 424-5937; www.wildlifepark.gov.ns.ca
- Springhill Miners' Museum, 145 Black River Rd, Springhill; 597-3449;www.town.springhill.ns.ca/Miners_Museum.htm

SUNRISE TRAIL
- Balmoral Grist Mill Museum, 660 Matheson Brook Rd, off Route 311, Balmoral Mills; 657-3016; www.museum.gov.ns.ca/bgm
- Northumberland Arts Council Fraser Cultural Centre, Main St, Tatamagouche; 657-3285, 657-3667 (off-season)
- Nova Scotia Museum of Industry, Hwy 104 at Exit 24, Stellarton; 755-5425; www.museum.gov.ns.ca/moi
- Hector Heritage Quay, 33 Caladh Ave, Pictou; 1-877-574-2868; www.townofpictou.com
- Hector Exhibit & Research Centre, McCulloch House, 100 Old Haliburton Rd, Pictou; 485-4563; www.rootsweb.com/~nspcghs
- Jost Vineyards, off Rte 6, between Tatamagouche and Pugwash at Malagash; 1-800-565-4567; www.jostwine.com.
- Northumberland Fisheries Museum, 71 Front St, Pictou; 485-4972; www.townofpictou.com/Fisheries
- Sunrise Trail Museum, Main St, Tatamagouche; 657-3007
- Sutherland Steam Mill Museum, off Rte 326, Denmark; 657-3365; www.museum.gov.ns.ca/ssm

MARINE DRIVE
- Canso Museum, Whitman House, Canso; 366-2170 or 366-2525; canconn@atcon.com.
- Fisherman's Life Museum, 58 Navy Pool Loop, Jeddore, off Rte 7 at Oyster Pond; 889-2053; www.museum.gov.ns.ca/flm
- Grassy Island National Historic Site, 1 kilometre off the coast of Canso; 295-2069; www.parkscanada.gc.ca
- Memory Lane Heritage Village, Route 7, Lake Charlotte; 845-1937; www.heritagevillage.ca
- Moose River Gold Mines Museum, Moose River Rd, Route 224; Moose River Gold Mines; 384-2006
- Musquodoboit Railway Museum, Main St (Rte 7), Musquodoboit Harbour; 889-2689; www.halifaxinfo.com/museums-galleries.php
- Nova Scotia Lighthouse Interpretive Centre, Rte 211, Port Bickerton; 364-2000
- Sherbrooke Village, off Route 7, near the modern village of Sherbrooke; 1-888-743-7845; www.museum.gov.ns.ca/sv

CABOT TRAIL AND CEILIDH TRAIL
- Acadian Museum, 744 Main St (at Co-operative Artisinale de Cheticamp Ltée.), Cheticamp; 224-2170; www.co-opartisinale.com
- Alexander Graham Bell National Historic Site, Baddeck; 295-2069; www.parkscanada.gc.ca
- *An Drochaid* (The Bridge), Main St, Rte 19, Mabou; 945-2311; androchaid@ns.sympatico.ca
- Les Trois Pignons and Elizabeth LeFort Gallery, 15584 Main St, Cheticamp; 224-2642 or 224-2612; www.lestroispignons.com.
- The Great Hall of the Clans at the Gaelic College of Celtic Arts and Crafts, South Gut St. Anns; 295-3441 or 295-2912; www.gaeliccollege.edu
- Giant MacAskill Museum, Rte 312, Englishtown; 929-2925
- Inverness Miners' Museum, in the old CNR station, Inverness; 258-3822; invhistsoc@ns.sympatico.ca
- L'Église Saint-Pierre (Church of Saint Peter), Cheticamp; 224-2062
- Lone Shieling, at the base of North Mountain, Cape Breton Highlands

National Park
- Margaree Salmon Museum, North East Margaree; 248-2848/2765/2623
- Highland Village Museum, 4119 Rte 223, Iona; 725-2272; www.museum.gov.ns.ca/hv
- Pleasant Bay Whale Interpretive Centre, Pleasant Bay; 224-1411; www.cabottrail.com/whales
- Scarecrow Theatre, Cap Le Moine (near Cheticamp); 235-2108

FLEUR-DE-LIS TRAIL, MARCONI TRAIL AND METRO CAPE BRETON
- Cossit House, 75 Charlotte St, Sydney; 539-7973 or 539-1572; www.museum.gov.ns.ca/ch
- Fortress of Louisbourg National Historic Site, Louisbourg; 733-2280, 733-3546 (off-season); www.parkscanada.gc.ca/louisbourg
- Marconi National Historic Site, Timmerman St, Glace Bay; 295-2069; www.parkscanada.gc.ca
- Miners' Museum, 42 Birkley St, Quarry Point, Glace Bay; 849-4522
- Sydney and Louisburg Railway Museum, Louisbourg; 733-2157; fortress.uccb.ns.ca/historic/s_l.html

FESTIVALS AND EVENTS

What follows is a listing by area of some of the best and most popular festivals and events in the province. For a complete listing, consult the *Nova Scotia Doers' and Dreamers' Guide* (see Travel Essentials). The scheduling of many of these events is subject to change; the Check In Reservation and Information Service will provide updated information (1-800-565-0000).

HALIFAX
Year-round
- Halifax Farmers' Market at the Brewery Market (Halifax). Saturday morning farmers' market where local crafts, baked goods and produce are available.

May/June
- Scotia Festival of Music. Internationally renowned festival of chamber music.

June
- Greek Festival. Three-day feast put on by the Halifax Greek community.
- Nova Scotia Multicultural Festival, Dartmouth. Food, music and dancing offered by Nova Scotia's different ethnic communities.

July
- Nova Scotia International Tattoo. A musical extravaganza with a military flavour.
- Atlantic Jazz Festival. Outdoor concerts and late-night sessions in city bars.
- Halifax Highland Games. A Scottish festival with pipes and drums, heavy events and more.
- Maritime Fiddle Festival, Dartmouth. Top-notch competitors from Canada and the United States.
- Africville Reunion. The spirit of the Black community of Africville is revived at a picnic, church service and dance.

August
- Halifax International Busker Festival. Street performers, including jugglers and clowns, provide 10 days of fun along the waterfront.
- Nova Scotia Designer Crafts Council Summer Festival. A juried market draws many of the province's best craftspeople.

September
- Atlantic Fringe Festival. Alternative plays performed around the city.
- Atlantic Film Festival. Independent films and parties celebrating the industry.
- Grou Tyme Acadian Festival. Music and food on the waterfront.
- Nova Scotia International Airshow. Atlantic Canada's largest demonstration of aerial acrobatics.
- Word on the Pier. Book sales, displays, author readings and entertainment.

October
- Studio Rally Weekend. Craft studios across the province open to the public.

Lighthouse Route
June
- Lights Along the Shore Lighthouse Festival at various sites along the South Shore.

June/July
- Privateer Days, Liverpool. Festival recalling the town's tumultuous early years.

July
- Lunenburg Craft Festival. Quality crafts from the province's top artisans.
- Mahone Bay Wooden Boat Festival. Boatbuilding competitions and demonstrations, and many other events recalling the town's shipbuilding era.
- Shelburne Founders' Days. Commemorates the arrival of thousands of United Empire Loyalists in the 1780s.
- South Shore Exhibition, Bridgewater. Century-old agricultural exhibition featuring ox-pulls among the many events.

August
- Chester Race Week. Atlantic Canada's largest regatta. The Front and Back harbours are crowded with sleek yachts.
- Lunenburg Fishermen's Picnic and Reunion. A festival for the fisheries that features unusual and entertaining competitions like net mending, scallop shucking and dory racing.
- Lunenburg Folk Harbour Festival. The Lunenburg waterfront provides an idyllic setting for a series of performances by folk musicians.
- Nova Scotia Folk Art Festival. Celebrates the work of Nova Scotia's best folk artists.

October
- Great Scarecrow Festival and Antique Fair, Mahone Bay. Dozens of vendors in three venues; music, food, activities for kids, and scarecrows everywhere.

Evangeline Trail
May/June
- Annapolis Valley Apple Blossom Festival Windsor to Digby. Community-based celebrations herald the arrival of another growing season.

July
- Bear River Cherry Carnival. Parade, auction, woodsmen's show and more in one of Nova Scotia's prettiest communities.
- Festival Acadien de Clare. Colourful Acadian celebration that runs the length of the Acadian Shore.
- Heart of the Valley Days, Middleton. Parade, concert and fireworks.

August
- Annapolis Valley Exhibition, Lawrencetown. Showcase of Valley agriculture, with top-name entertainment.
- Digby Scallop Days. A feast of Digby scallops, scallop-shucking competition.
- Natal Day Craft and Antique Show, Annapolis Royal. Fast-growing community of craftspeople displays its wares.

Sept/Oct
- Annapolis Royal Arts Festival. Best-selling Canadian authors are among the participants at this annual gathering.
- Berwick Gala Days, Berwick. Traditional end-of-summer celebrations with parades, family entertainment.
- Hants County Exhibition, Windsor. North America's oldest agricultural fair.
- Pumpkin Festival, Hants County Exhibition Grounds, Windsor. Growers of giant pumpkins vie for World's Biggest Pumpkin title.

Glooscap Trail
May
Truro International Tulip Festival

August
- Nova Scotia's Gem and Mineral Show, Parrsboro. An agate and amethyst hunt along Parrsboro-area beaches.

Sunrise Trail
July
- Antigonish Highland Games. Highland competitions from

dancing to caber tossing make this Nova Scotia's best Scottish festival.

- Festival of the Tartans, New Glasgow. Includes piping, dancing, drumming and Scottish heavy events.
- Gathering of the Clans and Fishermen's Regatta, Pugwash. A Scottish festival capped off by a lobster dinner.
- Pictou Lobster Carnival. Fishermen's competitions and Northumberland Strait lobsters are the highlights at this community festival.

August
- Hector Festival, Pictou. Celebrates the coming of the Scots to Nova Scotia aboard the *Hector*.

September
- Oktoberfest, Tatamagouche. Post-war immigration to the North Shore gave rise to this traditional German celebration.

MARINE DRIVE
July
- Stan Rogers Folk Festival, Canso. A celebration of the music of one of Canada's most celebrated folk musicians.

August
- Clam Harbour Beach Sand Castle and Sculpture Contest. The fine, white sand along one of Nova Scotia's best beaches is an ideal building material.

CAPE BRETON ISLAND
June/July
- Mabou Ceilidh. See for yourself why this village of 400 is home to several of Nova Scotia's best musicians. There are also Wednesday night ceilidhs throughout July and August.

July
- Judique-on-the-Floor Days. More of Cape Breton's best music.
- Big Pond Festival. Cape Breton music highlighting Big Pond's most famous resident, Rita MacNeil.
- Broad Cove Scottish Concert, near Inverness. A highlight of the summer ceilidh season.

July/August
- Festival de l'Escaouette, Cheticamp. An Acadian celebration featuring a special mass in Cheticamp's exquisite church.

August
- Baddeck Regatta. Highlight of Baddeck's summer sailing season since 1904.
- Feast of St. Louis. An 18th-century feast at the Fortress of Louisbourg.
- Gaelic Mod (South Gut St. Anns). Music and other Gaelic arts at the home of the Gaelic College.

Sept./Oct.
- Celtic Colours. An island-wide celebration of Celtic music featuring Cape Breton and international performers.

THEATRE

Halifax is home to Neptune Theatre, Nova Scotia's only professional live repertory theatre group. Also, a surprising number of communities throughout the province, including Halifax, are summertime venues for live theatre. Many productions are distinctly Nova Scotian — revealing much about the province and its people. The area code for all of Nova Scotia is 902.

- Astor Theatre, Gorham St, Liverpool; 354-5250. Featuring the Liverpool International Theatre Festival (bi-annually) in May.
- Atlantic Theatre Festival, Wolfville; 1-800-337-6661; www.atf.ns.ca (June-September).
- Bicentennial Theatre, 12390 Rte 224, Middle Musquodoboit; 384-2819.
- Centrestage Theatre, 363-R Main St, Kentville; 678-8040.
- The Chester Playhouse, Pleasant St, Chester; 275-3933; www.chesterplayhouse.ns.ca. Site of the Chester Theatre Festival April to December.
- Dartmouth Players Theatre, 5 Crichton Ave, Dartmouth; 465-7529; www.dartmouthplayers.ns.ca.
- deCoste Entertainment Centre, Water St, Pictou; 1-800-353-5338; www.decostecentre.ca.
- Eastern Front Theatre, Alderney Landing, Dartmouth; 466-2769;

www.easternfront.ns.ca.
- Evangéline, Université Ste-Anne; 769-2114; www.evangelinetheplay.com. Musical based on Longfellow's poem in Acadian French, live English translations; one performance a week in English (July-August.).
- Festival Antigonish, Bauer Theatre, St. Francis Xavier University, Antigonish; 1-800-563-7529; www.festivalantigonish.com (July-August).
- Grafton Street Dinner Theatre, 1741 Grafton St, Halifax; 425-1961; www.graftonstdinnertheatre.com.
- Halifax Feast Dinner Theatre, Maritime Centre, Barrington St, Halifax; 420-1840; www.feastdinnertheatre.com.
- Irondale Ensemble, 2182 Gottingen St, Halifax; 429-1370. Critical and thoughtful alternative theatre.
- Jest In Time Theatre, 1541 Barrington St, Halifax; 423-4647; www.jestintime.ns.ca.
- King's Theatre, Lower Saint George St, Annapolis Royal; 1-800-818-8587; www.kingstheatre.ca. Site of the Annapolis Royal Summer Theatre Festival in July and August.
- Louisbourg Playhouse, 11 Aberdeen St, Louisbourg; 1-888-733-2787 (June-Oct); www.artscapebreton.com.
- Mermaid Theatre, 132 Gerrish St, Windsor; 798-5841; www.mermaidtheatre.ns.ca. Touring puppet theatre for children.
- Mulgrave Road Theatre, 68 Main St, Guysborough; 533-2092; mrt@atcon.com.
- Neptune Theatre, 1593 Argyle St, Halifax; 429-7070; 1-800-565-7345; www.neptunetheatre.com.
- The Rebecca Cohn, Dalhousie Arts Centre, University Ave, Halifax; 494-3820. A variety of live performances including the Symphony Nova Scotia concert series.
- Savoy Theatre, 19 Union St, Glace Bay; 842-1577; www.savoytheatre.com. Highlights include the Cape Breton Summertime Revue, a lively blend of Celtic music and satire.

- Ship's Company Theatre, 38 Main St, Parrsboro; 1-800-565-7469; www.shipscompany.com. Innovative theatre aboard the MV *Kipawo*, a restored car ferry (July-September).
- Theatre Arts Guild, The Pond Playhouse, 6 Parkhill Rd, Halifax; 477-2663; www.theatreartsguild.com.
- Th'YARC, 76 Parade St, Yarmouth; 1-800-561-1103. Yarmouth Summer Stage is held in July and August.

SHOPPING

CRAFT SHOPS
- Arts North, just west of Cape North on the Cabot Trail. Specializing in Cape Breton pottery and jewellery, the gallery also features silk, weaving, prints, quilts and floorcloths by resident artisans. Open daily from mid-June to mid-October.
- Black Duck, 8 Pelham St, Lunenburg. A long-standing craft co-operative with adjoining art gallery and a fine selection of books on Nova Scotia and the Maritimes. Open year-round.
- Canadian Sterling Silver and Goldsmiths, Durham St, Pugwash. Hand-crafted silver jewellery made on the premises and a wide selection of other local crafts. Open Monday-Friday 8 am-8 pm, Saturday 9 am-6 pm, Sunday, 10 am-7 pm. Summer hours.
- Co-operative Artisanale de Cheticamp Ltée., 15067 Cabot Trail, Cheticamp. This is the place for hooked rugs in all shapes and sizes (as well as mats, coasters and wall-hangings). Watch how the hooking is done during one of the frequent daily demonstrations here or at any one of the numerous craft shops in Cheticamp. Open daily 8 am-9 pm, June 15-September 15, variable hours in off-season.
- Flight of Fancy, Main St, Bear River. Selling the work of over 200 craftspeople, this is a beautifully appointed shop in the picturesque village of Bear River — worth a trip just for the drive. Open May-October, Mon-Sat 9-5; Sun 11-5, July & August until 7 pm.

- Flora's, Point Cross (near Cheticamp) on the Cabot Trail. Large craft shop with a wide selection of hooked rugs. Open daily during tourist season.
- Glooscap Trading Post, Hwy 102, Truro. Traditional Mi'kmaq crafts, featuring woven baskets and twig furniture. The wonderful smell of sweet grass will make you want to browse just a little longer. Open year-round, 9 am-6 pm.
- Jennifer's of Nova Scotia, 5635 Spring Garden Rd, Halifax. Easy to find on Halifax's main downtown shopping street, Jennifer's features exclusively Nova Scotian crafts, especially pottery, pewter and knitted items. Also located on Route 333 between Halifax and Peggys Cove. Halifax store open 9 am-5:30 pm daily (Thursday and Friday to 9 pm). Store on Route 333 open 8 am-7 pm daily in summer, off-season 9 am-5 pm daily.
- Leather Works, at Indian Brook (between Baddeck and Ingonish) on the Cabot Trail. Historic reproductions and a variety of contemporary leather goods by John Roberts. Open daily May to October.
- Out of Hand, 135 Montague St, Lunenburg. Arts & crafts gallery, unusual gifts. Open May-December.
- St Ann's Lobster Galley Restaurant and Gift Shop, overlooking St. Anns Bay. Wide selection of fine Atlantic Canadian crafts. Open daily May to October, 9 am-9 pm.
- Suttles and Seawinds, 466 Main St, Mahone Bay. Brilliant colours and fine design in clothing that borrows from quilting methods to create high fashion. Also patchwork accessories including tote bags and jewellery rolls. Quilts. Open year-round.
- Weave Shed, 232 Main Street, Wolfville. Handmade rugs, pottery, pewter and quality crafts by local artisans. May-December.
- Wild Things, near Tarbotvale on the St. Anns Bay Loop. Fallen trees become creative wood turnings and carvings in the studio behind this shop. Open daily mid-June to mid-October.

FINE JEWELLERY AND CRYSTAL
- Fire Works Gallery, 1569 Barrington St, Halifax. An eclectic mix of silver and gold jewellery, some made by the shop's resident jewellers, and art glass, pottery by well-known local artists. Open daily except Sunday.
- Nova Scotian Crystal, 5080 George St, at Lower Water St, Halifax. Canada's only mouth-blown and hand-cut crystal in the centuries-old tradition of Waterford. Stemware, vases, bowls, giftware. Open daily except Sunday.

PEWTER
- Amos Pewter, 589 Main St, Mahone Bay. Interpretive workshop and studio. Contemporary designs including picture frames, goblets and jewellery. Open Monday-Saturday 9 am-5:30 pm, Sunday afternoons.
- Seagull Pewter, Route 6, 9926 Durham St, Pugwash. Full line of pewter products. Canada's largest giftware manufacturer, now international in scope. Open daily. Two locations in Barrington Place Shops, Halifax.

POTTERY
- Birdsall-Worthington Pottery Ltd, 590 Main St, Mahone Bay. Slip-decorated earthenware pottery, including commemorative plates and handmade earrings. Open Monday-Saturday 10 am-5 pm, Sunday 1 pm-5 pm, July to September; limited hours in off-season.
- Nova Scotia Folk Pottery, Front Harbour, Chester. Colourful platters, bowls, vases and serving dishes by Jim Smith. Open daily 10 am-6 pm, June-September; off-season by appointment, 275-3272.
- Shape Shift and Goose Cove Pottery, at St. Anns on the Cabot Trail. Carol MacDonald's stoneware and porcelain; studio on site. Open daily 9 am-5 pm, June to September.

FINE ART AND FOLK ART
- Folk Art by Reed Timmons, Pleasant Bay on the Cabot Trail. Specializing in hand-carved whales,

gulls, roosters and fishermen. Open daily June to October.

- Gallery Shop, Art Gallery of Nova Scotia, 1741 Hollis St at Cheapside, Halifax. Good selection of folk art, among the featured works of a wide variety of Nova Scotia artists and craftspeople. Open daily except Monday. Evening hours on Thursday.
- Harvey's Island Folk Art, 202 Island Centre Rd, Cheticamp Island; 224-1987. Vibrant, primitive land- and seascapes by Harvey Camus. Open May-October, 9 am until dark.
- Houston North Gallery, 110 Montague St, Lunenburg; 634-8869. Large selection of Inuit carvings and prints, Nova Scotia folk art, silk screens and intaglio. Open year-round.
- Le Motif, Main Street, Cheticamp. Specializing in rag rugs, carvings, twig baskets and other local folk art. Open daily, June to mid-October.
- Sunset Art Gallery, Cheticamp. Bright, whimsical wood carvings (lots of people and birds) by William Roach. Open daily May 24 to October 15 or by appointment.
- Water's Edge Gallery, Water St, Baddeck. A collection of artworks with a primarily maritime theme and featuring new and established artists of Atlantic Canada. 295-1209; www.thewatersedgegallery.com.
- Wood Studio, Hwy 1, Meteghan. New and restored quilts and local folk art. Open daily 10 am-6 pm, May 1-October 31.

GIFT SHOPS

- Kidston Landing, Chebucto St, Baddeck. Extensive selection of Nova Scotia crafts, Scottish woolens, men's and women's clothing, including wool and cotton sweaters. Open daily.
- Sea Shanty Crafts and Antiques, Beach Point at the Englishtown Ferry. Interesting collectibles, including vintage china and glassware, and a good selection of new and antique quilts. Open daily June to September.
- Seawinds Chandlery, on the Government Wharf, Baddeck. Fine handmade sweaters, gift items and marine supplies. Open daily during tourist season.
- Sou'wester Gift Shop, Peggys Cove. Large selection of Nova Scotia crafts including hand-knitted sweaters. Open year-round.
- Warp and Woof, Water St, Chester. Local art and crafts; fine gift items. Open daily, late May to October.
- The Teazer, Edgewater Rd (Route 3), Mahone Bay. Upscale local crafts and imported gift items, kitchen ware. Open daily (Sunday in afternoon only), April to Christmas; weekends in off-season.
- Treasures, Elm Avenue, Wolfville. A quirky gift shop featuring unusual gardening supplies and Victorian housewares. Open daily year-round.

SPECIALTY SHOPS

- The Book Room, 1546 Barrington Street, Halifax. Enjoy browsing in the city's oldest bookstore. Large selection of regional books. Open Mon-Sat.
- Box of Delights, Main Street, Wolfville. Good general bookstore with the valley's best selection of local titles. Open year-round.
- Grohmann Knives, 116 Water St, Pictou. Fine knives for every use made on-site. Plant tours Monday-Friday 9 am-3 pm. Open Monday-Saturday 9 am-8 pm, Sunday afternoons.
- Halifax Folklore Centre, 1528 Brunswick Street, Halifax. Large selection of traditional musical instruments and Nova Scotian recordings. Open Mon-Wed, noon - 5:30 pm, Thurs-Fri noon-9 pm, Sat 10 am-5 pm.
- Magasin Campus (Campus Bookstore), Université Sainte-Anne, Pointe de l'Église. Books dealing with the history and culture of the Acadians. Open Monday-Saturday 9 am-5 pm.
- The Outdoor Store, Chebucto Street, Baddeck. Quality outdoor clothing, equipment and gifts. All inclusive packages available.
- Sew Inclined, near Tarbot on the St. Anns Loop. Specializing in designer vests, hats and pants. Custom orders and sewing services available. Open daily June to October.

TREATS

- Clearwater Lobster Shops, 757 Bedford Highway, Bedford, Halifax International Airport, and other locations in metro Halifax. Live lobster packed for travel. Open daily.
- Domaine de Grand Pré Winery, Grand Pré. Stroll the grounds, taste the wine, enjoy Swiss cuisine at on-site restaurant.
- J. Willie Krauch and Sons Smoked Fish, Tangier. Danish-smoked Atlantic salmon, mackerel and eel; orders filled worldwide. Open daily from 8 am.
- Jost Vineyards, Rte 6, Malagash. Family-run winery on 10 hectares. Retail store, daily tours at 3 pm in summer. Open daily, to 6 pm (closed Sunday mornings) shorter hours in off-season.
- LaHave Bakery, Rte 331, LaHave. Whole grain and herb breads, and sweets. From Lunenburg, a short drive and cable ferry ride across the LaHave River; also at 3 Edgewater Rd in Mahone Bay.
- Sainte Famille Wines, corner Dyke Rd and Dudley Park Lane, Falmouth. Vineyard at site of early Acadian settlement. Daily tours 11 am and 2 pm. Wine, gift baskets and crafts at gift shop. Open daily to 6 pm (Sunday noon-5 pm).
- Spring Garden Place Market, Spring Garden Road, Halifax. Specialty foods available from a variety of shops. Open daily.
- The Tangled Garden, Rte 1, Grand Pré. Herb jellies and vinegars; also finely crafted natural dried flower wreaths and other arrangements. Open daily, 10 am-6 pm.

OUTDOOR RECREATION

PARKS AND NATURAL ATTRACTIONS

Included among the province's outstanding natural attractions are two national parks, Kejimkujik and Cape Breton Highlands. Nova Scotia also has 126 provincial parks. These range from sites of natural or historical significance to pleasant spots for a picnic or swim. Some have campgrounds. For more information on provincial parks, consult the detailed listings in the *Nova Scotia Doers' and Dreamers' Guide* (see Travel Essentials) or write to the Nova Scotia Department of Natural Resources, RR1, Belmont, NS, B0M 1C0. The area code for all of Nova Scotia is 902.

Halifax

- Point Pleasant Park, in the South End of Halifax. Shaded walking paths and views of Halifax Harbour and the Northwest Arm.
- Sir Sandford Fleming Park (The Dingle), off Purcells Cove Rd, overlooking the Northwest Arm in Halifax. Beautiful view of the Arm along walking trails. Dedicated in 1912, the Dingle Tower was built to commemorate 150 years of representative government for Nova Scotia.

Peggys Cove

- See the waves, the rocks and the lighthouse at Nova Scotia's most famous fishing village.

Lunenburg

- Blue Rocks, east of Lunenburg on Lunenburg Bay. This tiny, rockbound fishing village is a favourite haunt of local artists.
- Ovens Natural Park, Route 332 southeast of Lunenburg, near Riverport. Coastal caves and cliffside hiking trails highlight this privately owned park.

Liverpool and Shelburne

- Kejimkujik Seaside Adjunct National Park, off Route 3 between Port Joli and Port Mouton. This beautiful stretch of isolated coastline is accessible by hiking trails. This is a nesting area for the endangered piping plover and sections of the beach are closed mid-April to mid-August.

Annapolis Valley

- The Look-off, Route 358 north of Wolfville, on Cape Blomidon. Panoramic view of the Minas Basin and six river valleys.

Annapolis Royal

- Kejimkujik National Park, off

Route 8 between Annapolis Royal and Liverpool (park headquarters at Maitland Bridge). Situated in the interior of southwestern Nova Scotia, this 381-square-kilometre wilderness area is a favourite of campers and canoeists. For more information contact Kejimkujik National Park, Box 236, Maitland Bridge, NS, B0T 1B0; 682-2772.

Glooscap Trail
• Cape Chignecto Provincial Park, near Advocate Harbour. 48 kilometres of coastal wilderness trails: Nova Scotia's premier hiking destination.
• Cape d'Or Lighthouse Look-off, off Rte 209, Advocate Harbour. Breathtaking view of the Bay of Fundy and Minas Channel.
• Five Islands Provincial Park, Rte 2 east of Parrsboro, at Five Islands. Camp, hike or picnic in this beautiful park overlooking five islands in the Minas Basin.
• Joggins Fossil Cliffs, Joggins. Sandstone cliffs with 300-million-year-old fossil material. The cliffs themselves are off-limits but erosion ensures a steady supply of fossils on the beach. Tours available (see listing under Attractions).
• Victoria Park, Brunswick St and Park Rd, Truro. Recreational facilities, hiking trails and two waterfalls make this 400-hectare park ideal for family outings.

Marine Drive
• Taylors Head Provincial Park, Rte 7 east of Spry Bay. Hiking trails, wildlife habitat and coastal views along Taylor Head Peninsula.
• Tor Bay Provincial Park, Tor Bay (south of Larrys River). Contemplate the vastness of the Atlantic while picnicking on this rocky point.

Cape Breton and the Cabot Trail
* Cape Breton Highlands National Park, northern Cape Breton. Nova Scotia's most spectacular scenery. The 950-square-kilometre park affords abundant opportunities for camping and hiking. For more information contact Cape Breton Highlands National Park, Ingonish Beach, NS, B0C 1L0; 285-2691.

• Cabot's Landing Provincial Park, Cape North. Reputed to be the site where John Cabot landed in 1497. Picnic and enjoy the pleasant views of Aspy Bay.
• Marble Mountain, on the shores of the Bras d'Or, overlooking the village of the same name. After a steep hike, beautiful views of Cape Breton's inland sea. Swimming at the crushed marble beach.
• Uisage Bahn Falls Park, near Baddeck Bridge. A network of hiking trails leads through hardwood forest to a dramatic gorge and waterfalls.

GOLF

There are 60 golf courses in Nova Scotia that welcome green-fee players. Golf Nova Scotia members are committed to making tee times available to visitors. For a complete list of member courses contact www.golfnovascotia.com or for reservations call 1-800-565-0001. For more information on golf courses in Nova Scotia, visit the Nova Scotia Golf Association website at www.nsga.ns.ca.
• Abercrombie Golf Club (18 hole), New Glasgow; 755-4653
• Amherst Golf & Country Club (18 hole), Amherst; 667-8730
• Antigonish Golf Club (18-hole), Antigonish; 863-4797
• Bell Bay Golf Club (18 hole), Baddeck; 1-800-565-3077; www.bellbaygolfclub.com
• Bluenose Golf & Country Club (9-hole), Lunenburg; 634-4260
• Chester Golf & Country Club (18-hole), Chester; 275-4543
• Dundee Resort and Golf Course (18-hole), Dundee (on the south shore of the Bras d'Or); 1-800-565-1774; www.dundeeresort.com
• Glen Arbour Golf Course (18 hole), Hammonds Plains (near Halifax); 1-877-835-4653; www.glenarbour.com
• Grandview Golf & Country Club (18-hole), Dartmouth; 435-3767
• Granite Springs Golf Club (18-hole), Prospect Road (near Halifax); 852-4653; www.granitespringsgolf.com
• Highlands Links (18-hole), Ingonish Beach (at Keltic Lodge); 1-800-441-1118;

www.highlandslinksgolf.com
- Ken-Wo Golf & Country Club (18-hole), New Minas; 678-5388; www.ken-wo.com
- LePortage Golf Club (18-hole), Cheticamp; 1-888-618-5558; www.leportagegolfclub.com
- Liverpool Golf & Country Club (9-hole), White Point Beach; 1-800-565-5068; www.whitepoint.com
- Northumberland Links (18-hole), 1776 Gulf Shore Rd, Pugwash; 243-2808/3213; www.norlinks.pugwash.ns.ca
- Oakfield Country Club (18-hole), Grand Lake (near Halifax International Airport); 861-2658
- Osprey Ridge (18 hole), Bridgewater; 543-6666; www.ospreyridge.ns.ca
- Paragon Golf & Country Club (18-hole), Kingston; 1-877-414-2554
- Pictou Golf Club (9-hole), Pictou; 485-4435
- The Pines Resort Golf Club (18-hole), Digby;1-877-375-6343; www.signatureresorts.com
- River Oaks Golf Club (18-hole), Meaghers Grant (Rte 357 through the Musquodoboit River valley); 384-2033
- Sunrise Beach Golf Club (9-hole), Tatamagouche; 657-2666; www.sunrisebeachgolf.com
- Valley Vista Golf Club (18 hole), Aylsford; 1-866-735-4653

BOAT TOURS (SIGHTSEEING, WHALE- AND BIRD-WATCHING, FISHING)

- Atlantic Whale Watch, Ingonish Beach; 285-2320. Three trips daily. Sightings of whales, seals and seabirds.
- Bird Island Tours, Big Bras d'Or; 1-800-661-6680. Narrated tour to Bird Islands; see puffins, seabirds, eagles and seals from covered boat. Mid-May to mid-September.
- Brier Island Whale and Seabird Cruises, Westport; 1-800-656-3660; www.brierislandwhalewatch.com. Cruises two to five times daily, three to five hour cruises on the Fundy. Greatest variety of whales in Nova Scotia waters. Rainchecks are given on the rare occasions when no sightings are made.
- Captain Cox's Whale Watch Bay, St. Lawrence; 1-888-346-5556. Seabirds and whales in the waters off Cape Breton's northernmost tip; marine biologist guide. Three tours daily.
- Capt. Mark's Whale and Seal Cruise, Pleasant Bay; 1-888-754-5112; www.cabottrail.com/whalewatch Five trips daily (3 off-season). Hear and see whales, cruise past sea caves, waterfalls and pioneer settlements.
- Fan-A-Sea Charters, Baddeck; 295-1900; www.baddeck.com/fan-a-sea. Saltwater sport fishing and sightseeing charters.
- Four Winds Charters, Cable Wharf, Unit 4, Halifax and St. Margarets Bay; 492-0022. Whale-watching, history tours, ferry to Georges and McNabs islands.
- Fundy Voyager, Halls Harbour; 538-8199. Cruises of the Bay of Fundy and Minas Basin. Picnics and rockhounding.
- Jiggs & Reels Boat Tours, New Glasgow Riverfront Marina; 926-2305. Water taxi; sightseeing and entertainment tours by reservation.
- Murphy's on the Water, Cable Wharf, 1751 Lower Water St, Halifax; 420-1015; www.murphysonthewater.com. Harbour tours, some with commentary, aboard a variety of vessels.
- Peggys Cove Whale and Puffin Tours, Rte 333, Peggys Cove; 823-1060; www.peggys-cove.com. Two cruises daily. Whales, dolphins, seals, puffins and other seabirds.
- Seaquarium Whale Watching Tours, North Ingonish; 285-2103/2401; www.ingonish.com/seaquarium. See whales, marine life, bald eagles and seabirds with experienced captain and tour guide. Two or three cruises daily, June-September.
- Seaside Whale & Nature Cruises, Cheticamp; 1-800-959-4253; www.lauries.com. Three tours daily. Accommodation and cruise packages available through Laurie's Motor Inn (see Lodging).
- Sea Visions Whale Watch, Ingonish Ferry; 285-2628. Three trips daily. See whales and seabirds from the 11-metre sailing vessel *Resplendent*.

- Star Charters, 2 Bluenose Drive, Lunenburg; 634-3535. Harbour and bay tours by sail or lobsterman's skiff.
- Whale Cruisers (Cheticamp), Cheticamp; 1-800-813-3376; www.whalecruises.com. Frequent sightings of pilot, minke and finback whales. Landward view of the coastline of Cape Breton Highlands National Park. Two or three cruises daily.

HIKING

Hikers will find plenty to choose from in Nova Scotia — spectacular ocean views, desolate highland plateaus, thick boreal forest and more. There are trails suitable for family outings and trails to challenge the most serious hikers.

Useful information for hikers is available from a number of sources. *The Nova Scotia Atlas*, 5th edition (co-published by the Province of Nova Scotia and Formac Publishing) includes 90 pages of topographic maps that cover the whole of Nova Scotia at a scale of 1:150,000. Available from bookstores and online at www.gov.ns.ca/snsmr/consumer/publications/maps.stm. *Hiking Trails of Nova Scotia*, a publication of the Canadian Hostelling Association, is also available in bookstores. These publications can also be purchased at outfitters throughout the province.

For information on hiking trails in Nova Scotia's two national parks, Kejimkujik and Cape Breton Highlands, write Parks Canada, Atlantic Region, Historic Properties, Upper Water Street, Halifax, NS, B3J 1S9; 426-3436. *Walking in the Highlands* is a guide to the 28 marked and serviced trails in the Cape Breton Highlands park.

TIDAL BORE RAFTING

The tidal bore on the Shubenacadie River provides a unique rafting experience. Check ahead to find out when the bore is at its peak.

- Shubenacadie River Adventure Tours, South Maitland; 1-888-878-8687; www.shubie.com. Open May-October. Reservations recommended.
- Shubenacadie River Runners, 8681 Rte 215, Maitland; 1-800-856-5061; www.tidalborerafting.com.

Open May-October. Reservations recommended.
- Tidal Bore Rafting Park Limited, Urbania; 1-800-565-7238; www.tidalboreraftingpark.com. Open May-October.

BIRDING

Nova Scotia is an important stopover on the Atlantic flyway for many species of migratory birds. Late summer sees thousands congregate on Fundy shores. Whale-watching tours (see listings above) also provide an excellent opportunity to observe seabirds, guillemots, kittiwakes, gannets, cormorants and more. Atlantic puffins and bald eagles are special attractions. Serious birders can purchase Robie Tufts' beautiful guidebook, *Birds of Nova Scotia*, from local bookstores.

CANOEING AND KAYAKING

Opportunities for freshwater paddling and sea kayaking in Nova Scotia are practically unlimited. Much of the interior of the province is a wilderness area studded with lakes and creased by rivers and streams. There are also long stretches of sheltered coastline on both the Atlantic and the Fundy shores. The *Nova Scotia Doers' and Dreamers' Guide* lists a number of outfitters, as well as suppliers of equipment, maps and useful information.

BICYCLING

An extensive series of secondary roads has helped to make cycling one of the fastest growing sports in Nova Scotia. Serious cyclists can challenge the world-famous Cabot Trail while others may choose a gentler route like the Sunrise Trail along the shores of the Northumberland Strait. *Bicycle Tours in Nova Scotia,* which describes 20 of the province's best routes, can be purchased from the Touring Chairman, Bicycle Nova Scotia, Box 3010 South, Halifax, NS, B3J 3G6.

The Nova Scotia Bicycle Book, with extensive route information, is available from Atlantic Canada Cycling, Box 1555, Station C, Halifax, NS, B3J 2Y3; 423-2453; www.atlanticcanadacycling.com.

CAMPING

Nova Scotia's two national parks, Kejimkujik and Cape Breton Highlands, and many of the province's 126 provincial parks have campground facilities (see Parks and Natural Attractions for addresses and information). There are also close to 130 privately owned campgrounds in Nova Scotia. Exhaustive listings and information on camping facilities are provided in the *Nova Scotia Doers' and Dreamers' Guide* (see Travel Essentials).

FISHING

Deep-Sea Fishing

Options for saltwater fishing range from relaxing outings, often in combination with some cultural or historical commentary, where sedentary groundfish are the catch, to serious searches for large gamefish — bluefin tuna, shark and bluefish. Murphy's on the Water (see Boat Tours) is one of several charter companies that operate out of Halifax Harbour. For complete listings consult the *Nova Scotia Doers' and Dreamers' Guide* (see Travel Essentials).

Freshwater Fishing

Many species are caught in Nova Scotia lakes and rivers, but the province owes its lofty reputation among anglers to the speckled trout and the Atlantic salmon. The Margaree River in western Cape Breton and St. Marys River on the Eastern Shore have attracted anglers from around the world. These rivers and several others in the province are posted for fly-fishing only. Information on scheduled rivers, licenses, seasons and bag limits is available from outfitters and tackle shops or from all district offices of the Department of Natural Resources (Halifax; 424-5419). For information on the salmon fishery, write the federal Department of Fisheries and Oceans, Box 550, Halifax, NS, B3J 2S7; 426-5952.

SAILING

Nova Scotia is a popular destination for sailors. The island-studded bays and sheltered harbours of the South Shore and the unique sailing experience afforded by Cape Breton's inland sea, the Bras d'Or, have created yachting havens like Chester and Baddeck. Yacht clubs at these communities and several others, including Halifax, host colourful regattas during the summer months.

Operators of pleasure craft are required to report to Canada Customs by calling 1-888-226-7277 on arrival in the first Canadian port of call. Customs information concerning pleasure craft, and a list of Customs offices providing marine services, are available from Revenue Canada, Customs border services, PO Box 520, Halifax, NS, B3J 2R7; 426-2911, 1-800-461-9999; fax 426-6522.

For general information on boating safety write to the Rescue Co-ordination Centre, HMC Dockyard, Department of National Defence, Halifax, NS, B3K 2X0; 427-8200, 1-800-565-1582. The best source for charts and other nautical information is the Canadian Hydrographic Service, Bedford Institute of Oceanography, Box 1006, Dartmouth, NS, B2Y 4A2; 426-2373.

USEFUL ADDRESSES

It is possible to make detailed plans for your Nova Scotia vacation before leaving home by contacting Nova Scotia's Check In Reservation and Information Service. Travel counsellors will provide invaluable advice, reservation services and a wealth of written material to make travel planning easier. In North America, call 1-800-565-0000 or write to Nova Scotia Information and Reservations, Box 130, Halifax, NS, B3J 2M7; www.checkinnovascotia.com.

Once in Nova Scotia, the same services are available at any of the province's visitor information centres. These are indicated by a "?" on the Nova Scotia Scenic Travelways Map, and can be found at key locations throughout the province, including the New Brunswick – Nova Scotia border and the Halifax International Airport.

In Halifax, the International Visitor Centre on Barrington Street offers many services, including currency exchange, tour packages and reservations. The centre can provide you with a wealth of information about the province.

Visitors from the United States who need to contact home in case of an emergency may do so through the Consulate General of the United States of America, 1969 Upper Water St., Halifax, NS, B3J 3K1; 429-2480.

SPECIAL TRAVEL SERVICES

Visitors with Special Needs
The *Nova Scotia Doers' and Dreamers' Guide* indicates, with the international symbols, which lodgings and attractions are wheelchair accessible and non-smoking. To find out what additional services may be available, visitors are urged to make specific inquiries. Where possible, it is advisable to book in advance. For assistance, contact the Nova Scotia Check In Reservation and Information Service at 1-800-565-0000 (North America) or www.checkinnovascotia.com. The Abilities Foundation website (www.enablelink.org) and their magazine, *Abilities* (available online), offer some travel information.

Students
Student discounts are available for a variety of travel services. In order to qualify, students are advised to buy an International Student Identity Card. In Canada, cards may be purchased at Travel Cuts, a travel agency for students found on many Canadian university campuses. Halifax branches are located at St. Mary's University (494-7027) and Dalhousie University (494-2054) and at 1589 Barrington St. (482-8000). Students from the US can obtain cards from Council Travel, Council on International Educational Exchange, 205 E. 42nd Street, New York, NY, 10017; 212-661-1450, or from a local branch office.

To find out about hostelling in the province, contact Hostelling International–Nova Scotia, 1253 Barrington St, Halifax, NS, B3J 1Y2; 902-422-3863.

Seniors
There are discounts for seniors on many travel services including transportation and accommodation. Make inquiries before making reservations and have your senior citizen identification card at the ready.

Many of the private tour operators in the province offer coach tours at reduced rates for seniors (several companies are listed in the Getting Around section).

GENEALOGICAL SOURCES

✳ Nova Scotia Archives and Records Management, 6016 University Avenue, Halifax, B3H 1W4; 902-424-6060; www.gov.ns.ca/nsarm. Hours are 8:30 am-4:30 pm, Monday to Friday; 9 am-5 pm Saturday. Closed Sundays, holidays and Saturdays on holiday weekends.
• Genealogical Association of Nova Scotia, Box 641, Station Central, Halifax, B3J 2T3; 454-0322; www.chebucto.ns.ca/Recreation/GANS
• Acadia University, Vaughan Library, Wolfville, NS, B0P 1X0
• Argyle Township Courthouse and Goal, Box 10, Tusket, NS, B0W 3M0
• Cape Breton Genealogical Society, Box 53, Sydney, NS, B1P 6G4
• Centre d'Études Acadiennes, Université de Moncton, Moncton, NB, E1A 3E9
• Colchester Historical Society, 29 Young Street, Truro, NS, B2N 5C5
• Deputy Registrar-General, Box 157, Halifax, NS, B3J 2M9
• Kings Courthouse Heritage Museum, 37 Cornwallis Street, Kentville, NS, B4N 2E2
• Pictou County Genealogical Society, Box 1210, Pictou, NS, B0K 1H0
• Shelburne County Genealogical Society, 24 Dock Street, Shelburne, NS, B0T 1W0
• Yarmouth County Historical Society, 22 Collins Street, Yarmouth, NS, B5A 3CB

CONTRIBUTORS

COLLEEN ABDULLAH is a writer, visual communication designer and marketing consultant. Since her retirement from Nova Scotia Tourism and Culture she has travelled extensively. She lives in Mahone Bay on Nova Scotia's beautiful South Shore, where she has recently begun yet another career as an antique shop proprietor.

ELEANOR ANDERSON is president of Icon Communications, which has been actively involved in golf marketing in Nova Scotia for the past six years. Eleanor is the marketing director of Golf Nova Scotia and Cape Breton's Fabulous Foursome.

LINETTE CHIASSON is an actor and life-long theatre junkie. She recently returned to her native Halifax after studying theatre and English in Ottawa, where she appeared in a variety of roles. She is excited to be continuing her acting career in the dynamic theatre community of Nova Scotia.

SCOTT CUNNINGHAM, a biologist, is both a British Canoe Union (BCU) Senior Instructor and a Canadian Recreational Canoeing Association (CRCA) Instructor Trainer. He has developed a national sea kayaking program for the CRCA and is author of *Sea Kayaking in Nova Scotia*. He lives in Tangier, where he operates Coastal Adventures.

DALE DUNLOP is a native Nova Scotian who, after a 20-year absence, set out to explore every highway and byway in the province. In 1995, he and his wife Alison Scott published *Exploring Nova Scotia*, a comprehensive guide to Canada's Ocean Playground. When not travelling or writing, Dale puts in time at his day job as a litigation lawyer.

ELAINE ELLIOTT is the author, with her sister Virginia Lee, of the *Flavours* series of cookbooks and guidebooks, the most recent being *Summer Flavours*. She has an unparalleled knowledge of Nova Scotian restaurants and cuisine.

MICHAEL ERNST started Sail Mahone Bay in 1994. His fleet of Wayfarer dayboats, a 6-metre cruiser and a racer/cruiser, offer a variety of ways to sail on Mahone Bay. He has enjoyed sailing for 40 years, and for 20 years was a sailing instructor in Britain under the Royal Yachting Association. He has been involved in a number of tourism initiatives in Nova Scotia.

AL KINGSBURY is a journalist and author who lives in the Annapolis Valley.

ALLAN LYNCH is a freelance writer based in Nova Scotia's Annapolis Valley who focuses on travel, business and the business of travel. Lynch has contributed to eight books and written three, his latest being *All In The Family, Inc.: Insights from the Corporate Boardrooms and Kitchen Tables of Canadian Family Businesses*. In a perfect world his golf game would drop by 12 strokes.

ROBERT McCALLA is a geographer and author of *The Maritime Provinces Atlas*.

NIKKI MITCHELL is a communications specialist and freelance writer with expertise in arts and culture. She has had the benefit of seeing museums behind the scenes, having worked at the Royal Ontario Museum and the Ontario Science Centre. She loves to go on driving adventures, particularly with the windows down – when the sun shines.

TERRY PUNCH is Past President of the Royal Nova Scotia Historical Society and has written numerous books and pamphlets on genealogical research in Nova Scotia.

SUSAN RANDLES and DAVID STEPHENS wrote several books together, including *Lighthouses of Nova Scotia*.

ANTHONY RING is the Executive Director of the Music Industry Association of Nova Scotia and the former publisher of *Atlantic Gig*, a music newspaper for the Atlantic Canadian music scene.

JOAN WALDRON is an avid birder, and since her retirement from the Nova Scotia Museum she has been spotting birds around the world. "Whether I'm birding while visiting relatives in England and Ireland or checking birds on the beaches in the tropics, nothing compares to birding in Nova Scotia. It's as close to heaven as you can get!"

INDEX

Photo Credits

Legend: Top – T; Centre – C; Bottom – B
Photographs by Keith Vaughan, except as noted below:
Bay Ferries Limited: p.7, p.113 C; Mark Beaver: p.50; Julian Beveridge: p.18, p.21, p.35 C, p.86 T; Firefighters' Museum/Percy Cottreau: p.15; Freewheeling Adventures: p.48 T&B, p.49 T; Golf Nova Scotia: p.42, p.44 T&B, p.45 T, p.46 B; Steven Isleifson: p.104 B; Jocelyne Lloyd: p.120 B; Wendy MacGregor: p.57; Nova Scotia Tourism: p.2 C, p.26 T, p.51 B, p.71 C, p.73 T&B, p.84 B, p.109 T, p.121 C&B, p.129 B, p.145 T&B, p.158 B; Parks Canada: p.109 C; Port Bickerton and Area Planning Association: p.144 B; Gil Reynold: p.33 top; Ron Scott/scottwalking.com: p.51 T, p.52 T, p.53; Shakespeare by the Sea: p.27 B; Jamie Steeves: p.86 B; Richard Stern: p.68 T, p.69 B; Shimon Walt/Rhapsody Quintet p.31.
Maps by Peggy McCalla: pp.4-5, p.76, p.77, p.95, p.115, p.131, p.135, p.141, p.147, p.162.

Formac Publishing Company Limited
5502 Atlantic Street
Halifax, Nova Scotia B3H 1G4
www.formac.ca

Printed and bound in Canada

Distributed in the United States by:
Casemate
2114 Darby Road,
2nd Floor
Havertown, PA 19083

Distributed in the United Kingdom by:
Portfolio Books Limited
Unit 5, Perivale Industrial Park
Horsenden Lane South
Greenford, UK, UB6 7Rl